THE COMPLETE
ENCYCLOPEDIA OF
DOGS

THE COMPLETE
ENCYCLOPEDIA OF
DOGS

Includes caring for your Dog and
descriptions of breeds from around the world

ESTHER J. J. VERHOEF-VERHALLEN

REBO
PUBLISHERS

© 1996 Rebo International b. v., The Netherlands

Text: Esther J. J. Verhoef-Verhallen
Cover design: Minkowsky Graphics, Enkhuizen, The Netherlands
Production: TextCase, The Netherlands
Translation: Stephen Challacombe for First
Edition Translations Ltd, Great Britain
Typesetting: Hof&Land Typografie, The Netherlands

ISBN 90 366 14996

Contents

Foreword

This book sets out to present dog breeds in a clear and logical manner which has wide international acceptance.Therefore the classification system used is the one adopted by the International Cynological Federation (FCI, Fédération Cynologique Internationale). This organization's grouping of breeds is widely accepted although the Kennel Club in Great Britain and the American Kennel Club have slightly different classifications, as do certain other countries. It is therefore quite possible that a breed may not appear within the grouping familiar to you. The national breed registration organization or specific breed society will be able to information about the group in which your chosen breed is recognized in your own country. Because many specific breed books and other encyclopedias on dogs deal in depth with the history and origins of breed families, this book concentrates instead on the practical considerations of each breed since these are the points most often raised with breed societies and breeders alike. The intention is to enable you to judge from the breed descriptions whether a specific type of dog is suitable for your home, and your particular requirements.When this basic choice has been made, helped with the practical information, detailed matters about the specific dog, such as the breed standard, can be found both in existing publications and from the relevant breed society.

Esther J. J. Verhoef-Verhallen

Introduction

A pedigree dog is more than just another dog

Almost everyone who is looking for a pedigree dog will be influenced initially by the outward appearance of the breed. This is fine provided that it is remembered that each breed has its specific character. Many breeds have existed for centuries and have been used for a very wide range of purposes, mainly to work for humans and to make their tasks easier, or even to take them over.

Originally the outward appearance of the dog was of little significance, although early on men realized that certain types and colours of coat, and the build of a dog were better suited to specific tasks. It was not just coincidence that led to uniformity among dogs doing the same work in the same part of the world. True pedigrees did not of course exist then yet those early standardized dogs are not far removed from today's pedigree animal.

Today, particularly in the West, most of these dogs no longer perform the tasks for which they were originally bred. Except for a few breeds, dogs have adapted perfectly to their new role as pets.

Grooming to keep the coat in condition is an important part of keeping a dog

The primitive instincts are carried in the genes through the generations. Centuries of selective breeding cannot be eradicated in a few decades. This needs to be considered when deciding on your choice of breed. Cliché it may be, but the look of a particular dog is something to which you will become accustomed; its character is harder to adapt to. The dog's character has to please you throughout its life. The careful, and correct choice is very important. The purchase and care of a pedigree dog should be a rewarding and pleasurable experience for both the dog and the family of which it will form part.

The purchase of a pedigree dog

Not a spur of the moment decision

Clearly the decision to buy a pedigree dog is not one to be made lightly on the spur of the moment. The dog which you choose will probably be a part of your family for more than ten years, with you every day and will make a significant impression upon your daily life. It is necessary to separate the wheat from the chaff, since there are good and bad breeders.

Consider first your reason for acquiring a dog. Do you intend to breed with it? Is it your intention to show the dog? Or do you not want anything to do with such matters and are you merely seeking a family pet? In this case, a dog with a small imperfection in colour or coat will be much cheaper to buy, but do not expect to walk away with the prizes at a dog show, or to breed a future champion. Such a dog, though, might be a perfect family member. If the need is for a hunting dog, then seek out a breeder who specializes in the line breeding of hunting dogs.

You are then more likely to obtain a puppy which will hunt well than if you buy a dog of the same breed with only show championships in its pedigree. The opposite is also true of course.

If it is possible, first make contact with the society which promotes the welfare of the particular breed. Visit and talk with a number of breeders and enthusiasts and join the breed association so that you will receive newsletters, usually about twice a year, full of useful information.

Whatever you do, consider it carefully and never buy a dog from puppy farms, traders, pet shops, or from a market. It is impossible to know from these sources whether the dog is healthy, the appearance and character of its parents, and, most importantly, how it has been handled during the crucial imprinting phase of its development. Such a puppy may well be much cheaper but the apparent "gain" can be wiped out after several months of heavy vet's bills with a sickly animal.

Should your choice be an uncommon breed, it will be much more difficult to find the best breeder.

The national breeds' registration organization should be able to assist your search. Occasionally an unusual breed will have to be imported. If so ensure that all the necessary papers are in order and ask your national organization if they know of anyone with previous experience of importing the breed in question.

An unusual breed need not be more expensive than a popular one; in some cases the dog can be cheaper, since the breeder of a relatively unknown breed has greater difficulty in finding good homes for the offspring.

Dog or bitch

Both dogs and bitches have their advantages and disadvantages. Dogs are generally more uniform in character than bitches. This is due to the action of the hormones on bitches during the periods when they are "on heat." This happens on average twice each year, making them eager to be with dogs and causing them to leave blood spots on your carpet. There are, however special diapers or nappies available, or you can ask your vet to give your bitch a hormone injection to prevent the onset of ovulation. It is of course possible to have a bitch's ovaries removed, with the additional benefit that she becomes more equable.

Dogs are usually more independent by nature and less gentle.

This is especially noticeable with the more dominant breeds such as the Rottweiler. The difference between the sexes is generally far less pronounced with the more gentle breeds, but there are countless exceptions to this rule.

The choice between dog or bitch is a personal one. For those interested in the more dominant breeds but who have little experience in bringing up dogs, a bitch will be a better choice. Ask the breeder for advice. He or she will have spent every day with the dogs and will know their characters like none other. A good breeder will agree to select from the litter the puppy that is most suitable for your wishes and situation.

This book provides hints on the characters of different breeds. Remember though, that these are general character traits of the average member of the breed. Within specific lines of breeding of the same breed, character can vary widely. Above all, every dog is unique, even dogs from the same litter.

Older dog or puppy?

The majority of people will choose a puppy in preference to an older dog. That is not surprising, considering that a puppy is comparatively easy to train. Most people enjoy watching a young dog grow up. In spite of this, an older dog can be an ideal choice. The mature dog has already developed its character and has finished growing. Normally, they have had at least rudimentary training and are house-trained.

The exuberance of puppy-hood is behind them and they adapt readily to the new circumstances. It is possible to develop as equally strong a bond with an older dog as with a puppy. Many breed associations have a special department to find new owners for fully grown or almost fully grown dogs that, for whatever reason, need a new home; this might be because their owners are emigrating, but divorce can also lead to a dog requiring a new place to live.
The breed association will be wholly honest about the reason why a new home needs to be found. If your thoughts do not immediately fly to

the notion of a puppy, then contact the organization for your preferred breed without obligation.

Training

Socializing

Various scientific studies have shown that the influences and experiences which a puppy undergoes during the first twelve to fourteen weeks of its life are the most formative in its upbringing.
This period is also known as the imprinting phase and if during this time a dog learns that strangers, children, cats, and busy urban traffic mean it no harm, it will then react in a stable way to them throughout its life. The opposite of this is equally true: a puppy which has spent the entire period of fourteen weeks in a kennel with its mother and the other members of the litter for company, apart from the one human who looks after them, finds it difficult to adapt to human society.
The way in which these experiences occur has an enormous influence upon the young dog. If the puppy is attacked by a cat during this period, it is likely that it will react badly towards cats for the rest of its life.
It is clearly best to buy a puppy from a breeder who gives you the confidence that they spend sufficient time and energy in ensuring the puppies are well socialized. When a puppy is seven to twelve weeks old, you may take it home. Now it is your responsibility to complete what the good breeder has begun.

Consistent and logical

Consistent handling in its upbringing is essential with every dog, irrespective of the breed. This means, for example, that a dog is only told what a "good dog" it is when it has obeyed a command. This may seem rather obvious but it is apparent that people find it difficult to remain consistent and logical in daily life. If you want your dog to lie down, only show you are pleased with it when it has actually lain down.

Often people find it satisfactory if after countless efforts, the dog finally decides to sit. This is not consistent logic. When people leave a dog, they often say "stay in your basket." Since it is impossible to verify whether the dog actually does so, it is better not to give such an order. If you decide not to allow the dog on to the sofa, then it must never be permitted, even when your dog is unwell.

In such a case, place an old cot mattress on the floor. The same applies if you do not want your dog to jump up enthusiastically to greet people; never permit it, not even on occasions when you find it fun as you happen to be wearing old clothes. A dog cannot understand the subtle difference that makes a certain behaviour acceptable at one time and not so on another and it will become confused and unhappy.
Remaining consistent as a dog grows up is of course difficult, particularly in a large family in which everyone has his or her own idea about the best way of bringing up a dog. It is highly confusing for a dog not to know where it stands. Some breeds are so sensitive to this that they exhibit disturbed behaviour either in the form of domination or by becoming highly submissive. Do not permit the family to adopt flexible rules. Before a dog joins the family, every member

must know what the rules for the dog are and understand the importance of sticking rigidly to them.

Punishment

Only ever punish a dog immediately if it does something wrong, never when the mischief happened some time ago. Imagine that, in your absence, the dog has played havoc with the contents of your home. When you discover this on returning home, you punish the dog, verbally or physically.

It may seem obvious to you that the dog is at fault and you may think from the expression on the dog's face that it knows this. Nothing could be less true. Most dogs will have forgotten entirely what they have done but will react to your manner and either become submissive or try to escape. The only lesson the dog will learn is that punishment is associated with your returning home and consequently it will anxiously anticipate what will happen when you enter the room.

Depending upon the breed, a dog may become aggressive or very nervous and submissive; it will lose trust in the - to its eyes - fickle and unpredictable pack leader. If your dog misbehaves whenever you are away, then it is best to put it in a kennel outdoors or restrict it to a room where it can do no harm. This ensures that it will always be a "good dog" on your return. Most dogs grow out of the destructive urge once out of puppyhood but a few continue because they get insufficient exercise or attention. Sometimes it is the result of pure boredom.
It is essential to punish the dog

immediately for any misbehaviour during the early days of upbringing. Perhaps you call your dog to you and eventually it comes to you after much dithering. Since it has obeyed your command, the dog now deserves a reward. Unfortunately dogs are often punished by owners for failing to come quickly enough. The likely consequence will be that the dog learns to associate your orders with punishment and will most certainly have no desire to react quickly to you the next time. The scope of this book does not extend to a full explanation of the training and upbringing a dog. You are advised to consult one of the many excellent books on this subject. If you have no experience in training and upbringing of a dog, it is a good idea to join a puppy course - with the puppy of course! In this way your puppy's education can be well guided but bear in mind that every dog is different and that there are considerable differences between breeds. Ensure that the instructors are familiar with the characteristics of your dog's breed.

Association with dogs, other pets, and children

How well the dog mixes with dogs, other pets, and with children is partially dependent upon the individual dog and its breed and partially upon its imprinting and socializing. When a dog is badly imprinted from a breed once kept in packs - such dogs need to be sociable - there is a high risk that it will display disturbed behaviour towards other dogs, pets, and children.

Association is very important. These Dobermanns leave the poultry alone because they have been correctly socialized in their upbringing

13

The character descriptions in this book are generalized; they assume that a dog will have enjoyed good socializing and be well brought up. A word of caution is appropriate though.

However lovable and patient a dog is with children, it should never be left unsupervised with children. It is important for children to understand that a dog must be left in peace when in its basket or while it is eating. Clearly, a dog must be left alone in its domain; children must never be permitted to pester it! Teach your children never to approach the dog but to call it to them instead in order to establish the correct hierarchy.

Caring for your dog ears, claws, and teeth

Every type of dog's coat has specific requirements for its care. These specific points are dealt with in the sections on the breeds. To clean the ears, it is important never to use cotton buds since these will only push any dirt further into the ear with all the consequences that may bring. Use instead a recognized brand of ear cleaner; let the drops enter the ears and massage them. Afterwards clean away surface dirt with a tissue.

Some dogs have excessive growth of hair in the ears which should be removed regularly to avoid infection. Avoid removing too much at once but also do not clip one hair at a time because this will be painful for the dog; try to find a middle way. Sometimes too much hair grows between the pads of the feet. In this case the best method is to cut the hair growing between the pads. Curved scissors are the safest to use; keep the curve facing away from the dog's foot so that you will not cut a pad.

Keep your dog's claws short. When a dog walks regularly on hard or rough ground, its claws will wear themselves down but some dogs have very quick-growing claws and in such cases the claws must be clipped. In order to keep your dog well groomed and cared for, it is important to get it used to this ritual when young. An older, and stronger dog which is not accustomed to it will try to resist, so that regular grooming could become a major problem. If you find it unpleasant to do these kinds of jobs yourself, you can take your dog to a professional salon where they trim and groom dogs. They can explain and demonstrate to you the best way to do the more difficult tasks so that you may then be able to cope with them yourself. General care also includes care of the teeth; provided that your dog is fed with hard biscuit and regularly has a good quality bone to chew on, the teeth should require little attention.

The excess of hair between the pads of the feet must be regularly trimmed back

Dogs which on the contrary are mainly fed soft food and seldom if ever get the chance to use their teeth are far more likely to develop tartar - with all the wretchedness this causes. Check regularly to see if your dog is developing tartar scale because prevention is always better than cure.

The coat

Some coats, especially the long-haired varieties, require intensive grooming. This can mean at least an hour of brushing and combing. Teach your dog to stand or lie on a table with a hard surface for this ritual. This will prevent you from getting backache and make it easier to do the job thoroughly. Brush dogs with long hair at least once a week. This is not an unnecessary luxury even for smooth-haired breeds.

During grooming you may notice things that would otherwise be overlooked such as small wounds, ticks, and other parasites. To shampoo a dog, use only a recognized brand of dog shampoo that will not affect the skin's natural oils. Never leave a wet dog outdoors, or in a cold draughty place. Make sure your dog is fully dry before letting it out of the house.

With a number of breeds it is necessary to have the coat trimmed regularly. This may be a simple task which can be learned from the breeder, but more usually it is a complex job best left to the professionals in the grooming salon. These salons know the right way to deal with the coats of most breeds; if your dog is unusual, it is best to take an illustration of the right style of trimming for your breed. A visit to such a salon is an excellent idea if you intend to show your dog. The correct trimming style can usually be obtained from the breed association or from your dog's breeder.

Exercise

A breed to suit you

On warm sunny days or lovely autumn ones people often think how nice it would be to take a dog for a walk with them to play in the woods, or on the beach. Walking the dog has been rather over-romanticized. Once a dog is established in the home, it usually falls to just one person to "take the dog out." When it is howling a gale, raining, or freezing, the eagerness to walk the dog is reduced to nil.

A year consists of 365 days, on every one of which a dog will need to be exercised a minimum of four times, whatever the weather. There are breeds that require considerable exercise. In these cases four times is certainly not sufficient; it may be necessary to cycle with the dog. It is clear then that choosing a breed which - so far as exercise is concerned - suits the life-style of your family is essential. If you are sporty, enjoy cycling, or run for pleasure, then highly active dogs make perfect companions. When you loathe these activities, choose a less active breed.

Dog sports

Sports for dogs, such as fly-ball and agility skill trials have become increasingly popular.
Certain breeds - specifically the sheepdogs - enjoy this form of exercise tremendously. Other less developed breeds can also participate in training classes.
The important point is that both you and your dog should enjoy the activity. This does not have to be a competitive activity, although competition can become addictive if you dis-

cover that you and your dog form a good team. Another well-known sporting activity is defence or security classes for highly trained dogs. Only certain breeds are permitted to participate or are considered for the mandatory training. Competing forms a key part of this activity and is taken very seriously.

Often the organizers will insist that your dog has gained diplomas for obedience classes before they will accept it. This is understandable in view of the role dogs play in such competitions where they grab hold of "suspects" wearing protective suits with their teeth to "arrest" them. It is essential for the dogs to be strictly controlled. A brave and intelligent dog is essential, but it is of equal importance for the dog to be equable and good-natured.
Considerable effort, patience, and dedication are also demanded from the owner. With appropriate training your dog will be no less trustworthy than before the course, and probably more so. The notion, which some people have, that these dogs become unreliable is baseless.

This is an extremely disciplined activity in which there is no room for initiative on the part of the dog, on or off the training ground. This sport becomes a way of life to many of the human participants rather than just an interest.
This is equally true of hunting. The bond between you has to be good if you go hunting with your dog. The dog must be well under control. Consequently, not every breed is suitable to be used as hunting dog. In the group of hunting dogs there are numerous sections, each of which has a breed regarded to be the best in

its category. Hunting need not necessarily include hunting wild game and killing it. Drag hunts use dummies bearing a scent for the dogs to nose. This can be an exciting multi-faceted sport for both you and your dog.

Dog racing is the best known way for a greyhound to really stretch its legs, although in some countries coursing is permitted. Both sports are generally restricted to greyhounds or dogs of the same group.

In mild climates it is rather difficult to exercise sledge dogs; hence many owners take their dogs to higher, and colder places where snow can be usually guaranteed. The dogs can then carry out the work for which they were originally bred, although generally not in competitive circumstances. In countries with little or no snow the practice sledge on wheels forms a means of training and exercising the dogs.

Showing dogs is an art in itself. First and foremost, your dog must be an outstanding specimen of its breed; secondly, its coat must be faultless. That is unfortunately not the end of it. Not every dog, however beautiful, is prepared to stand as the centre of attention, and not every owner knows how best to accentuate his dog's best points. Every national breed registration organization runs courses on showing dogs and preparing them.

This summary of sporting activities for dogs is far from comprehensive. Taking part in a sport with your dog is an enjoyable way for both of you to be active together. You will understand your dog better from it and the same is true for it, and the bond between you will be strengthened. It is important that both of you should enjoy the activity.

If your dog is not suited for a particular activity, this does not devalue its other qualities.

Adapted exercise

Many of the fast-growing breeds require adapted exercise in the first year of their life. With these breeds it is inadvisable to walk or play too much with the dog during its growing phase because the joints, bones, and limbs would be too highly stressed, leading to problems later in life. Hip displacement, knee, and back problems are in part inherited disorders, but the wrong upbringing can cause harm.

Such breeds will not be happy either to be wrapped in cotton wool! Take them for a short walk, twice per day. Movement straight ahead at a tempo suitable for the dog is a good way to develop the muscles. Running next to a cycle is ideal for many breeds as exercise. After the dog is fully grown, the distance can be gradually increased. A winter break is quite acceptable in this routine but do not then begin straight away in the spring with long distances.

The dog also needs to regain its condition. Not everyone will be able to find a safe place to exercise their dog alongside a cycle, although there are probably more opportunities in your area than may at first be apparent. The chosen track must enable you to cycle safely with the dog alongside away from other traffic.

1. Sheepdogs and cattle herders

Sheepdogs and herding dogs

Australian Shepherd

COUNTRY OF ORIGIN
United States.

APTITUDE
Sheepdog.

SIZE
The shoulder-height is 50 – 57cm
($19^1/_2$ – $22^1/_2$ in) for dogs and 45 – 52cm
($17^1/_2$ – $20^1/_2$ in) for bitches.

COAT
The coat consists of medium to long hair that has either pronounced or loose waves and a dense undercoat. The Australian Shepherd's colourings can be blue-black marbled, red marbled (liver-coloured), plain black or brown, possibly with tan markings and some white.

CARE REQUIRED
Relatively little grooming is needed for its coat. During moulting the under layer of the coat is shed, requiring a good combing to remove loose hairs.

CHARACTER
This intelligent, astute, eager to learn dog is level-headed, vigilant, alert, active, tough, very loyal, has ample stamina, and bonds closely with the family.

TRAINING
Training is easy because the Australian Shepherd learns so quickly and eagerly.
If condemned to an outing just three times a day, the Australian Shepherd may behave very tediously. In addition to a certain level of regular exercise, this breed also requires to be kept occupied. It is sensible to involve it in agility skills training, fly-ball, or obedience competitions – for which it is ideally suited.

Long-haired Border Collie

SOCIAL BEHAVIOUR
Provided that it has been well socialized, the Australian Shepherd causes no problems with other dogs and pets. They are also generally good with children but can be a bit shy with strangers.

EXERCISE
This dog needs lots of exercise, but above all it needs to be kept occupied to keep it happy. Perhaps the best home for it is with sporty people who are able every day to spend time doing things with it.

Australian Shepherd

Head of an Australian Shepherd

Bearded Collie

COUNTRY OF ORIGIN
Scotland.

APTITUDE
Sheepdog and family pet.

SIZE
The shoulder-height is 53 – 56cm ($20\frac{1}{2}$ – 22 in) for dogs and 51 – 53cm (20 – $20\frac{1}{2}$ in)for bitches.

COAT
The undercoat is dense and woolly; the outer coat is straight, tough, long, and rough. Permitted colours are black, blue, slate-coloured, reddish-brown, all shades of grey with white markings on the nose, chest, legs, and feet or neck. The white markings are not permitted beyond the shoulder.

Bearded Collie

CARE REQUIRED
The Bearded Collie requires lots of grooming. The hair must be brushed and combed a couple of times each week to avoid tangles. Remove excessive hair between the pads and keep inside the ears clean.
The hair of a Bearded Collie should be parted along the back.

CHARACTER
This is a high spirited, cheerful, and clever dog that is eager to learn, lovable, gentle, sociable and companionable, extremely independent, active. A Bearded Collie belongs to the family and is not a suitable dog to banish outdoors to a kennel.

TRAINING
The Bearded Collie is an intelligent dog who learns quickly. Treating it severely during its of the training does not work; you can achieve better results by a playful, soft-handed approach. Give it ample praise and plenty of cheerful commands and avoid pressurizing it, because that spoils its receptive and friendly disposition.

SOCIAL BEHAVIOUR
These dogs can get very on well with children, household pets, and other dogs. Even strangers are normally greeted exuberantly.

EXERCISE
The Bearded Collie will adapt itself to the situation but you can give it no greater pleasure than to take it on long country walks. Bearded Collies have no tendency to run away (in common with most dogs in this group); on the contrary they stay close by you. This breed usually performs well in obedience trials and agility competitions.

SPECIAL POINTS
Because of its gentle nature the Bearded Collie is most ideal for those with little experience of bringing up a dog; with its great adaptability it fits in just as happily in town as in the country. Bear in mind that the coat requires extensive grooming.

Bearded Collie

Clipped harlequin-coated Beauceron

Unclipped Beauceron

Beauceron

France.

Aptitude
Herding dog and family pet.

Size
The shoulder-height is 65 – 70cm
($25^1/_2$ – $27^1/_2$ in) for dogs and 63 – 68cm ($24^1/_2$ – $26^1/_2$ in) for bitches. The weight can vary from 30 to 40 kg (66 to 88 lb).

Coat
The short, tough, and smooth coat has both a dense and soft undercoat. There are two recognized colours: black with brand marks and black-grey brindle. The latter colour is fairly rare.

Care required
The coat of the Beauceron does not require a great deal of attention. An occasional grooming with more attention during the moult is sufficient.

Character
The dog is clever, attentive, active, intelligent, and sometimes stubborn, and loyal to its owner and the family. It has considerable stamina and is very watchful.

Training
A consistent and loving upbringing with plenty of exercise and ample contact with its owner are indispensable for the well-balanced development of a young Beauceron. If it is denied this, then it can become neurotic or aggressive. Let it make acquaintance as a puppy in a positive way with different people, animals, things, and situations.

Social behaviour
A Beauceron that has been well socialized and brought up gets on fine under normal circumstances with children, and that also ensures that other dogs and pets will present no problems.

Exercise
This breed is not satisfied with a circuit of the block three-times-a-day. Take it for regular long walks during which it can run free off the lead and play. If both of you enjoy it, enrol it for a course to train for fly-ball or to compete in agility skills classes, although in competition it is likely to be less successful than other more suitable breeds.

Head of a Laeken Belgian Shepherd

Belgische Herder

Laeken Belgian Shepherd

• Laeken Belgian Shepherd

COUNTRY OF ORIGIN
Belgium.

APTITUDE
Historically a cattle-driving dog, in present times a guard-dog and family pet.

SIZE
The shoulder-height is about 62cm (24^1/$_2$in) for dogs and 58cm (22^1/$_2$in) for bitches. The breed standard permits variation in height of 2cm (^{1}/$_2$in) shorter and 4cm (1^1/$_2$in) taller.

COAT
The coat is rough-haired and a drab sandy colour with darker streaks around the nose and tail.

CARE REQUIRED
This rough-haired dog needs to be trimmed about twice each year, depending upon the quality of the coat from which dead and excessive hair should be removed. Ignore suggestions to have your dog close trimmed as this ruins the coat for several years. In addition to the occasional light trim, use a coarse-toothed comb for grooming. The Laeken Belgian Shepherd can manage perfectly well in an outdoor kennel provided it receives sufficient attention and exercise.

CHARACTER
This breed is attentive, tough, and brave, eager to work, a good guard-dog, has great stamina, is lively, intelligent, dominant, and bonds with its family.

TRAINING
For the right owner the Laeken Belgian Shepherd is not difficult to bring up. This breed requires a well-balanced and confident handler. Generally these dogs are very intelligent and eager to learn.
nsure there is plenty of variety in training sessions.

SOCIAL BEHAVIOUR
Generally these sheepdogs get on with children but they can be rather dominant towards other dogs.
Provided they are correctly socialized with cats and other pets, these should present no problems.

EXERCISE
This breed demands a significant level of exercise. They make excellent guard- and defence dogs. Even when this direction of activity is not to your taste, these dogs must be taken out regularly to burn off their surplus energy.

• Mechelen Belgian Shepherd

COUNTRY OF ORIGIN
Belgium.

Mechelen Belgian Shepherd

APTITUDE
Historically a cattle-driving dog, today a guard-dog, defence dog, and family pet.

SIZE
The shoulder-height is about 62cm (24$^1/_2$in) for dogs and 58cm (22$^1/_2$in) for bitches. The breed standard permits both sexes to be 2cm ($^1/_2$in) shorter and 4cm (1$^1/_2$in) taller.

COAT
The coat is short-haired, drab sandy-coloured with black tips to the hairs and a black muzzle.

CARE REQUIRED
The Mechelen Belgian Shepherd does not require much in the way of grooming for its coat. The occasional brushing, particularly during moulting, is sufficient. They are quite happy in an outdoor kennel provided they get sufficient exercise and attention.

CHARACTER
This breed is attentive, brave, tough, a good guard dog, intelligent, eager to work, has considerable stamina, bonds with its own people, is dominant, and temperamental.

TRAINING
The dog learns relatively quickly. Its potentially dominant character demands a handler who is confident.

SOCIAL BEHAVIOUR
Generally this breed gets on with children. Provided it has been correctly socialized, contact with other pets should present no problems. Some are rather aggressive to their own kind.

EXERCISE
This breed is ideally suited to defence dog- and security-training and performs well in such competitions. Even if you have no interests in this direction, you will need to take the dog for long walks to burn off its energies.

Most Mechelen Belgian Shepherds enjoy playing ball games, swimming, retrieving, running beside a cycle, and playing.

• *Tervueren and Groenendael Belgian Shepherds*

COUNTRY OF ORIGIN
Belgium.

APTITUDE
Historically herding dogs, now family pets.

SIZE
The shoulder-height is about 62cm (24$^1/_2$in) for dogs and 58cm (22$^1/_2$in)for bitches. The breed standard permits both sexes to be 2cm ($^1/_2$in) shorter and 4cm (1$^1/_2$in) taller.

Mechelen Belgian Shepherd, study of the head

Groenendael Belgian Shepherd

COAT

This breed has a long-haired coat with an undercoat. Groenendael Belgian Shepherds are black with perhaps some white on the chest and feet. Tervueren Shepherds are red, mealy brown-grey, and every variety of brown to grey, with a black muzzle.

Groenendael Belgian Shepherd

CARE REQUIRED

Do not brush or comb these dogs too much since this can damage the under layer of the coat. During moulting use a coarse-toothed comb to make the coat more respectable in appearance.

CHARACTER

These dogs are energetic, alert, intelligent, eager to work, very lively, and attentive.
Both breeds like to be close to their owner in the home.

TRAINING

Both breeds need to have their confidence strengthened as puppies. Take them to new places and let them, under control, make acquaintance with different people and animals. Make sure these meetings are positive in nature.

They learn quickly and react well to the voice of the handler. Hitting and screaming is both unnecessary and likely to have an adverse effect. A gentle but determined hand works wonders with them. They are suitable for various types of sports, particularly agility competitions, and fly-ball.

SOCIAL BEHAVIOUR

These breeds get on well with their own kind, cats, and other pets provided they have met them when young. So long as children treat them well, they present no problem with children.

They tend to be rather shy with strangers. (Photograph of Tervueren Belgian Shepherd: see page 25).

EXERCISE

When both breeds get sufficient outdoor exercise, they are calm. Most examples of the breed are crazy about retrieving and playing with a ball.

Bergamasco

COUNTRY OF ORIGIN
Italy.

APTITUDE
Sheepdog, guard-dog, and family pet.

SIZE
The dogs weigh 32 – 38kg (70$^1/_2$ – 83$^1/_2$lb) with a shoulder-height of 60cm (23$^1/_2$in). The bitches weigh 26 – 32kg (57 – 70$^1/_2$lb) with a shoulder-height of 56cm (22$^1/_2$in).
The breed standard permits both sexes to be 2cm ($^1/_2$in) shorter.

Fully-grown Bergamsco bitch

COAT
The Bergamsco has a thick under layer to its coat and has a tendency for the outer layer to become felt-like; the hair on the head and shoulders is free from this problem. The coat is plain grey or speckled grey, plain black, or greyish-yellow with fawn markings. White markings

Young Bergamsco male

are permissible provided they do not represent more than 20 per cent of the area of the coat.

CARE REQUIRED
During its first year merely comb the Bergamsco. Thereafter, the coat will start to felt-up and to prevent this you will need to pluck bunches of about 3cm (1^1/$_2$in) diameter out by hand. The hair on the head must be combed. A bath now and then does no harm but it is best given in the summer since it can take more than a day for the coat to dry.

CHARACTER
Intelligent and extremely eager to work, independent, well-balanced and calm, brave and alert, friendly, and bonds very closely with its human family.

TRAINING
Bergamsco is not a difficult breed to bring up and to train. Socialize them well when they are young and remain consistent and clear in your dealings with them.

SOCIAL BEHAVIOUR
Provided they have been correctly socialized, they get on well with other pets.

This breed is generally fine with children; indeed it has a tendency to protect them against being pestered by other children. They make first-class guard-dogs and an extremely unpleasant surprise for anyone who should break into your house. They are rather reserved with those whom they do not know.

EXERCISE
They require plenty of exercise. This is best done with regular walks. Within a large enough, well-fenced area the Bergamsco will happily take care of its own exercise.

They are still used daily to herd livestock, making them true working dogs which do not belong in a small flat.

Maremma Sheepdog

COUNTRY OF ORIGIN
Italy.

APTITUDE
Family pet and guard-dog for herds.

SIZE
The shoulder-height is 63 – 73cm (24^1/$_2$ – 28^1/$_2$in) for dogs and 60 – 68cm (23^1/$_2$ – 26^1/$_2$in) for bitches.

COAT
The coat is long-haired and wiry with a dense under layer. Colours of white with markings of ivory, light yellow, or pale orange are permitted by breed standards.

CARE REQUIRED
This breed requires regular thorough grooming with both brush and comb to remove all the

Maremma Sheepdog

They can be slightly reserved with strangers but not strongly so. Someone with no right to be on your property gets no chance to step on to it.

EXERCISE
This breed needs space, mentally as well as physically. Do not condemn this dog to a walk-around three times a day. Long and alternating walks are necessary for this breed. It must indulge itself freely from time tot time. When it gets enough freedom and space, it will be quiet in the house.

Maremma Sheep dog

dead and loose hairs. This requires particular attention during the moulting period.

CHARACTER
This dog is friendly and loyal, sober, determined, brave, intelligent, dignified, well-balanced, and a very good guard-dog without being a constant barker.
They are correctly described as affectionate but not dependent.

TRAINING
This breed is not one to follow your every command slavishly and absolutely never when it cannot see the point in it! Its education and training require mutual respect in handling and voice, and above all consistency.

SOCIAL BEHAVIOUR
This breed gets on well with other dogs and pets, and in general is patient and forgiving with children.

Border Collie

COUNTRY OF ORIGIN
England.

APTITUDE
Sheepdog and cattle-herder.

SIZE
The shoulder-height is 53 – 55cm
($20^{1}/_{2}$ – $21^{1}/_{2}$in) for dogs; bitches are slightly smaller.

COAT
The thick undercoat is medium length and shiny. All colours are permissible but white should not be predominant. Black and white coats are the most usual..

Border Collie

CARE REQUIRED
The Border Collie's coat does not require much attention. Weekly brushing will keep it in good condition.

CHARACTER
This dogs is very eager to work, intelligent and astute, a quick learner, attentive, lively, alert, it forms a very close bond with his handler and family. It is also determined and brave.

TRAINING
The Border Collie is famous throughout the world for its tremendous intelligence and its desire to please. They quickly learn new commands and almost all of them have a natural aptitude for herding sheep.

Border Collie, study of the head

SOCIAL BEHAVIOUR
Provided it gets sufficient activity to keep it occupied and ample exercise, the Border Collie will get along quite happily with other dogs and pets, and children.
If there is insufficient, activity then it will find work to do, which could be herding your children.

EXERCISE
The idle Border Collie will become extremely badly behaved and even aggressive. Physical exercise alone is not sufficient for this breed. They want to work and must do so, with body and mind as one, carrying out different tasks. It is not surprising that at competitive level in various sports - agility skills, obedience, and sheepdog trials, or fly-ball - Border Collies are represented among the top in the sport. They are perfectionists with a permanent will to please. In brief, this breed lives for serving you day in day out.

SPECIAL REMARKS
• This breed is fine in a kennel provided it has daily activity and sees plenty of its handler.
• For those who wish to reach high levels in dog sports, the Border Collie is a gift from heaven. Farmers, for whom the dogs perform the work for which they were bred, are also happy with them. They are not ideal pets.

Briard

COUNTRY OF ORIGIN
France.

APTITUDE
Herding dog, guard-dog, and family pet.

SIZE
The shoulder height is 62 - 68cm (24½ - 26½in) for dogs and 56 - 64cm (22 - 25½in) for bitches.

COAT
The Briard has a long wavy coat of rather dry hair and a light undercoat.
All plain colours are permitted with the exception of white and chestnut. The most usual colours are black and fawn.

CARE REQUIRED
Briards require regular grooming with brush and comb once a week. The inside of the ears must be kept clean and any excessive hair in the ears should also be removed.

This is equally true of the excessive hair which grows between the pads of their feet.

CHARACTER
Intelligent and prepared to work, tough, brave, alert, loyal, slightly dominant, and totally unsuitable for a life in a kennel.
The Briard has no sense of humour, so do not pester it.

TRAINING
Training of the Briard must be consistent, with much patience and love combined with a firm hand. Severe, unjust training will have the same result as none at all.
With poor handling and training the Briard becomes withdrawn and even aggressive. They are happiest in the home as part of the family.

SOCIAL BEHAVIOUR
With the right handler the Briard blossoms as a first-class pet who can happily coexist with other pets.
They can be slightly aggressive towards other dogs. Strangers are viewed with suspicion.

EXERCISE
This breed needs reasonable amounts of exercise. This could be a country walk but swimming and running alongside a cycle are also excellent forms of exercise for them.
They are ideally suited to defence dog/police dog trials.

SPECIAL REMARKS
In countries outside France the Briard will be a novelty who will protect you and your family but this is definitely not the dog for everyone.

Cao da Serra de Aires
(Serra de Aires Mountain dog)

COUNTRY OF ORIGIN
Portugal.

APTITUDE
All-round herding dog, guard-dog, and family pet.

SIZE
The shoulder-height is 45 - 55cm ($17^1/_2$ - $21^1/_2$in) for dogs and 42 - 52cm ($16^1/_2$ - $20^1/_2$in) for bitches.

COAT
The coat is long and smooth or sometimes there is a slight wave; there is no under layer to the coat. The most usual colour is black, but grey, yellow, and brown are also to be found, preferably with tan markings.
A few white hairs are permissible but patches of white hairs are not, except for a white patch on the chest.

CARE REQUIRED
Check regularly for tangles but do not brush the coat too much because it is not good for the tex-

Cao da Serra de Aires

ture of the hair. Trim any excess hair between the pads of the feet. It is said that this breed should be shampooed as little as possible.

CHARACTER
This high spirited, animated, and intelligent dog is eager to work, very loyal and bonds with its own people, is sober, alert, easily learns, but is also stubborn, and dominant.

TRAINING
The Cao da Serra de Aires demands an extremely consistent and well-balanced training. They learn quickly and easily, but can exhibit stubbornness and dominance. It requires a confident handler.

SOCIAL BEHAVIOUR
These dogs mix well with other dogs, and live happily alongside other pets, provided they have been correctly socialized.

They are usually patient with children but the dogs in particular can be possessive of their territory. This breed tends to be reserved with strangers and makes a good watchdog.

EXERCISE
The Cao da Serra de Aires has an extreme stamina. If it gets enough exercise, it will be calm in the house. This breed achieve very well in agility.

German shepherd

COUNTRY OF ORIGIN
Germany.

APTITUDE
Family pet, suitable for a number of other purposes.

SIZE
The shoulder-height is 60 - 65cm ($23^1/_2$ - $25^1/_2$in) for dogs and 55 - 60 cm ($21^1/_2$ - 23 $^1/_2$in) for bitches.

Cao da Serra de Aires

Head of a German Shepherd.

German Shepherd

COAT

The German Shepherd can have three kinds of coat: coarse straight-haired, long coarse straight-haired, and wavy long-haired. The last of these three is less desirable. The coat can be black, iron-grey, ash-coloured, or can be one of these colours with regular brown, or yellow-to-light-brown markings. An upper layer of black is very common.

CARE REQUIRED

The coat has relatively little attention required. During moulting the use of a special comb for their hair will help to remove dead and loose hairs.

CHARACTER

This very intelligent and eager pupil is an obedient, sociable, and friendly dog that is temperamental, attentive, alert, protective, brave, self-assured, independent, and unconditionally loyal towards its handler and family.

TRAINING

Throughout the world these dogs are used as guide dogs, avalanche rescue dogs, tracking dogs, watchdogs, defence dogs, and police dogs. In some of these roles, the German Shepherd is almost the only breed used. In obedience competitions they stand head and shoulders above over breeds. It is therefore unnecessary to explain what the possibilities are with this breed.

It is eager to learn from you, intelligent and quick to get the hang of things. Work principally with your voice. The great majority of the breed worship their handler and has an enormous need for contact with it. If you do not have the time to devote to them, it is not ad-

visable to purchase a German Shepherd. In its Country of origin, the German Shepherd is still used for herding livestock.

SOCIAL BEHAVIOUR

German Shepherds get on well with their own kind, other animals, and children provided they have been correctly socialized, but unwanted visitors are halted. They are territorial by nature which means that they have no tendency whatever to run away.

EXERCISE

People who keep German Shepherds frequently overlook the fact that they are eager to work for their handler. It is not sufficient for them to be companions in the home with nothing else to occupy them.

Join a breed group or other organization so that you can participate together in agility, obedience, defence and police trials, tracking, or whatever else is available, in order to keep your dog both physically and mentally fit. For all

German Shepherd

large dogs, and that includes the German Shepherd, all their energy is needed during the growing stage for healthy bones, joints, and muscles. Damage which cannot be put right can be done by over-exercising or inadequate diet. They can happily live in an outdoor kennel provided they get sufficient exercise and regular attention.

SPECIAL POINTS
The German Shepherd is the only breed for which there is a world-wide umbrella organization engaged in matters relating to the breed. Based in Germany, the WUSV has more than half a million members, distributed through sixty countries.

Dutch Shepherd

COUNTRY OF ORIGIN
The Netherlands.

APTITUDE
Sheepdog and family pet.

SIZE
The shoulder-height is 57 - 62cm ($22^1/_2$ - $24^1/_2$in) for dogs and 55 - 60cm ($21^1/_2$ - $23^1/_2$in) for bitches.

COAT
There are three different types of coat for the Dutch Shepherd: short-haired (silver and gold streaks), rough-haired (blue-grey pepper-and-salt-coloured, or silver and gold streaked), and long-haired (silver and gold streaked).
With all varieties, dogs for the show ring should not display too much white on their chest and feet.

CARE REQUIRED
Both short- and long-haired coats require regular grooming with brush and comb, to remove dead a loose hairs.
The rough-haired coat should never be brushed, although combing is fine, but in moderation, otherwise the coat suffers. Always use a coarse comb. Have the coat plucked by a dog salon twice a year The hair can be clipped in a few places as a finishing touch and the excessive hair in the ears should be removed.

Short-haired Dutch Shepherd

CHARACTER
This affectionate dog is eager to learn, intelligent and obedient, sober, very loyal to its handler and family, incorruptible, active, lively, and alert.

TRAINING
Dutch Shepherds are happy to be all-round dogs. They can and will learn new commands quickly. In certain branches of sport such as agility, fly-ball, and obedience competitions, they can eclipse their rivals. The short-haired type is the most usual sort for defence/police dog trials.

SOCIAL BEHAVIOUR
Dutch Shepherds enjoy the company of their own kind and get along fine with other animals. Provided children allow the dogs to have peace, they can also make good play-mates for children.

Unwanted visitors are halted in their tracks, while known family friends will be greeted enthusiastically.

Rough-haired Dutch Shepherds

EXERCISE

It is good for this breed to let them regularly run beside the cycle, or take it into the woods or open countryside where it can run to its heart's content.

Because Dutch Shepherds want to work, it is advisable to drill them at least twice per week to keep them both physically and mentally fit.

Komondor

COUNTRY OF ORIGIN
Hungary.

APTITUDE
Guard-dog for the herd.

SIZE
The shoulder-height is a minimum of 65cm (25$^1/_2$in) for dogs and a minimum of 60cm (23$^1/_2$in) for bitches.
It is generally preferred to see heights much taller than this. There is no maximum height.

COAT
The coat is the most important distinguishing feature of this breed. This consists of felt-like strands which form and become longer over the years. It can take up to three years for the eventual coat of the Komondor to be formed. The coat is always white.

CARE REQUIRED
Generally this breed is never brushed or combed since it is intended that the felting of the coat will occur. The strands are formed because the soft undercoat is not shed but catches in the tougher, and longer outer hair. To encourage development of the felt strands, they can be teased out by hand. Bathing is best left until summer, since it can take several days for the coat to dry.

CHARACTER
These are independent, dominant, and very alert dogs that are brave, incorruptible, determined, social, very loyal to their handler and family, sober, well-balanced, and calm. They do not naturally bark much. They have the amazing ability to judge whether a person has harmful intentions.

TRAINING
The Komondor is a dog whose natural instincts are still close to nature and it will often rely upon its own instinct. Its training must be consistent and based upon mutual respect.
The Komondor has an uncomplicated charac-

Komondor

country will more to its liking. If the Komondor is kept outdoors, it will naturally inspect its territory and meet its needs for exercise itself. They can be extremely lazy and will sleep and rest for hour upon hour.

Damp and chilly or even cold weather will not harm this breed, they are so well protected by their impenetrable coat.

Kuvasz

COUNTRY OF ORIGIN
Hungary.

APTITUDE
Family pet and guard-dog for the herd and property.

SIZE
The shoulder-height is 71 - 75cm (28 - 29$^1/_2$in) for dogs and 66 - 70cm (26 - 27$^1/_2$in) for bitches. Dogs weight 40 - 52kg (88 - 114$^1/_2$lb), while bitches are somewhat lighter.

COAT
The hair is short on the head and the front of the legs; on the rest of the body the hair is longer. The texture is course and the hair is wavy, with a soft undercoat. The coat is always plain white.

Kuvasz

ter and, once he understands your rules, it will not overstep them. Despite its honest nature, the Komondor needs a confident handler. Because it will only obey an order in which it can seen any point, it is not suitable for obedience courses and similar activities.

SOCIAL BEHAVIOUR
The Komondor will get along fine with other animals and with children provided they are part of your household and family. It will protect your children from being pestered by other children.

Strangers are instinctively mistrusted and unwanted visitors get no chance to step on to your property. Regular visitors with no harm in them will be treated as one of you and treated accordingly.

EXERCISE
It is as possible to keep this breed in an urban environment as in the country, although the

CARE REQUIRED
The Kuvasz has a very thick coat which protects it from all kinds of weather. During moulting this breed loses significant volumes of hair. It is

therefore sensible to brush the Kuvasz thoroughly and regularly and especially during moulting.

CHARACTER

A good watchdog, which is intelligent, barks only when necessary, very independent, brave, dominant, honest, well-balanced, determined, and loyal to the family. The Kuvasz is affectionate but not dependent.

TRAINING

This breed requires a balanced and consistent training and upbringing. The Kuvasz is no breed for beginners; the owner needs to be a confident person.

This also means that a severe hand cannot be used in its training. This dog will learn best in a harmonious environment which provides scope for its own initiative.

SOCIAL BEHAVIOUR

The Kuvasz can be rather dominant towards its own kind, but if it is properly socialized with other animals when young, there will normally be no problems with it towards these animals. Its high pain threshold and stable nature make it tolerant with children but given its independent initiative and large size, it is best not to leave it to look after the children. It is important to know that the Kuvasz will protect people and animals who belong to its family which includes protecting your children from their friends if play becomes a little rough.

EXERCISE

Since the Kuvasz will patrol and inspect its borders a number of times every day, it keeps itself in good condition. If you do not have the space, it will be necessary to take it out regularly because the Kuvasz needs space for its mental well-being as much as the exercise.

Mudi

COUNTRY OF ORIGIN
Hungary.

APTITUDE
Hunting dog (principally for large wild game), herding dog, guard-dog, and family pet.

SIZE
The shoulder height is 35 - 47cm
($13^1/_2$ - $18^1/_2$in).

Head of a Kuvasz

COAT

The hairs of the coat are 3 - 7cm long (1½- 2½in); they are thick and curly or wavy. The length of the hair varies on different parts of the body.

Mudis are coloured black or white or a combination of the two.

CARE REQUIRED

They are very easy to care for. A regular combing is sufficient to keep the coat in good condition.

CHARACTER

This watchful and animated dog is alert and

Head of a Mudi

brave, it barks gladly, learns willingly, is intelligent, slightly independent, and sober. The Mudi has a strong urge to protect the family to which it belongs. Within the family it also has the tendency to bond with one person in particular.

TRAINING

If you take their independent nature into account, Mudis are usually not difficult to educate.

SOCIAL BEHAVIOUR

The Mudi usually gets on well with other dogs and animals, and with children. They are excellent guard-dogs which will protect the entire family without being unduly suspicious of strangers. When circumstances demand courage, the Mudi will display it.

EXERCISE

This breed adapts to any form of exercise. They are suitable for various sporting activities such as agility and fly-ball.

Mudi

Old English Sheepdog

COUNTRY OF ORIGIN
England.

APTITUDE
Sheepdog and family pet.

SIZE
The shoulder-height is a minimum of 60cm (23½in) for dogs and 56cm (22in) for bitches.

COAT
The coat is luxuriant, rough, tough, and long, with a waterproof under-layer. Permitted colours are blue or different shades of grey. The head, neck, front quarters, and belly are white, with or without markings. White patches in the blue on the back are not permissible.

CARE REQUIRED

These dogs require regular grooming: brush them thoroughly at least once a week, not overlooking the places where tangles form. During moulting it is quite possible to collect half or even a whole rubbish bag full of hair that you have brushed off it.

Keep the inside of its ears clean and remove both dirt and hair. The claws must be kept short so clip them regularly. Excessive hair between the pads of the feet should also be trimmed. For successful showing, the rear of the dog must be higher than the shoulders and this is sometimes accentuated for the show ring.

Sometimes they are trimmed, which, however unpopular with some enthusiasts, is better than a mass of tangled hair. It begs the question why anyone should acquire a long-haired dog and then have it clipped.

Old English Sheepdog

CHARACTER

Intelligent, considerable adaptability, amiable, social, not particularly alert, boisterous, uncomplicated nature, and likes to be part of the family.

TRAINING

This breed needs gentle and consistent handling during training. It wants to please you and rarely displays dominant behaviour, making it suitable for people with little experience of the upbringing of dogs. Because grooming forms so important a part of the general care for this breed, it is important to brush it as young as possible.

This prevents grooming degenerating into a wrestling match when it is much larger and stronger.

SOCIAL BEHAVIOUR

The Old English Sheepdog gets on exceptionally well with other animals, dogs, and children. Visitors too will be greeted warmly.

EXERCISE

This breed needs a fair amount of exercise but it will not misbehave if you miss a day through a shortage of time.
Most of the breed are crazy about playing with a ball and are well represented as competitors in various sports.

Old English Sheepdog groomed ready for a show

Picardy Shepherd

Picardy Shepherd

COUNTRY OF ORIGIN
France.

APTITUDE
Watchdog, sheepdog, and family pet.

SIZE
The shoulder-height is 60 - 65cm
(23$^1/_2$- 25$^1/_2$in) for dogs and 55 - 60cm
(21$^1/_2$ - 23$^1/_2$in) for bitches.

COAT
The coat consists of coarse and wiry, medium-length hair.
The colours are grey, grey-black, blue-grey, red-grey, and light or darker fawn. A small white patch on the feet is not desirable but is permissible.

CARE REQUIRED
The Picardy Shepherd requires regular grooming with both brush and comb. The coat should on no account be trimmed.

CHARACTER
Energetic, intelligent, alert, loyal, amiable with children, and a little wilful. Usually they behave rather detachedly towards strangers. They like to bark and do so frequently which is a disadvantage if you live surrounded by other people.

Picardy Shepherds

Head of a Picardy Shepherd

Head of a Picardy Shepherd

To really please this dog, enrol it for an agility skills course, for fly-ball, or obedience training.

They do not do well in competition, because they find it impossible to perform consistently.

Polish Lowland Sheepdog

Polish Lowland Sheepdog

TRAINING
The Picardy Shepherd must be properly socialized when young if it is to grow up as a well-balanced dog. Training this breed, which is full of character, is not an easy matter since they can be wilful and can sometimes be subject to fits of bad humour.
If you decide on this breed, then you must learn to accept these moods; try hard not to break the dog's resistance because this can really harm its character.

They are very sensitive to the voice and it is necessary to tread carefully as you first begin to train them. Cheerfully given commands generally work best.

SOCIAL BEHAVIOUR
Contact with other animals and children is not generally a problem. The Picardy Shepherd wants lots of attention from its handler and is not happy to share it with other dogs.

EXERCISE
This breed of dog requires lots of exercise. Running alongside a cycle, swimming, and walking are all ideal ways to channel their energy in a positive direction.

COUNTRY OF ORIGIN
Poland.

APTITUDE
Sheepdog and family pet.

SIZE
The shoulder-height is 45 - 50cm ($17^1/_2$ - $19^1/_2$in) for dogs and 42 - 47cm ($16^1/_2$ - $18^1/_2$in) for bitches.
Dogs weigh about 20kg (44lb), while bitches are in the region of 18kg ($39^1/_2$lb).

COAT
This breed has a long, wire-haired coat with a soft under-layer. All colours are permitted - the most usual being white with grey or black, or plain grey.

CARE REQUIRED
The coat needs to be groomed thoroughly with a brush once a week to prevent tangles.

CHARACTER
This animated, happy, and alert dog has a good memory, is obedient and intelligent, affectionate, and slightly lacking in confidence with strangers.

TRAINING

This breed is easy to educate. The dog learns quickly and is happy to do things for its handler.

SOCIAL BEHAVIOUR

The Polish Lowland Sheepdog is a breed that is excellent with children, dogs, and other pets. Visitors will be announced at the top of its voice.

EXERCISE

This dog's origins are as a working dog. Previously it watched over the herds and flocks on the extensive Polish plains and it remains a herding dog in heart and mind.

Consequently it is not a town dog which will be content with three little outings per day. Its brain needs stimulating with changes of scenery and preferably with something to do.

Join a dog group where it can join in agility training, or fly-ball which are both activities it will relish.

Polish Lowland Sheepdog

Thirteen year-old Hungarian Puli

Puli

Hungarian Puli

COUNTRY OF ORIGIN

Hungary.

APTITUDE

Sheepdog or family pet.

SIZE

The desired shoulder height is 40 - 44cm (15^1/$_2$ -17^1/$_2$in) for dogs and 37 - 41cm (14^1/$_2$ - 16^1/$_2$in) for bitches. The weight is 10 - 15kg (22 - 33lb).

COAT

The coat of the Puli is its trademark. These dogs are richly covered in long cords of felted hair. The Puli is usually black, but white, broken white, and black with apricot are also known.

CARE REQUIRED

The Puli's distinctive coat does not fully develop until the third year. The soft under layer does not fall out but becomes felt on the outer, and harder hairs. If required, the felted strands are teased to encourage the development of the felt strands or cords.

An advantage of this coat is that the Puli does not moult, but there is the disadvantage that all manner of dirt and small objects can become caught up in the hairs. Wash the Puli in the summer because the long coat will take several days to dry fully.

CHARACTER

This intelligent dog learns easily, is full of character, animated, a good watchdog, and loyal to the family.

This breed is very adaptable to the circumstances surrounding it although the dogs can be somewhat independent. A Puli will rarely run away.

Hungarian Pumi

TRAINING
This breed requires a very consistent approach to training which needs to take place within the first year. They do not like boring drills, preferring a challenge.

Vary the training routine constantly and ensure plenty of play within the exercises. This breed usually learns quickly.

SOCIAL BEHAVIOUR
They normally get on well with their own kind, other animals, and generally like children. They have the tendency to bond closely with one member of the family.

EXERCISE
This breed is in its element if it can romp and play and with its unusual coat this is delightful to watch.

If you enjoy it, you could enrol both of you for agility skills or fly-ball courses. The Hungarian Puli usually does well in both activities.

Hungarian Pumi

Hungarian Pumi

COUNTRY OF ORIGIN
Hungary.

APTITUDE
Sheepdog or companion.

SIZE
The desired shoulder height is 35 - 44cm ($13^1/_2$ -$17^1/_2$in).

COAT
The coat consists of medium length hair in tufts. In some places the hairs are shorter and rougher; in others they are longer and tangled. The coat has a rather unkempt look about it. The most common colours are slate-grey and other tints of grey; black and white also exist, but patches are not permissible.

CARE REQUIRED
The Pumi requires relatively little grooming. Brush the coat right through about once a week and remove excessive hair from inside the ears. For showing, the Pumi is specially prepared.

CHARACTER
Attentive, alert, likes to bark, dapper, energetic, temperamental, intelligent, learns readily, and sober.

TRAINING
This is not a difficult breed to train. They are intelligent enough to grasp what you mean quickly.
If you live surrounded by neighbours, it is sensible to teach the dog that after a couple of barks it must be quiet.

SOCIAL BEHAVIOUR
The Pumi can be shy and rather mistrustful of strangers. There are breeds that are better for families with children but a well brought-up Pumi will cause no problems with children provided they do not pester it.

EXERCISE
This is an outdoors dog and at its best living on a farm where it will find work enough to do for himself, such as guarding the entrance, and keeping the livestock together.

If it is to live in an urban environment then you must find replacement activities to keep it occupied.
They do well in both fly-ball and agility skills classes.

SPECIAL POINTS
Not widely known in areas where there is insufficient work and outlet for this active, free-booting workaholic.

Pyrenean Sheepdog

Pyrenean Sheepdog

COUNTRY OF ORIGIN
France.

APTITUDE
All-round herding dog and family pet.

SIZE
The shoulder height is 40 - 50cm (15^1/$_2$ - 19^1/$_2$in) for dogs and 38 - 48cm (15 - 18^1/$_2$in) for bitches.

COAT
The coat consists of fairly long, or at least medium length hair with either a strong curl or lighter wave. They can be sandy-coloured, with or without black hairs, streaky grey, or black with white markings.

CARE REQUIRED
They need little attention to their coats. The breed is supposed to look natural and rather rustic and the coat is of such a texture that at most a quarter of an hour a week with a brush is sufficient.

Do not forget to remove excessive hair regularly from inside the ear. Wash its short beard from time to time unless you can find another way to keep it clean.

CHARACTER
An intelligent dog that is ready to work, alert and quick, vigilant, animated, with good scenting powers, and which is loving with children but not smotheringly so. The Pyrenean Sheepdog enjoys an outdoor life.

TRAINING
Requires consistent, strict and honest training that is not too tough. It is ready to work and can and will learn. The Pyrenean Sheepdog who is condemned to its basket with nothing to look forward to other than a trot around the block three times a day will become troublesome. They are ideally suited for training as rescue dogs and also do well in activities such as fly-ball and agility classes.

SOCIAL BEHAVIOUR
This breed gets on well with families, including the children. There is also no problem with other pets provided it has had good experien-

Pyrenean Sheepdogs

ces with them as a young dog. They are some-what cautious with strangers.

EXERCISE
It is advisable to spend at least an hour each day in activity with the dog; walking is fine, so are dog sports.

Saarloos Wolfhound

COUNTRY OF ORIGIN
The Netherlands.

APTITUDE
Family pet.

SIZE
The shoulder height is 65 - 75cm ($25^1/_2$ - $29^1/_2$in) for dogs and 60 - 70cm ($23^1/_2$ - $27^1/_2$in) for bitches.

COAT
The coat is smooth and to be found in wolf grey, forest brown, cream, and white.
The most usual colours are wolf grey and forest brown.

Wolf grey Saarloos Wolfhound, study of the head

CARE REQUIRED
The coat is easily looked after. The type of comb available for German Shepherds is ideal for their grooming. Comb regularly and keep the inside of the ears clean.

CHARACTER
This intelligent, careful, and alert dog has a good scenting nose, and affectionate.

This breed is patient with children. They bark rarely and come into season only once per year.

TRAINING
Early mixing with other dogs, animals and people is necessary - before the tenth week - if this breed is to grow up as a well-balanced dog. Let it be acquainted with all manner of situations in a positive way.
They learn commands easily but this is not a breed from which to expect absolute obedience.

SOCIAL BEHAVIOUR
These are really sociable dogs and they present no problem with other dogs or with children if you have heeded the advice given in the previous paragraph.
If the early contacts have been well handled, the Saarloos Wolfhound will behave perfectly. They tend to be cautious about both strangers and new situations.

EXERCISE
The breed has a fairly average need for exercise. If the occasion arises in which you are forced to miss a walk one day, it will accept it without fuss.

SPECIAL REMARKS
Saarloos Wolfhounds are healthy dogs. For a dog of its size it can live to be quite old - thirteen or fourteen years old is not uncommon. The breed is little known outside its native country and is a comparatively recent arrival, having been bred by crossing German Shepherds with Wolves.

The Czech Wolfhound is an apart breed that also came into existence in a similar way. Both dogs have similar characters, although it is considered that the Czech breed is rather tougher and more independent in character.

Schapendoes

COUNTRY OF ORIGIN
The Netherlands.

APTITUDE
Sheepdog and family pet.

SIZE
The shoulder height is 43 - 50cm (17 - 19½in) for dogs and 40 - 47cm (16 - 18in) for bitches. The weight is about 15kg (33lb).

COAT
The Schapendoes has a double coat: the outer layer is long, dry-textured, and wavy, while the inner layer is thick and soft. All colours are permissible, but blue-grey to black is generally the most popular.

Schapendoes

CARE REQUIRED
It is not intended that the Schapendoes should appear to be highly groomed but it is necessary to brush and comb them regularly to prevent tangles. When this is done, clean in the ears as well but do not use cotton buds. It is quite normal for the hair to cover the eyes and certainly this should not held clear with a hair band. Check the eyes regularly for both dirt and loose hair.

CHARACTER
This happy, cunning dog is eager to learn, alert, brave, attentive, very loyal to the family, very playful and lively, and affectionate.

TRAINING
The Schapendoes will feel at home in a sporty family in which it can have a well-balanced upbringing.

It will enjoy obedience classes, and greatly value subsequent agility classes and competition.

SOCIAL BEHAVIOUR
It is this breed's nature to get on well with its own kind, other pets, and with children. They give voice if they detect trouble.

EXERCISE
Just as with countless other breeds, the Schapendoes needs exercise to rid it of its abundant energy.

It is advisable to let it run and play off the lead for at least an hour a day. Provided it gets sufficient exercise, it is extremely peaceful indoors.

Most Schapendoes love to play, swim, and retrieve.

Schapendoes

Schipperke

COUNTRY OF ORIGIN
Belgium.

APTITUDE
Vermin destroyer and family pet.

SIZE
The shoulder-height is 25 - 30cm ($9^1/_2$- $11^1/_2$in).
In Belgium and France they are classified in
two groups by weight: those of 5 - 8kg (11 -
$17^1/_2$lb), and others of 3 - 5kg ($6^1/_2$ - 11lb). In
other countries the weight for the breed standard is usually 5 - 8kg (11 - $17^1/_2$lb).

COAT
A tough coat with a soft under layer. Around
the neck, or mane, and by the hindquarters, the
hair is much longer. The normal colour is black;
some countries permit other colours including
blonde.

CARE REQUIRED
This breed has little grooming needed. An occasional brushing will keep them in excellent condition.

CHARACTER
These are attentive, self-confident, cunning and
high spirited dogs that are lively, determined,
constant, tireless, alert, and loyal to the family.

TRAINING
This breed is easily alerted and barks at the first
sign of trouble.
Where you are surrounded by other homes, it is
good neighbourly to teach it that a couple of
barks are sufficient.

Generally they are easy to train; they are intelligent and eager to learn.

SOCIAL BEHAVIOUR
This breed will defend its territory - whether
that is a flat or a large area of land - against both
two-legged and four-legged intruders.
If someone new visits, they will adopt a watchful position. The pet cat will be happily accepted. Generally they are quite good with children.

EXERCISE
The Schipperke is a bundle of dynamite. To be
happy, it needs to be able to play and run about
a great deal.
In addition to daily walks, let it run about in the
garden or park off the lead.

Short-haired Border Collie with blue marbling

Border Collie, short-haired

COUNTRY OF ORIGIN
Northern England and Scotland.

APTITUDE
Sheepdog and family pet.

SIZE
The shoulder-height is 56- 61cm (22 - 24in) for
dogs and 51 - 56cm (20 - 22in) for bitches.

COAT
The coat is dense and short-haired. They can be sable with white, a blue-black, or triple-coloured (mainly black with white and tan markings).

CARE REQUIRED
They need regular grooming with a brush and comb and lose copious amounts of hair during moulting.

CHARACTER
These are happy, very intelligent dogs which are eager to work, cunning, sociable, protective, energetic, alert, loveable, watchful, sensitive, affectionate, they bond closely with their family members.
Like most dogs in this group, they have no tendency to run away. They would rather stay close to you.

TRAINING
A fairly quick learner who is pleased to work for you. The best results are achieved by variations in intonation of your voice. Never scream at it or punish severely.

Short-haired Border Collie, sable and triple-coloured

SOCIAL BEHAVIOUR
This breed gets on well with its own kind, other pets, and children. Visitors whom you wish to see are given a friendly welcome.

EXERCISE
The adult of this breed needs plenty of exercise although it is capable of adapting itself if you fail to take it for a long walk on the odd day. Most of them enjoy retrieving and playing with a ball and they perform well in obedience and agility classes, and at fly-ball.
Care needs to be taken with young dogs during the growing stage so that their energy is directed into growing healthy bones, joints and muscles.

Long-haired Border Collie

Border Collie, long-haired

COUNTRY OF ORIGIN
Northern England and Scotland.

APTITUDE
Sheepdog and family pet.

SIZE
The shoulder-height is 56 - 61cm (22 - 24in) for dogs and 51 - 56cm (20 - 22in) for bitches.

COAT
The long-haired coat is very close; a definite collar "ruff" is a desired feature for showing. They are available in sable, blue-black, and three-colours.
The three-colours are chiefly black with white and tan markings.

Long-haired Border Collie

prevent tangles. During moulting, daily brushing and combing is necessary.

CHARACTER
These happy, very intelligent dogs are eager to work, sociable, cunning, protective, energetic, attentive, loveable, watchful, sensitive, affectionate, and bonds very closely with their family.

TRAINING
The Border Collie learns quickly and is best trained using the intonation of your voice.

SOCIAL BEHAVIOUR
Most Border Collies get on well with other pets, their own kind, and with children. Visitors you wish to see will be enthusiastically welcomed.

EXERCISE
They are very adaptable but you are hardly fair to your dog if you expect it to suffice on a quick turn around the block three times a day. Allow it to run and play off the lead. Most of them are fond of playing with a ball and retrieving. They can compete on level-terms at activities such as agility skills, fly-ball, and obedience competitions. During the growing stage it is important to ensure that their energies are available for building healthy bones, joints and, muscles.

CARE REQUIRED
They required regular grooming about once a week consisting of a thorough brushing. In the areas of the coat that are thickest, the brushing should be worked right through to the skin to

Long-haired Border Collies

Shetland Sheepdog

COUNTRY OF ORIGIN
Scotland.

APTITUDE
Sheepdog or family pet.

SIZE
The shoulder-height is 37cm (14^1/$_2$in) for dogs and 35.5cm (14in) for bitches. Deviation of 2.5cm (1in) above and below these standards is permissible.

COAT
They have a double coat: the outer layer consists of long wiry hair, whilst the inner layer is soft, short, and close. Shetland Sheepdogs are bred in sable (light sandy-coloured to mahogany), with and without black tips to the hairs, and also in three-colours (black with tan and white markings), blue-black, and black-white. The most attractive look is the three-colours with white feet, white chest, collar ruff, blaze, and tip of the tail.

CARE REQUIRED
The care of the Shetland Sheepdog is not demanding; grooming with brush and comb are needed, especially during moulting. Tangles

Blue-black Shetland Sheepdog

form, particularly behind the ears, the hindquarters, and beneath the shoulders. Make sure these areas are attended to during grooming.

CHARACTER
This extremely intelligent, and cunning dog is loyal to its handler and family, affectionate, obedient, responsive, happy, considerable stamina, and fairly robust.

Shetland Sheepdogs

TRAINING

Not a difficult breed to train. The Shetland Sheepdog learns happily and enjoys being busy. For this reason it is an excellent idea to enrol in obedience training classes and to follow a course for agility competition. You will see how much enjoyment it gets from these activities.

SOCIAL BEHAVIOUR

These are extremely sociable dogs who usually get on extremely well with their own kind, cats, and small animals. Provided children leave the dog in peace, there will be no problems. They are cautions and watchful with strangers.

EXERCISE

They will readily adapt to the circumstances but you will harm an intelligent and workaholic animal if you do not engage it in plenty of activity.

They enjoy learning and love to be out with their handler. They are high performers in various areas of dog sports.

SPECIAL REMARKS

This breed is known to get too big. If you wish to show it, bear this in mind.

Tatra Mountain Sheepdog

COUNTRY OF ORIGIN

Poland.

APTITUDE

Watchdog, herding dog, family pet.

Tatra Mountain Sheepdog

SIZE

The shoulder-height is 65 - 70cm ($25^1/_2$ - $27^1/_2$in) for dogs and 60 - 65cm ($23^1/_2$ - $25^1/_2$in) for bitches.

COAT

The hair is short on the head and on the front of the legs; elsewhere, it is thicker and longer. Both straight and curly hair are permitted by the breed standard. The colour is always very white without markings.

CARE REQUIRED

Except during moulting little attention is needed to maintain the coat, which does not readily tangle.

During moulting they need regular grooming with brush and comb to remove loose and dead hair.

CHARACTER

Quiet, well-balanced, sociable, brave, obedient, intelligent, loyal, watchful, affectionate, they are not independent.

TRAINING

The Tatra requires a handler who radiates an air of calm control. Training needs to be consistent and conducted in peace and harmony. Treating them severely works counter-productively. The breed can be independent-minded to the extent that they will only obey commands in which they can see any point.

SOCIAL BEHAVIOUR

Tatra Mountain Sheepdogs generally get on with other pets, dogs, and children. Bear in mind they will take the side of your children if play with other children becomes rough.
They are somewhat reserved towards strangers.

EXERCISE

This is an outdoor dog which never is not suitable for a flat or even a terraced house with a small garden. The coat protects it from all kinds of weather. Regular long walks are much to its liking but it is not interested in playing ball games or such like.

The Tatra Mountain Sheepdog can cope perfectly well in a kennel provided it gets sufficient daily exercise and attention.

Tatra, study of the head

Welsh Corgi (Cardigan)

no extensive walks before the dogs is fully grown, and do not let it go up and down stairs too often during this time.

SOCIAL BEHAVIOUR
The Cardigan can be rather reckless with other dogs. It is important to socialize them early with cats and other animals, to prevent some problems in the future. Usually they get on well with children.

EXERCISE
This breed likes to be outdoors. Take it regularly for long and varied walks. With such a dog there are a number of sporting activities to involve both of you, for example fly-ball and agility skills trials.
Cardigans have been used as avalanche search and rescue dogs.

Welsh Corgi (Cardigan), brindle

Welsh Corgi (Cardigan)

COUNTRY OF ORIGIN
Wales.

APTITUDE
Herding dog and family pet.

SIZE
The ideal shoulder-height is 30.5cm (12in). Cardigan dogs are permitted to weigh 15 - 18kg (33 - 39 1/2 lbs); bitches are somewhat lighter.

COAT
The short-haired coat is weather-resistant. Any colour is permitted provided that white areas do not exceed 30 per cent. Widely found colours are brindle, black with white, beige and blue-black.

CARE REQUIRED
The Cardigan will be satisfied with as little grooming as possible. Brush occasionally to remove dead hairs.

CHARACTER
This intelligent dog is eager to learn, hardy and brave, bonds with its handler and family, fairly calm by nature, and has an especially good sense of humour.

TRAINING
Generally this is a problem-free breed to bring up; it will gladly learn from you, and is quick to understand. This makes it successful in several of the sporting activities for dogs. Care is needed during the growing stage, which means

Welsh Corgi (Pembroke)

COUNTRY OF ORIGIN
Wales.

APTITUDE
Herding dog and family pet.

SIZE
The shoulder-height is 25 - 30.5cm (9 1/2 - 12in). The dogs weigh 9 - 11kg (20 - 24lb).

COAT
The coat consists of hard straight hairs and is water-resistant. They can have coats of red, beige (or sable), and black-and-tan, with and without white markings on the chest, neck and, legs. Some white markings are permitted on the head and muzzle.

Welsh Corgies (Pembroke) with undocked tail

CARE REQUIRED
The Pembroke's coat requires very little grooming; use a good brush from time to time in order to remove any dead hair.

CHARACTER
Full of energy, this dog bonds with its handler and family, and is alert, hardy, very self-assured, intelligent, eager to learn, and sometimes is too brave.

TRAINING
These are not difficult dogs to train and to bring up because of their high intelligence and quick learning ability.

SOCIAL BEHAVIOUR
Pembrokes get on well with children provided they do not tease them, for they have no tolerance whatever of such treatment.
The breed is alert but not over-suspicious of strangers. They can be rather dominant towards their own kind.

EXERCISE
Give Pembrokes the chance to burn off their energy; three times a day quickly around the block is not sufficient exercise for them.

They usually have no tendency to wander, even if your property is not fenced, since they become attached to your house and garden.
It is advisable to ensure varied "work" for them; this might include agility skills, and fly-ball, which are very suitable for this breed.

Welsh Corgi (Pembroke), study of the head

South Russian Owtcharka, study of the head

nant, but it is sober, alert, cannot be led astray by bribes, is honest, loyal, demanding of itself, very brave, and intelligent.

They have razor-sharp reactions, unusual for such a large dog. They are somewhat independent and make their own decisions.

TRAINING

Training needs to be founded on mutual respect and it is essential to treat the dog fairly and with careful consistency.

SOCIAL BEHAVIOUR

This dog gets on with children but they must avoid plaguing it because this definitely does not amused it.

If it grows up among other dogs and household pets, or cattle, the South Russian Owtcharka will accept and protect these animals from people who would harm them.

They do not usually form good relationships with cats - their ancestors were fleet-footed hunting dogs.

The South Russian Owtcharka eyes strange visitors suspiciously, and unwanted ones will get no chance to step onto your property. Regular visitors will be recognized and adopted by it as one of its own.

South Russian Owtcharka

COUNTRY OF ORIGIN
Ukraine.

APTITUDE
Sheepdog and watchdog.

SIZE
The shoulder-height is a minimum of 65cm (25$^1/_2$in) for dogs and 62cm (24in) for bitches.

COAT
The South Russian Owtcharka has a weather-resistant coat which is long, coarse, and bristly, with a thick under-layer.

The colours are white or grey-cream (in various possible tints), or white with grey markings.

CARE REQUIRED
This breed requires relatively little grooming. A weekly brushing will keep the coat in good condition.

CHARACTER
This breed is full of character and rather domi-

South Russian Owtcharka

EXERCISE
The South Russian Owtcharka will take care of its own needs for exercise if it lives on a well-fenced property.

They tend to inspect the boundaries of their territory, which keeps them fit. These are not suitable dogs for a small plot in a busy neighbourhood or for a flat. This breed is happy to be outside and is not troubled in any way by bad weather.

SPECIAL REMARKS
The South Russian Owtcharka is suitable for people with enough room and space, preferably in remote regions. It is a good watchdog without presenting itself too much. This breed bonds strongly to its territory and usually has problems in adapting itself to an new boss and new surroundings.

Cattle drivers

Australian Cattle Dog

COUNTRY OF ORIGIN
Australia.

APTITUDE
Cattle driver and family pet.

SIZE
The shoulder-height is 46 - 51cm (18 - 20in) for dogs and 43 - 48cm (17 - 18^1/$_2$in) for bitches.

COAT
The outer layer of the coat is weather-resistant, short and fairly rough; the under-layer is short and thick. Two colours are permitted: the first is blue, by which is meant plain blue, but also blue speckled with and without black, and blue with tan markings.
The other colour is described as speckled red, which may include dark speckled red markings on the head.

CARE REQUIRED
The coat of the Australian Cattle Dog does not require much attention. An occasional grooming with brush or comb is sufficient.

CHARACTER
The Australian Cattle Dog is very intelligent and willing to work, well-balanced, barks little, is loyal to its handler, brave, hardy, alert, optimistic, and active.

TRAINING
The Australian Cattle Dog is a very intelligent dog which is eager to learn and ready to work. Training it is therefore easy. You will be unfair to it if you do not work with it. Agility skill trials are an ideal activity, but the dog will equally enjoy fly-ball, or other sports. Provide

you keep it intensively active, it will not disappoint you.
A bored Australian Cattle Dog will be a major problem and will find ways to amuse itself that will not endear it to you.

SOCIAL BEHAVIOUR
This breed's behaviour towards its own kind, other pets, and children is a perfect example for other dogs. This model behaviour can only be achieved though if the dog is adequately socialized when very young.

EXERCISE
This breed needs lots of exercise and plenty to occupy it to keep it in good physical and mental health, and in top condition.

If you are seeking a family dog with which you do not have to be very active, then forget this breed.

Australian Cattle Dog

Bouvier des Flandres

COUNTRY OF ORIGIN
Belgium.

APTIDUDE
Historically a cattle driver, nowadays guard dog, defence dog, and family pet.

SIZE
The shoulder height is 62 - 68cm (24^1/$_2$ - 26^1/$_2$in) for dogs and 59 - 65cm (23^1/$_2$ - 25^1/$_2$in) for bitches. The ideal shoulder height is 65cm (25^1/$_2$in) for dogs and 62cm (24^1/$_2$in) for bitches.

COAT
The rough-haired coat is dry-textured, without a sheen. The hair, which may not be too long, has light whirls but is not curly. Permitted colours are dun or grey, streaked or highlighted. Plain black is not favoured for showing but is permissible. Blonde Bouviers are not considered acceptable.

CARE REQUIRED
A Bouvier needs to be trimmed at least three times a year. Between trims remove any excess of hair inside the ears and trim hair between the pads of the feet.
Do not let the hair grow too long close to the feet but trim it so that the Bouvier has nice round feet. A well groomed Bouvier sheds little hair in the home.

CHARACTER
The Bouvier des Flandres is very loyal, bonds with both its handler and family. This alert, brave, hardy, equable, and intelligent dog enjoys working, and is sensible.

TRAINING
The Bouvier requires well-balanced training which remains consistent in nature. It is important to make the dog aware, without being too hard with it, that you are and will remain the boss.

This is an intelligent breed which learns new commands relatively fast, though not quite at the tempo of a German Shepherd. Once they have learned something, they will remember it for the rest of their lives.

SOCIAL BEHAVIOUR
Bouviers are generally sociable animals and provided they have been well socialized with cats when young, they get on well with other pets, and their own kind. Children and Bouviers generally form a good combination. They regard strangers with suspicion and are very protective for the family; their loyalty is world-famous.

EXERCISE
This dog has an average demand for exercise. Take it regularly for a long walk, or let it run beside you on a cycle as a good form of exercise. During the growing stage exercise needs to be carefully regulated so that growing bones, joints and muscles are not to strenuously stressed. The dog requires all its energy to build a strong frame.

Bouvier des Flandres

Bouvier des Flandres puppies

2. Pinscher, Schnauzer, Molossian, Mastiff, and Swiss Sennenhund breeds

Pinschers and Schnauzers

Affenpinscher

COUNTRY OF ORIGIN
Germany.

APTITUDE
Vermin destroyer, watchdog, and family pet.

SIZE
The shoulder-height is 25 - 30cm ($9^1/_2$ - $11^1/_2$in).

COAT
The Affenpinscher has coarse hair which grows in whirls. The coat is usually plain black, but russet brown and grey markings are accepted.

CARE REQUIRED
It may be necessary to pluck the Affenpinscher's coat. This is usually done by a dog trimming specialist but it is possible to learn how to do it yourself. The hair should never be clipped because this ruins the coat for many years. Hairs sometimes grow in the corners of the eyes, causing irritation; these should be dealt with promptly.

CHARACTER
Lively, cheerful, friendly, alert, undaunting, dependent, and sharp-witted.

TRAINING
Affenpinschers learn commands fairly quickly. Ensure consistency in the training but make sure there is ample variety in the drills.

SOCIAL BEHAVIOUR
Affenpinschers get on well with children, and can also be fine with their own sort, and other household pets. If you get visitors who are unknown to him, the Affenpinscher will refuse them entry.

Affenpinscher

EXERCISE
This breed is happy if you take it for a quick trot around the corner three times a day. If you also play with it regularly, then its happiness is complete.

Dobermann

COUNTRY OF ORIGIN
Germany.

APTITUDE
Guard- and defence-dog, and family pet.

SIZE
The shoulder-height is 68 - 72cm ($26^1/_2$ - $28^1/_2$in) for dogs and 63 - 68cm (25 - 27in) for bitches.
The weight is between 32 - 45kg ($70^1/_2$ - 99lb) for dogs.

Clipped brown Dobermann

COAT

The colour of the sleek smooth coat of short hairs is often black and tan, or brown and tan. Coats of blue and tan, or grey-yellow and tan are not recognized in every country.

CARE REQUIRED

A Dobermann's coat does not require much attention. During moulting use a rubber glove with knobbled surface to remove dead and loose hairs. Keep the claws short and check the teeth from time to time for tartar.

CHARACTER

This active, cunning dog bonds closely and is brave, intelligent, a good guard-dog, loyal, dependent, occasionally noisy and boisterous, and has tremendous stamina. Dobermann's have a tendency to become a one-person's-dog.

TRAINING

This strong, handsome dog requires very careful and consistent training. Strive to ensure everything is harmonious throughout the training. If you have little experience of training dogs, then you are seriously advised not to acquire one of this breed. Many Dobermanns are neurotic if wrongly brought-up (and unfortunately this is all too frequent), making them fearful and/or snappy - while their natural character is straightforward and reliable.

Always act clearly and fairly with a Dobermann; never hit it and make absolutely sure it is not pestered. They are ideally suited to defence-dog training, but do not start too young and avoid too much pressure on the dog in the early stages - never force it! Wait for really serious activity until a Dobermann has matured somewhat.

SOCIAL BEHAVIOUR

A properly socialized Dobermann can get along fine with dogs, other household pets, and children. Unwanted visitors are stopped in their tracks.

EXERCISE

A Dobermann cannot be fobbed off with a daily trot around the neighbourhood. It is built for speed and has tremendous stamina. Take it swimming, or let it run alongside a cycle, or run free in the woods.

This breed is ideal for a variety of sporting activities.

Dobermanns are excellent working dogs

German Pinscher

COUNTRY OF ORIGIN
Germany.

APTITUDE
Vermin destroyer, watchdog, and family pet.

SIZE
The shoulder height is 45 - 50cm ($17^1/_2$ - $19^1/_2$in).

COAT
The German Pinscher's coat is smooth-haired and plain red, or black and tan.

CARE REQUIRED
The German Pinscher requires little grooming; an occasional brushing to remove dead hairs is all that is necessary.

CHARACTER
This happy, very intelligent and cunning dog is vigilant, alert, friendly, playful, patient with children, loyal to its own family, a sense of humour, brave, not squeamish, sober, and has considerable stamina. German Pinschers only bark when necessary.

TRAINING
This breed learns quickly and makes a keen pupil. It is necessary to be firm to some extent, but in a loving and consistent way. German Pinschers are capable of doing well in various sporting activities.

SOCIAL BEHAVIOUR
German Pinschers usually get on very well with children. Visitors will be announced with loud barking but then things usually calm down quickly.
The dog will defend its territory, handler and the family to the end against those intent upon harm. Normally they get on without problems with other household pets.

EXERCISE
This breed has an average need for exercise. They enjoy running alongside you when you cycle, but should you perhaps be too busy then it will be happy with three turns around the locality, provided you also take time to play with the dog in the garden.

German Pinschers

German Pinscher

Miniature Pinscher

COUNTRY OF ORIGIN
Germany.

APTITUDE
Family pet.

SIZE
The shoulder height is 25 - 30 cm ($9^1/_2$ - $11^1/_2$in).

COAT
The Miniature Pinscher has a very short-haired

Black and tan Miniature Pinscher

coat. The colour is basically brown but can vary through various shades of brown, including deer red to black and tan.

CARE REQUIRED
The Miniature Pinscher requires little grooming. During moulting, use a rubber brush to remove dead and loose hairs; follow this by wiping the coat with a damp cloth to encourage the hair to shine.

CHARACTER
This lively, alert and vigilant dog likes to bark, is intelligent, sober, somewhat (over)courageous, dependent, loyal to its handler and learns quickly.

TRAINING
Many people seem to feel that just rudimentary training is sufficient with a small dog. This is a pity because the Miniature Pinscher can learn extremely well and wants very much to do so. It is certainly valuable for its socialization to take the dog to puppy courses where it can meet other people and dogs.

You will be dumbfounded by the speed at which the little Pinscher understands and obeys. Pay particular attention to house training since a puddle from such a small dog can easily be overlooked, so that the Miniature Pinscher gets the idea that you are happy to accept it fulfilling its natural needs indoors.

SOCIAL BEHAVIOUR

The Miniature Pinscher can get along well with other household pets and children, provided they do not pester it. They can be rather suspicious towards strangers, but their behaviour will depend entirely upon how they were broughtup as young dogs.

EXERCISE

A Miniature Pinscher is perfectly happy living in a flat provided it gets at least three outings a day when it can run and play.

They are not really happy to spend their entire life in a basket or as a lap-dog.

White Miniature Schnauzer

Black and silver Miniature Schnauzer

Miniature Schnauzer

COUNTRY OF ORIGIN
Germany.

APTITUDE
Vermin destroyer, watchdog, and family pet.

COAT
The coat is rough-haired and salt-and-pepper coloured (with dark face), or black (with black and silver markings on the head, legs and belly). There are also, more rarely, white examples.

CARE REQUIRED
The rough-haired coat of the Miniature Schnauzer needs to be plucked by hand or with a blunt trimmer at least twice a year. They must never, in any circumstances, be clipped because this spoils the coat for many years.
The excessive hair between the pads of the feet should, however, be clipped, and comb the embellishments regularly to prevent tangles. By embellishments is meant the beard, moustache, and long eye-brows.
When necessary, remove excessive hair growth within the ears.

CHARACTER
This lively, attentive, intelligent dog can be wilful and stubborn, and is vigilant , untiring, loyal to the family, and is not led astray by bribes.

TRAINING
The Miniature Schnauzer needs a confident handler despite its size, and also needs to be handled fairly and with consistency. Schnauzers are quick and bright pupils, although they frequently have their own ideas about your commands.
Vary the drills with play and do not repeat them too frequently.

SOCIAL BEHAVIOUR
In general the Miniature Schnauzer gets on well with other household pets and children. They are very uncertain about strangers and will announce visitors with full throated barking.

EXERCISE
The Miniature Schnauzer has enormous amounts of energy.
Country walks and romping in your garden please them. Take them out of doors as much as possible.

Dutch Smoushond

COUNTRY OF ORIGIN
The Netherlands.

APTITUDE
Stable dog, rat-catcher, and family pet.

SIZE
The shoulder height is 37 - 42cm ($14^1/_2$ - $16^1/_2$ in) for dogs and 35 - 40cm ($13^1/_2$ - $15^1/_2$in) for bitches. Dogs weigh about 10kg (22lb).

COAT
The coat of the Dutch Smoushond is rugged, coarse, and wiry. The colour is straw yellow.

CARE REQUIRED
Depending upon the quality of the coat, the Dutch Smoushond generally requires the hairs to be plucked by hand about twice a year, leaving the hair on the head alone so far as possible.

Between these grooming sessions, remove any excess hair from inside the ears. They can also be troubled by too much hair between the pads of the feet, so ensure this is regularly trimmed.

CHARACTER
These friendly, engaging, cunning, and intelligent dogs have considerable adaptability, are dependent, sober, sensitive, companionable, alert, and have a sense of humour.

TRAINING
The Dutch Smoushond is an intelligent dog which is eager to do things for you. The training is therefore quite easy.

Dutch Smoushond

It is important, though, to ensure that you are consistent towards them because some can assert themselves if they get an idea that their handler is rather easy-going.

SOCIAL BEHAVIOUR
They get on well with children and happily accept the family cat.
Most Dutch Smoushonds get on well with their own kind.

EXERCISE
This breed is untiring and enjoy long walks, and swimming. Decide to enrol it for its agility skills or fly-ball courses because it is ideal for both and will enjoy the activity enormously.

When a week occasionally passes without a good long walk, the Dutch Smoushond will accept it without difficulty.

Standard Schnauzer with salt-and-pepper coat

Standard Schnauzer

COUNTRY OF ORIGIN
Germany.

APTITUDE
Vermin destroyer, watchdog, and family pet.

SIZE
The shoulder-height is 45 - 50cm
($17^1/_2$ - $19^1/_2$in).

COAT
The rugged wire-haired coat is black or salt-and-pepper coloured with a dark face.

CARE REQUIRED
The coat of this Schnauzer needs to be plucked about twice a year. Such plucking is necessary with most wire-haired breeds because it is the only way to keep both coat and skin in the best condition. When necessary, remove any excess hair within the ears and between the pads of the feet.
The beard, moustache, and eyebrows require regular combing to prevent tangles.

CHARACTER
This is a temperamental and intelligent breed which is eager to learn, sober, dependable, very dependent on its own family, it is not easily led astride with bribes, is observant, and vigilant.

TRAINING
Schnauzers learn quickly and are eager pupils but they possess a fair amount of stubbornness. They respond best to fair and consistent handling, with the sound of your voice being normally sufficient.

SOCIAL BEHAVIOUR
Standard Schnauzers naturally get on well with dogs, other animals, and are extremely tolerant with children.

They are mistrustful of people they do not know.

EXERCISE
This breed has an average need of exercise. Despite this, it likes to be busy doing things such as swimming, running beside a cycle, agility skill competitions, fly-ball, playing in the garden, or running in the woods.
These are all suitable activities for this dog of character.

Standard Schnauzer, tolerant of children

Austrian short-haired Pinscher

COUNTRY OF ORIGIN
Austria.

APTITUDE
Vermin destroyer and family pet.

SIZE
The shoulder-height is 35 - 50cm
($13^1/_2$ - $19^1/_2$in).

COAT
This breed's short-haired coat is most commonly found in the colours russet-brown,

Austrian short-haired Pinscher

Austrian short-haired Pinscher

yellow, streaked brown, with and without white markings.

CARE REQUIRED
No major requirements are demanded to care for an Austrian Pinscher.
It is sufficient to keep the coat in good condition if you will brush it from time to time to remove loose and dead hairs.

CHARACTER
It is constantly alert, lively, and very active, demanding of itself, intelligent, and an outstanding rat-catcher. This dog bonds extremely closely with its family.

TRAINING
Give the Austrian Pinscher a caring, fair, but somewhat firm-handed training. They learn quickly and perform well in skill competitions. With the right handler they can also do well in obedience trials.

SOCIAL BEHAVIOUR
The Austrian Pinscher can be rather dominant towards other dogs. There are usually no problems with cats and other household pets, provided of course the usual advice to socialize when young is heeded.
They can keep themselves rather remote and watchful with strangers.

EXERCISE
The Austrian Pinscher is by origin a farm dog so that a home in the country where it can get all the exercise it needs on its own is the ideal place for this dog.

If this does not match your circumstances then take it for long walks regularly.

Giant Schnauzer

COUNTRY OF ORIGIN
Germany.

APTITUDE
Watchdog, guard-dog, and family pet.

SIZE
The shoulder height is 60 - 70cm ($23^1/_2$ - $27^1/_2$in).

COAT
The coat is rough-haired. The most usual colour is salt-and-pepper; a dark face is desirable with any colour.

CARE REQUIRED

About twice a year the hair needs to be plucked. Check regularly that there is not too much hair in the ears and snip it if necessary. Excessive hair growth between the feet pads must also be dealt with. Comb the long decorative hair embellishments that are a feature of its head to prevent tangles.

CHARACTER

An alert, vigilant, hardy, and sober dog that does not wander, is very loyal to its handler and family, intelligent and eager to learn, thoughtful, good-natured, considerable stamina, and is not led astray by bribes.
Giant Schnauzers bond closely with the family of which they form part.

TRAINING

This breed, which is full of character, requires a sound upbringing. If the training is consistent, fair, and full of variety, it will like it. Provided you bear in mind that a Schnauzer has its own ideas and will not follow every command slavishly, it can do well in various sporting activities - especially defence dog trials.

SOCIAL BEHAVIOUR

The Giant Schnauzer causes few problems with dogs and other pets. The usual caveat applies that he must be correctly socialized when young. They are naturally loving with children.

They are not interested in strangers and tend towards shyness, although to what extent depends largely upon the upbringing and socializing process.

EXERCISE

This is a breed that requires quite a lot of exercise. Ensure it gets plenty of outdoor exercise and it will be quite peaceful.

Black Giant Schnauzer, study of the head

Black Giant Schnauzer

Russian Bear Schnauzer, study of the head

Russian Bear Schnauzer

COUNTRY OF ORIGIN
Former Soviet Union.

APTITUDE
Watchdog, guarddog, and family pet.

SIZE
The shoulder-height is 66 - 72cm (26 - 28$^1/_2$in) for dogs and 64 - 70cm (25$^1/_2$- 27$^1/_2$in) for bitches.

COAT
The breed has a thick under-layer to the upper rough-haired coat.
Their colours are plain black, or black with some grey mixed in.

CARE REQUIRED
The coat requires plucking about two to three times each year. This is necessary to maintain a good tough coat. Between these occasions the excess hair in the ears and between the pads of the feet should be trimmed.
Comb the beard and moustache regularly to prevent tangles.

CHARACTER
This dog is vigilant and protective without barking greatly, quiet in the house, intelligent, cunning, obedient, loyal to its handler and family, and sober.
Russian Schnauzers like to show their own initiative.

TRAINING
This interesting breed likes to work and quickly grasps what is required. The training has to be clear and consistent in nature to succeed. The dogs react very well to the voice and punishment is rarely necessary.

Russian Bear Schnauzer

SOCIAL BEHAVIOUR
The Russian Bear Schnauzer is very friendly with children and can get along fine with cats and other household pets. Family friends will be enthusiastically greeted but strangers will be halted in their tracks.
The breed is naturally reserved with strangers but after its handler says they are all right, this is accepted.

EXERCISE
Russian Bear Schnauzers likes to be kept busy but they do not misbehave if you do not have time to take them for a long walk. The breed is suitable for a wide variety of dog sports and particularly for defence dog trials.

SPECIAL REMARKS
A Russian Bear Schnauzer is an ideal family pet but is not a dog for beginners. Dogs which are imported from their Country of origin or surrounding countries can often have sharper and harder characteristics than similar breeds bred in Western Europe or North America.

Mastiffs

Argentinian Mastiff, or Dogo Argentinof

COUNTRY OF ORIGIN
Argentina.

APTITUDE
Hunting dog.

SIZE
The shoulder-height is 60 - 65cm (23$^1/_2$ - 25$^1/_2$in).

COAT
The Argentinian Mastiff has a short-haired coat which is always white, sometimes with pigment flecks in the skin. A small black patch between the ears is permissible.
There is also an extremely rare version with a long-haired coat.

CARE REQUIRED
The coat of the Argentinian Mastiff is very easy to keep in condition. Remove dead and loose hairs during moulting with a rubber brush. Keep the claws short and, as is necessary with all other dogs, make sure the ear passages are kept clean.

Unclipped Argentinian Mastiff

CHARACTER
This brave, temperamental dog is loyal to its handler and family, barks little, is demanding of itself, has considerable stamina, and a strongly developed hunting instinct. The dogs in particular can be very dominant towards their own kind.

TRAINING
This is definitely not a breed for beginners. It requires a well-balanced, loving, but very consistent upbringing. Try to reward it when things go well and when they go wrong punish the dog solely with your voice. A combination of isolation in a kennel, and a tough training regime can lead to unpredictable behaviour.

SOCIAL BEHAVIOUR
They usually get on with children although some of them can be rather boisterous. It is possible to socialize them to tolerate cats and other pets but it is not advisable to expect an Argentinian Mastiff to share a house with them. Remember that this is a hunting dog which will regard a cat or sheep as prey.

They are not an ideal choice as watchdogs because of their hunting instincts although they are likely to frighten away most wrong-doers.

EXERCISE
A daily turn around the block is definitely not enough for this breed. To really please this dog, take it regularly for long walks. In a large enough fenced garden it will burn-off its energy itself.
Because of the strong hunting instincts and dominant behaviour towards other dogs, an Argentinian Mastiff must be firmly controlled when walked on the lead.

SPECIAL REMARKS
This breed is banned as a dangerous breed in Great Britain. For countries where they are permitted, they are not suitable for beginners. Deafness is prevalent in this breed.
Purchase puppies only from a trustworthy recognized breeder.

Dogue de Bordeaux

Dogue de Bordeaux

COUNTRY OF ORIGIN
France.

APTITUDE
Watchdog and family dog.

SIZE
The shoulder-height is 60 - 70cm ($23^1/_2$ - $27^1/_2$in) for dogs and their minimum weight is 50kg (110lb). The shoulder-height is 58 - 66cm ($22^1/_2$ - 26in) for bitches and their minimum weight is 45kg (99lb).

COAT
The coat consists of soft short hair of mahogany red, or red-brown, with a red or black face. White markings are considered unacceptable.

CARE REQUIRED
Brush the coat regularly during moulting with a rubber brush to remove dead and loose hairs. If necessary, clean the folds in the face.

In common with other large dogs, the Dogue de Bordeaux grows quickly and needs all its energy to build a healthy body. Do not allow a young dog to tire itself and ensure it gets ample food of sufficient nourishment.

CHARACTER
An equable, calm dog which rarely barks and is friendly, attentive, curious, very brave, demanding physically of itself, this dog bonds closely with its handler and family. The Bordeaux will protect the family and guard the house and grounds.

TRAINING
Give the Bordeaux a consistent training in a fair and calm manner. This dog becomes very attached to, and wants to please its handler.

Make a fuss of the dog and let it see you are pleased when it behaves well, and do speak encouragingly to it. This dog requires a handler who naturally has command over it .

SOCIAL BEHAVIOUR
When the Bordeaux has had lots of positive experiences in its youth, enabling it to develop as an equable dog, its behaviour with other pets will probably be fine.

They are usually kindly and protective with children. Visitors are initially eyed mistrustfully but once its handler signifies approval, they are accepted. This breed can be rather dominant towards other dogs.

Dogue de Bordeaux are sociable animals

EXERCISE
This breed has average exercise demands. Two walks (on the lead) each day together with running and playing off the lead a few times each week are sufficient for it .

SPECIAL REMARKS
This strong dog bonds figuratively and almost literally to the family. Separation will be regarded as punishment. Do not choose this breed if you have to be away from the house for long periods.

Boxer

COUNTRY OF ORIGIN
Germany.

APTITUDE
Working dog and family pet.

COAT
The Boxer has a short smooth-haired coat. They are either brindle or yellow, possibly with white markings and a dark face.
The white should not cover more then a third of the dog.

CARE REQUIRED
The coat can be kept in condition by grooming occasionally with a rubber brush. Do this particularly during moulting.

CHARACTER
This happy, friendly, spontaneous, and intelligent dog is eager to learn and curious, learning quickly, it is also vigilant, boisterous, uncomplicated, straight forward, lively and constantly on the move, bonding very closely with the family.

TRAINING
Teach the Boxer not to be so boisterous (not to

Boxer

71

Bullmastiff

jump up at people). Since it learns quickly and has substantial intelligence, the Boxer is ideal for various sporting activities from defence trials to skill trials.

SOCIAL BEHAVIOUR
Boxers are known for the way they get on so well with children. A well brought-up and properly socialized Boxer will also get on with his own kind and other household pets.

The Boxer's nature is to protect you, your family, and your home. Known visitors will be welcomed boisterously.

EXERCISE
Try to give a Boxer plenty of exercise. When it has grown-up, you can carefully let it run beside a cycle.

They love playing and romping with their own kind but it will happily leave its basket to play with a ball with you.

Bullmastiff

COUNTRY OF ORIGIN
England.

APTITUDE
Watchdog and family pet.

SIZE
The shoulder height is 63.5 - 68.5cm (25 - 27in) for dogs and 61 - 66cm (24 - 26in) for bitches.

COAT
The coat is short-haired and the colours, which may be streaked, are tan or red-brown, always with darker muzzle and ears. A little white on the chest is permitted.

CARE REQUIRED
There is little to the grooming of a Bullmastiff. Occasionally remove dead and loose hairs with a rubber brush or massage glove.

TRAINING
This breed reacts best to a fair, stable, and consistent approach carried out in a harmonious manner.

The Bullmastiff is very sensitive to the tone of your voice and is not really difficult but does require a handler who can assert his authority. The Bullmastiff is quite unsuitable for banishing to a kennel.

SOCIAL BEHAVIOUR
Bullmastiffs are very tolerant towards children but can be rather dominant towards their own kind. Provided they are properly socialized when young, they can learn to get along with other household pets. Friends of the family will be accepted, especially if the handler signifies approval, but unwanted visitors will be halted in their footsteps.

EXERCISE
The Bullmastiff has an average demand for exercise. A couple of outings every day with several opportunities to run and play (on the lead) give it sufficient freedom of movement.

Bullmastiff, study of the head

Estrela Mountain Dog

Estrela Mountain Dog

COUNTRY OF ORIGIN
Portugal.

APTITUDE
Guarding the herd and the household, and family pet.

SIZE
The shoulder height is 65 - 72cm ($25^1/_2$ - $28^1/_2$in) for dogs and 62 - 68cm ($24^1/_2$ - $26^1/_2$in) for bitches. Dogs weigh 30 - 50kg (66 - 110lb).

COAT
There are two types of coat for this breed: long-haired and short-haired. Both types of coat should be abundant, with an under-layer of fine, short hairs. Reddish-brown, wolf-grey, and yellow, plain or with white markings, are all permitted.

CHARACTER

This breed is vigilant (sometimes rather noisily alert), sober, equable, intelligent and eager to learn, but it can also be stubborn, independent but affectionate, and it bonds very closely with the family and with people it knows.

This breed can find it difficult in later life to accept a new handler or owner.

TRAINING

The Estrela Mountain Dog learns quite quickly; some examples of the breed have excelled at obedience trials. They are intelligent and agile enough to perform well in skills trials but only if both of you enjoy the activity. At competition level the Estrela will be overtaken by faster breeds.

Stubbornness and making up their own mind are characteristics of the Estrela but they will only appear if the dog finds the drills boring or that it is pressurized. An equable and quiet approach with consistency is the key to successful upbringing of this breed.

Do not over-tire the dog and adapt the extent and nature of exercise during the growing stage when it needs all its energy to build healthy bones, muscles and joints.

SOCIAL BEHAVIOUR

Those who are known to the family and all the people and animals of the household will be seen as its responsibility to look after; strangers will be extremely suspiciously regarded.

EXERCISE

The Estrela Mountain Dog is happiest with plenty of space, indoors as well as out. They adore going for walks with you, but if that is not always possible, they will accept the situation without fuss.

Blue Great Dane with clipped ears

Unclipped Black Great Dane

Great Dane

COUNTRY OF ORIGIN
Germany.

APTITUDE
Previously hunting dog for large game, now watchdog, and family pet.

SIZE

The shoulder-height is a minimum of 80cm ($31^1/_2$in) for dogs and 72cm ($28^1/_2$in) for bitches. There is no maximum standard and generally people like the dogs to be well over the minimum height. These dogs weigh 50kg (110lb) and upwards, depending upon the size and sex.

COAT

They have short smooth-haired coats which have three accepted colours: yellow (which can be streaked) with a black face; black, perhaps with a little white, or white with black spots (known as harlequin and the only variety permitted to have blue eyes and partially flesh-coloured muzzle); and blue.

Two other colours are accepted in some countries. These are the "Mantel" which has a black coat covering almost all the dog like a mantel, with white showing on just the chest, neck, blaze, belly, legs, and tip of the tail; with the other variety, this mantel is broken with white. Both are considered as black in some countries. The different colours are not interbred.

CARE REQUIRED

The Great Dane's coat requires very little attention. During moulting it is best to remove dead and loose hairs with a rubber brush.
The Great Dane must always be allowed to lie somewhere soft to avoid causing pressure marks. Fast-growing breeds like the Great Dane require care during the growing stage. The first essential is the right nutrition. The other point to watch is to limit exercise, avoid pressurizing and over-tiring, which can cause serious problems for the development of bones, joints and muscles.
They do not belong in a kennel and are rather fond of comfort.

CHARACTER

These are affectionate, calm, and intelligent dogs that are sensible, sensitive, very loyal to the handler and family and not easily led astray by "bribes"these curious dogs. Despite the fact that they do not bark much, these dogs make excellent watchdogs.

It is said that a housebreaker can easily get into a house watched over by a Great Dane but can never get out. Like other Mastiff types, the Great Dane is not very susceptible to pain and so it is possible that an illness or injury may be overlooked for some time.

TRAINING

The Great Dane grows in a very short period into a very large dog. You must therefore teach it as a very young dog that it must not pull on the lead.
Train it with understanding in an harmonious manner and with great consistency. They are very sensitive to the intonation of the voice and

your friendly request is often sufficient to get them to do what you require.

SOCIAL BEHAVIOUR
Generally Great Danes get on perfectly well with their own kind, other household pets, and children.
Most of them are rather uncertain of strangers but friends of the family will be warmly greeted.

EXERCISE
These strong and elegant dogs require significant levels of exercise. They will enjoy being able to run free and romping, off the lead, in open country or woodland. They can also be exercised running alongside a cycle provided they stay strictly to heel.

Great Danes that get sufficient outdoor exercise will be very peaceful indoors.

English Bulldog

English Bulldog

COUNTRY OF ORIGIN
England.

APTITUDE
Family pet.

WEIGHT
The English Bulldog weighs 22 - 25kg (48$\frac{1}{2}$ - 55lb).

COAT
The coat is short-haired and is found in beige, red-brown brindle (with or without a black face), white (with lots of dark pigment on the muzzle and eye) and piebald. Black, liver, and black and tan are not acceptable colours.

CARE REQUIRED
When the Bulldog moults, it is easy to remove dead and loose hairs with a rubber brush. When necessary clean the folds in the face with a special lotion made for this purpose.
The English Bulldog prefers to lie in a draught-free, soft, dry place, and a kennel is definitely unsuitable.

CHARACTER
The Bulldog is animated, spontaneous, uncomplicated, and equable with a sense of humour, gentle-natured, sensitive but demanding of

English Bulldog puppy and adult puppy and adult

itself, and is intrepid if necessary, intelligent in a thoughtful way, and peaceful in the house. They are very affectionate and prefer to be close to the family.

TRAINING
This breed is usually easy to train. They are very sensitive to your voice or voices and will often respond to a friendly but determined request. In no circumstances should they be severely treated but do not let them take liberties either. Remain at all times consistent and clear with them.

SOCIAL BEHAVIOUR
Mixing with other dogs and household pets is usually problem-free. They make ideal friends for children and are very tolerant. Most also have a well-developed sense of humour. Some English Bulldogs are extremely wary, while others are friends with everybody.

EXERCISE
This is not a breed requiring long walks. The English Bulldog will be quite happy with three

short outings a day. For the rest of the time they will be pleased to stay in the house or garden, provided the family is close by.

This makes them ideal for less active people. Bulldog puppies have a tendency to keep on running and playing when they are exhausted.

Make sure that they get sufficient rest and limit their exercise so that their energy can be used to build healthy bones, joints, and muscles. They are not able to withstand the heat, so make sure that they have somewhere cool to lie on hot days.

Fila Brasileiro

Fila Brasileiro or Brazilian Molosser

COUNTRY OF ORIGIN
Brazil.

APTITUDE
Watchdog and tracking dog.

SIZE
The shoulder-height is 65 - 75cm ($25^1/_2$ - $29^1/_2$in) for dogs and 60 -70cm ($23^1/_2$ -$27^1/_2$in) for bitches.

COAT
The short-haired coat of the Fila Brasileiro is known in many different colours of which only white, mouse-grey, and spotted or piebald coats are not accepted. The most usual coat is brindle.

CARE REQUIRED
This breed requires relatively little care. Let them lie somewhere soft to prevent callouses forming on the leg joints.

CHARACTER
The Fila Brasileiro can be very affectionate and it always subjects itself to its handler, which it obeys totally. They are suspicious of strangers and this can manifest itself as aggression or they can be evasive.The reaction depends upon the person in question. Regular visitors are usually accepted. The breed has an exceptionally well developed sense of smell so that the dogs are very aware of whatever approaches. They can act quite independently, depending upon the situation. They also have very strong territorial instincts.

TRAINING
The owner of a Fila Brasileiro needs to be confident and have a well-balanced nature in order to train this breed successfully. Many find the dog's character to be difficult and unfathomable. Training needs to be calmly carried out in a harmonious manner and with understanding for the dog's character.
An occasional correction is acceptable but this breed is very sensitive to the intonation of your voice.
The potential owner must be aware that they react very quickly. For the right handler they are obedient.

Head of a Fila Brasileiro

SOCIAL BEHAVIOUR

For the children of its family, the Fila Brasileiro presents no problems but this is not true of their playmates. It will also accept some other household animals which it has met while young. New pets joining the family are not generally accepted.

EXERCISE

It is best to keep this breed in a large, securely fenced garden where it can take care of its own exercise needs.
From time to time take it to new places to provide a change of scene for it.

SPECIAL REMARKS

The Fila Brasileiro or Brazilian Molosser is banned as a dangerous breed in Great Britain. For countries where they are permitted, this is definitely not a breed for beginners, nor one to be kept in an urban environment.

Black and tan Hovawart

Hovawart

COUNTRY OF ORIGIN

Germany.

APTITUDE

Watchdog and family pet.

SIZE

The shoulder-height is 63 - 70cm ($24^{1}/_{2}$ - $27^{1}/_{2}$in) for dogs and 58 - 65cm (23 - 26in) for bitches.

COAT

The Hovawart has a long-haired, wavy coat which lies flat.
The colours are plain black, black with a marking, and blonde.

CARE REQUIRED

The coat does not require a great deal of attention. An occasional brush and comb (particularly in places where tangles might form) is sufficient.

CHARACTER

Good-natured, equable, demanding of itself, loyal to the family but with the tendency to become a one-person's dog, affectionate, vigilant and protective, attentive, and a good watchdog.
The Hovawart has a good scenting nose and remains playful until old age.

TRAINING

The Hovawart learns quickly what you expect of it. The best results are achieved with extremely consistent, loving, and a well-balanced training.
Hovawarts are ideally suited as tracking-, avalanche-, watch-, and defence dogs.

SOCIAL BEHAVIOUR

Behaviour towards other household animals is good regardless of whether it is a cat or poultry. This is true provided the dog has met these animals when it was young. They are generally very patient with children but sometimes reserved towards strangers.
It will protect your property against intruders with great zeal. When its handler indicates that visitors are approved, then it accepts them immediately.

EXERCISE

The Hovawart adapts itself to the circumstances. Take the dog for regular long walks and let it enjoy running and playing off the lead. A great advantage of this breed is that it has a highly developed sense of territory and will not readily desert your property.

Blonde Hovawart

Anatolian Shepherd Dog or Karabash

COUNTRY OF ORIGIN
Turkey.

APTITUDE
Sheepdog and protector for cattle herds.

SIZE
The shoulder-height is 74 - 81cm ($29^1/_2$ - $31^1/_2$in) for dogs and 71 - 79cm (28 - $31^1/_2$in) for bitches. The dogs weigh 41 - 64kg (90 - 141lb).

COAT
The outer protective coat is smooth-haired with a sheen and mainly short, but longer around the collar and tail.
Any colour is permitted, but the most acceptable are plain cream to fawn with a black face and ears.

CARE REQUIRED
The Anatolian Shepherd Dog requires little grooming. During moulting use a comb with a double row of metal teeth to remove the dead and loose hairs of the under-layer of the coat.

CHARACTER
This equable dog is brave and demanding of itself, unsure of strangers, can be stubborn and dominant, is reasonably independent, and very vigilant.

TRAINING
The Anatolian Shepherd is not a dog for beginners. It needs a handler who naturally radiates leadership.
The best results are achieved with a determined, consistent, and loving approach. It is very important to begin training quite early because fully grown dogs are too strong and too big to be corrected.

SOCIAL BEHAVIOUR
The breed generally gets on well with other animals provided it has been introduced to them when young.
They are rather reserved towards strangers but there are seldom problems with children from its own family.

They can be rather dominant towards other dogs. Much depends upon introducing the puppy early in its life to its own kind, other animals, and people.

EXERCISE
Anatolian Shepherds require quite considerable exercise. When they can run free in their own garden with a fence surrounding it, they can decide upon their own exercise needs. This breed is not suited to a flat or maisonette.

Anatolian Shepherd Dog, study of the head

Caucasian Owtcharka or Caucasian Sheepdog

COUNTRY OF ORIGIN
Former Soviet Union.

APTITUDE
Watchdog.

SIZE
The shoulder-height is a minimum of 65cm (25$^1/_2$in) dogs and 62cm (24$^1/_2$in) for bitches.

COAT
The Caucasian Owtcharka has three different kinds of coat: long-haired with a collar and longer-haired hindquarters; short-haired; and medium-length hair without the collar and the long hairs on the hindquarters.
The main colours are different shades of grey with light to rust-coloured markings; yellow, white, dun, rust-brown; they can be multicoloured and patterned.

CARE REQUIRED
The long-haired kinds require grooming from time to time with brush and comb, especially where tangles might occur. The coat of the short-haired variety needs less grooming .

CHARACTER
The Caucasian Owtcharka's original role was to protect livestock from four-legged and two-legged predators.
It is a very brave, vigilant, strong dog, which is hardy, and distrusts people it does not know, possessing a powerful urge to defend.

TRAINING
The potential owner of a Caucasian Owtcharka needs to be strong in character and physique. The breed has a distinct sense of right and wrong and you must therefore never treat it severely or punish it unfairly.

The right handler can achieve a Caucasian Owtcharka which is obedient and very loyal through mutual respect, that will protect the family and home with its life.

Caucasian Owtcharka, study of the head

SOCIAL BEHAVIOUR
Everything and everyone who belongs to the family - and that includes children, cats and chickens or whatever, will be regarded as "its", and respected and protected.

Do not leave it alone with your children because if play should become rough when they play with other children, the Caucasian Owtcharka will defend your children.
It has no time for strangers but will greet family friends warmly. It can be rather dominant towards other dogs.

EXERCISE
This breed is best suited to a family with lots of space surrounding the home where it can attend to its own exercise needs.
Because its thick coat protects it so well, this breed can happily cope with living out of doors.

Landseers

Landseer E.C.T. (Europees Continentaal Type)

COUNTRY OF ORIGIN
Canada/Europe.

APTITUDE
Family pet.

SIZE
The shoulder height is 72 - 80cm
($28^1/_2$ - $31^1/_2$in) for dogs and 67 - 72cm
($26^1/_2$ - $28^1/_2$in) for bitches.
Small variations above and below these standards are permitted.

COAT
The under-layer of the coat is soft, the outer coat is long, thick, and without curls. The colour is white with black patches, and a black head with white blaze is much preferred. For showing, it is preferable not to have black spots on the coat.

CARE REQUIRED
Regular brushing and combing is sufficient, specifically paying attention to the places where tangles are likely to occur, such as between the hind and front legs.

Keep the ear passages clean and snip away excessive hair between the pads of the feet. The Landseer, in common with other big dogs, grows fairly quickly and needs high quality nutrition. Adapt exercise during this phase to prevent overworking a growing body.

CHARACTER
The Landseer is an amiable, soft-natured, straight forward, affectionate, docile, sociable,

self-aware, and equable dog which is friendly towards people and animals, and is a keen swimmer. It will protect the members of the family and the house and garden if necessary. The Landseer rarely barks.

TRAINING
Normally this breed is not difficult to train. Teach the young dog to walk to heel and not to pull on the lead, because when fully grown they are much too strong to control.

SOCIAL BEHAVIOUR
The Landseer is a fine family dog, which will live in harmony with other dogs and household pets.

Children often receive special attention from them (in a positive sense). Visitors who have no evil intentions will be treated in a friendly manner.

EXERCISE
Do not take it on exhausting long walks until it is fully grown. They love to swim and this is an ideal form of exercise for them.

SPECIAL REMARKS
The Landseer is well protected against poor weather and it is not therefore necessary for it to have to be indoors in the warm.

Landseers E.C.T.

Leonberger

Leonberger

COUNTRY OF ORIGIN
Germany.

APTITUDE
Family pet.

SIZE
The shoulder height is 72 - 80cm
(28^1/$_2$ - 31^1/$_2$in) for dogs and 65 - 75cm (25^1/$_2$
- 29^1/$_2$in) for bitches. The ideal height is 76cm
(30in) for dogs and 70cm (27^1/$_2$in) for bitches.

COAT
The Leonberger has a soft to firm coat of medium-length hair with a thick under-layer. The
most usual colours range from golden-yellow to
red-brown, with a dark face.
The tips of the hairs should be black. The lack
of a black face is accepted but not preferred.

CARE REQUIRED
Brush and comb the coat regularly to remove all
the dead hair. In addition keep the ear passages
clean. Because this breed grows so rapidly, you
must never economize on a good well-balanced
diet.

Bear in mind that the bones, muscles, and joints
of the young dog must not be too heavily taxed
with long walks or by letting it run up and down
stairs too often.

CHARACTER
A peaceful, self-confident, and equable dog
which is straight-forward, loyal, intelligent, a
quick learner, it will alert you to visitors.

TRAINING
This breed responds best to a well-balanced
training programme in a harmonious manner. It
learns quickly and will rapidly grasp what is
expected of it.

SOCIAL BEHAVIOUR
Leonbergers get on well with dogs and other
household pets, and mixing with children presents no problems. It makes little difference to
it whether visitors have evil intentions or not.
Once it has alerted you the Leonberger con-
siders its job done.

EXERCISE
The Leonberger requires extensive exercise.
Take it with you regularly for long walks during
which it can have an opportunity to run and
play off the lead.

Leonbergers

Mastiffs

Mastiff

COUNTRY OF ORIGIN
England.

APTITUDE
Previously a hunting dog for large game and a watchdog, now a watchdog and family pet.

SIZE
The shoulder height is a minimum of 76cm (30in) for dogs and 70cm (27$^1/_2$in) for bitches.

COAT
The Mastiff's coat is short-haired and can be apricot, silver, yellow, or streaked. With all of them, the face should be black.

CARE REQUIRED
During moulting the loose and dead hairs can best be removed by using a rubber brush. Give the Mastiff a soft place to lie down to avoid ugly pressure marks. Economies must not made with the young and growing dog's diet. Good nutrition is essential to optimum growth. Like other mastiff types, the Mastiff has a high pain threshold and since it is very demanding of itself, injuries and illnesses can be overlooked until they are truly serious.

CHARACTER
The Mastiff is a calm, self-confident, watchful, and patient dog who is soft-natured towards his family, intelligent, and dignified.
It rarely barks but it is in its nature to defend its territory and the family who go with it against wrongdoers.

TRAINING
Training a Mastiff must be enjoyable, conducted calmly and in an harmonious manner.

Mastiff

Consistency, lots of love, and plenty of understanding work wonders.

SOCIAL BEHAVIOUR
Provided correctly socialized, the Mastiff presents no problems mixing with other dogs, and household pets.

Normally its behaviour with children is good-tempered and friendly. When strangers visit, it determinedly refuses them access unless they are accepted by its handler.

EXERCISE
Do not let a young Mastiff run about and play to its heart's content. Control exercise during puppyhood and youth, because this rapidly growing animal needs all its energy for development.

If the dog is too strongly pressured or becomes over-tired, it can have an adverse effect upon the development of bones, joints, and muscles. An adult Mastiff has an average need for exercise. In general they do not really enjoy playing with a ball and similar activities.

Young Spanish Mastiff

Spanish Mastiff

COUNTRY OF ORIGIN
Spain.

APTITUDE
Guard-dog for livestock.

SIZE
The shoulder-height is a minimum of 78cm

(30$^1/_2$in) for dogs with a preferred height of 80cm (31$^1/_2$in). The shoulder-height is a minimum of 74cm (29$^1/_2$in) for bitches with a preferred height of 76cm (30in).

COAT
The Spanish Mastiff has straight hair with a dense under-layer. The centre of the back and the tail have longer hair. The colours can be plain yellow, red, black, wolf-grey, and red-brown, or broken colours or spotted. White should not be too dominant.

CARE REQUIRED
Groom the Spanish Mastiff regularly with a brush, especially during the moult, and examine the ear passages for dirt.

CHARACTER
This breed is very gentle-natured for the members of its family, but it is very mistrustful of strangers. This dog is also self-confident and independent, intelligent, and very alert, and it will protect you and your family against unwelcome visitors to its full ability.

TRAINING
It is important to train the Spanish Mastiff with an equable, consistent, and loving approach. A tough or unjust approach to training will bring undesirable characteristics to the surface. Its handler needs to be a well-balanced, calm person who naturally exudes leadership.

Spanish Mastiff, study of the head

SOCIAL BEHAVIOUR
Its own family is always the most important for a Spanish Mastiff. This dog takes its responsibilities as watchdog very seriously and will allow no person or no other animal onto the property where it lives.

This is a role it assumes naturally without training or commands. When its handler indicates that visitors are indeed wanted, it accepts them without difficulty. It is always friendly towards other animals regardless of whether they are cats or large or small livestock. It is usually extremely patient with children.

EXERCISE
These dogs are in their element if your home is surrounded by plenty of land. Take them occasionally for an outing to the woods or open countryside for a change of scene.
The breed's thick coat protects them from cold and wet so that they can happily live out of doors.

Unclipped Neopolitan Mastiff

Neopolitan Mastiff

COUNTRY OF ORIGIN
Italy.

APTITUDE
Watchdog and family pet.

SIZE
The shoulder-height is 65 - 75cm (25$^1/_2$ - 29$^1/_2$in) for dogs and 60 - 68cm (23$^1/_2$ - 26$^1/_2$in) for bitches.

COAT
The coat is short-haired and most usually blue-

Head of an unclipped Neopolitan Mastiff

grey; they can also be grey, black, brown, and fox red. All colours may be broken. A little white on the chest or feet is permitted.

CARE REQUIRED
During moulting the dead and loose hairs are best removed with a rubber brush.
The breed likes a draught-free and dry place to sleep which must be soft to prevent pressure marks.

CHARACTER
A dominant, watchful, equable, and peaceful dog which is brave, intelligent, not aggressive, affectionate, demanding of itself, and does not really bark.

TRAINING
This large Mastiff requires a good, well-balanced training. Ensure you are consistent in approach and do not keep repeating commands that it has failed to obey.
These are not dogs for beginners but it is an exaggeration to describe them as difficult in

their association with others. A calm handler with natural leadership will achieve the best results with this breed. It is in their nature to protect you and your possessions - it does not need to be reminded.

SOCIAL BEHAVIOUR
The dogs can be somewhat dominant towards other dogs that they meet, but with regard to children they are generally always loving, provided the children do not tease them. If the dog has had positive experiences with cats and other household pets when young, there should be no problems in this direction.

EXERCISE
Do not let the young Neopolitan Mastiff run and play too much. Limit its exercise because it must on no account be over-tired. Avoid rough games in the growing stage and ensure that all its energy is available to make healthy bones and muscles.
When full-grown the Neopolitan Mastiff has an average demand for exercise.

Newfoundland

Newfoundland

Newfoundland

COUNTRY OF ORIGIN
Canada.

APTITUDE
Originally a fisherman's dog, now a family pet.

SIZE
The shoulder-height is about 71cm (28in) for dogs and about 66cm (26in) for bitches. Their weight is 50 - 69kg (110 - 152lb).

COAT
The Newfoundlander has a water resistent, double, medium-length, greasy and dense coat. Permitted colours are brown or black, with some white on the chest, toes and tip of the tail. Black and white Newfoundlanders exist, but are seldom seen.

CARE REQUIRED
Brush and comb this breed regularly with special attention to the hindquarters and other areas where tangles quickly form.
Trim any excessive hair growth between the pads of the feet.

CHARACTER
Good humoured, sociable, gentle-natured, straight forward, affectionate, and tractable, this breed is friendly with people and animals, loves to swim, is not particularly vigilant yet protects its family if it should become necessary.
The Newfoundland rarely barks, is self-assured, and has an equable nature.

TRAINING
Training must be conducted in a calm and well-balanced manner. They are very sensitive to the tone of your voice.

SOCIAL BEHAVIOUR
The Newfoundland is a through and through household companion. Any dog, other animal, child, or visitor who has no evil intentions will receive a friendly welcome.

EXERCISE
Avoid all exhausting day-long hikes until the dog is fully grown. They love to swim and this is an ideal form of exercise for the Newfoundland. The thick coat protects them against cold and rain so that they can happily be kept out of doors.

Pyrenean Mountain Dog

Pyrenean Mountain Dog

COUNTRY OF ORIGIN
France.

APTITUDE
Sheepdog (to protect flocks and herds of cattle), and family pet.

SIZE
The shoulder-height is 70 - 80cm (27$^1/_2$ -

31$^1/_2$in) for dogs and 65 - 72cm (25$^1/_2$ - 28$^1/_2$in) for bitches. The weight is 45 - 60kg (99 - 132lb).

COAT

The coat is abundant and tightly packed with fairly long hair that is even longer around the neck and tail. Pyrenean Mountain Dogs are plain white with markings on the head, ears, and root of the tail.
These markings can be grey, badger-coloured, pale yellow, or wolf-grey. Some markings on the body are permissible.

CARE REQUIRED

This breed requires fairly thorough grooming to keep the coat in good condition. It is certainly necessary to brush or comb the dog thoroughly once or twice a day in order to remove loose hairs. This is even more important during moulting.

CHARACTER

An equable, attentive, vigilant, brave and intelligent dog that is reasonably independent and hardy, and can sometimes be stubborn. The Pyrenean Mountain Dog rarely barks.

TRAINING

It is essential to make this breed aware of everything it must and must not do when still very young because when fully grown they are far too strong and would be too independent if not properly trained. Pyrenean Mountain Dogs require an equable handler who can be consistent and loving.

SOCIAL BEHAVIOUR

The Pyrenean Mountain Dog can act aggressively towards dogs that might be a match for him but usually displays no aggression towards smaller dogs. Normally they mix well with children, but strangers are mistrusted, and it will protect you, your family, and your home against unwanted visitors. There are not any problems with regard to cats and other household animals.

EXERCISE

The Pyrenean Mountain Dog requires extensive exercise. Take it for long walks regularly and give it the opportunity during the walk to run and play off the lead.

The breed belongs really with a family that has plenty of space - indoors and out - but it will adapt to smaller homes provided it gets sufficient exercise. In common with all the rapidly growing breeds they must not be exhausted during the growing stage.

Rottweilers

Rottweiler

COUNTRY OF ORIGIN
Germany.

APTITUDE
Watchdog, guard-dog, and family pet.

SIZE
The shoulder-height is 61 - 68cm (24 - 26$^1/_2$in) for dogs and 56 - 63cm (22 - 24$^1/_2$in) for bitches.

COAT
The breed has not very long, thick and coarse outer-layer of hair with a thick under-layer. The coat is always black with brown markings. Long-haired examples occur occasionally but are not so highly considered. A white chest marking is also not desirable.

CARE REQUIRED
The Rottweiler is relatively easy to care for. For the removal of loose and dead hairs during moulting it is best to use a rubber glove which works better than a normal brush. If you wish to make the coat shine, there are special lotions which can be used. Keep the claws short and the ear passages clean.

CHARACTER
The Rottweiler is intelligent, obedient, unconditionally loyal to its handler and family, and is vigilant, protective, brave, strong, imposing, and can be jealous if attention is given elsewhere than to him.
A Rottweiler will defend its family and property to the end. Most of them have a tendency to become a one-person's-dog.

Rottweilers can be rather dominant in nature and therefore require an equable, calm handler, who is confident and always fair. Teach the puppy what it may and what may not do and hold consistently to this. The breed is extremely sensitive to your voice: use this therefore also to praise it when it does well.

A varied training programme gives the best results. Generally it is necessary to be a bit more forceful with the dogs than the bitches, which have a slightly gentler nature. Rottweilers are ideally suited for security work and defence dog training and sports, although success will not come as quickly as with the Mechelen Belgian Shepherd.

SOCIAL BEHAVIOUR

When a Rottweiler has been consistently brought up and trained, it will be loyal to its family and a good playmate for your children. Cats and other household animals will be accepted unquestioningly, provided it has had positive experiences with them when young. Some Rottweilers can be rather dominant towards other dogs and want to assert themselves.

Friends and relatives of the family are normally enthusiastically welcomed, whereas strangers can get no nearer than the garden fence. The Rottweiler is an outstanding watchdog.

EXERCISE

Make sure that a Rottweiler gets plenty of exercise because it needs it. Running in the woods and in open country makes it very happy and it has no desire to wander far from you. Swimming or running beside a cycle are perfect activities for this dog and it also adores retrieving a ball.

Rottweiler

Young Shar Pei

Shar Pei

COUNTRY OF ORIGIN
China.

APTITUDE
Family pet.

SIZE
The shoulder-height is 48 - 58cm ($18^1/_2$ - $22^1/_2$in) and the weight is about 18kg ($39^1/_2$lb).

COAT
The coat is very hard and is intended to be very short and bristly (the "horsecoat" variety). There is also a variety with longer hair (the "brushcoat") but these are not preferred. Permitted colours are black, brown, red, and fawn. A cream-coloured coat is also known but is not highly regarded. Lighter tints of the main colours are permitted but never white or multi-coloured. Shar Pei dogs have a blue tongue and blue pigment.

CARE REQUIRED
The Shar Pei has folds of skin over his entire body, especially when young. Check them regularly and clean if necessary. Some examples have a tail which lies very close to the body and this too needs to be inspected and cleaned to prevent infections.
Put drops in the eyes as necessary and groom the coat with a soft brush.

CHARACTER
This breed is loyal to its handler, playful, active, dominant, brave, and is an intelligent dog

St. Bernard

that does not follow slavishly, and is reasonably vigilant.

TRAINING
The training needs to be extremely consistent. Whenever you are too uncertain, too inconstant, too soft, or too lenient in the dog's eyes, it will reverse roles. The Shar Pei needs a confident handler.

SOCIAL BEHAVIOUR
The Shar Pei bonds with the people who form its family but they are not unfriendly towards strangers. Normally they are fine with children and cats present no problems if they have met them when young.
Mixing with other dogs can sometimes present problems. This is because the Shar Pei is by nature ready for a fight.

EXERCISE
The breed has a fairly considerable need for exercise. Provided they get enough outdoor exercise, they will be very peaceful indoors.

Shar Pei

COUNTRY OF ORIGIN
Switzerland.

APTITUDE
A long established search-and-rescue dog, now principally a family pet.

SIZE
The shoulder-height is a minimum of 70cm (27$^1/_2$in) for dogs and 65cm (25$^1/_2$in) for bitches. The weight depends upon the height and build of the dog but should be at least 60kg (132lb).

COAT
There are both short-haired and long-haired St. Bernards. The colour is red with white or white with red, or white with streaked patches. The St. Bernard must have white legs, a white chest, and white tip to his tail, a white blaze, and a white neck patch or collar.

Short-haired St. Bernard, study of the head

Short-haired St. Bernard

Long-haired St. Bernard

CARE REQUIRED
Groom with brush or the comb every day to remove loose hairs. Keep the ears clean and check the eyes of dogs that have drooping eyelids regularly.

CHARACTER
Good-humoured, friendly, and equable, the St. Bernard is marvellous with children, loyal to its handler, careful, and not given to barking. It will defend you and your possessions if necessary although this is not its primary role.

TRAINING
Young dogs must be taught early not to pull on the lead because this will be hard to teach them later.

In common with all mastiff types, the St. Bernard requires considerable understanding in its training from you.
Ensure also that they are not too physically stretched in the growing stage.

SOCIAL BEHAVIOUR
St. Bernards get along fine with children, and other dogs and household animals normally present no problems.

EXERCISE
An average level of exercise is sufficient for the St. Bernard.
Three times a day around the block with regular longer walks when it can run free, off the lead, are all that it needs.

Long-haired St. Bernard in traditional rescue harness

Tibetan Mastiff

Tibetan Mastiff

COUNTRY OF ORIGIN
Tibet.

APTITUDE
Watchdog and family pet.

SIZE
The shoulder-height is a minimum of 66cm
(26in) for dogs and 61cm (24in) for bitches.

COAT
This breed has a long, thick coat with a heavy
under-layer. The Tibetan Mastiff is known in
plain black, black and tan, golden brown or
grey, with and without tan markings.

CARE REQUIRED
The breed requires regular grooming with a
brush. In the winter the Tibetan Mastiff has an
abundance of hair forming a very thick coat, but
at the beginning of the summer much of the
hair falls out, During this period the owner must
spend half an hour daily pulling out the loose
hair with a brush and comb. The Tibetan Mastiff becomes adult somewhat later than other
breeds.

CHARACTER
Equable, calm and thoughtful, the Tibetan Mastiff is dignified, very loyal to its own family,
reserved towards strangers, and can be both
stubborn and of its own mind, is also dominant, and self-confident. It comes naturally to

this Mastiff to guard its family and the property.

TRAINING
This special dog has to be raised to adulthood
in a carefully well-balanced manner. Strong
words and a readiness to hit the dog will only
cause it to ignore its handler. The objective is
to achieve a bond of mutual respect between
you.

SOCIAL BEHAVIOUR
The Tibetan Mastiff is by and large loving with
children but he will distrusts strangers. If it has
gained confidence in contact with other animals when young, it will accept them. Contact
with other dogs is also usually without difficulty.

EXERCISE
The dogs of this breed have an average demand
for exercise and will enjoy going with you to
woods and open countryside but they are not
particularly keen on playing games with a ball
and such things. Take care that the bones, muscles, and joints of the young dog are not very
overtaxed during the growing stage.

Head of a Tibetan Mastiff

Tosa Inu or Japanese Tosa

COUNTRY OF ORIGIN
Japan.

APTITUDE
Watchdog and family pet.

SIZE
The shoulder-height is a minimum of 61cm (24in) for dogs and 55cm (21^1/$_2$in) for bitches. As no maximum shoulder height is prescribed these heights are substantially exceeded.

COAT
The short-haired coat of the Tosa Inu is found in a number of colours including red-brown, black, yellow, streaked, and black and tan. Multi-coloured is also permissible.

CARE REQUIRED
The Tosa Inu is fairly easy to look after. The coat can be kept in good condition by an occasional brushing to remove dead and loose hairs. These dogs do not slobber.

CHARACTER
The Tosa Inu is quiet and self-aware, patient, brave, and a very good watchdog which only barks when necessary, has a strong protective urge, and is exceptionally intelligent.

They are very affectionate towards their family members but more reserved with strangers.

TRAINING
The Tosa Inu requires an equable and consistent but amiable approach to its training. It is very sensitive to your voice.

It is not sensible to take a hard line with the Tosa Inu although a commanding and confident approach is essential. This is not a breed for beginners.

SOCIAL BEHAVIOUR
The Tosa Inu places its family first and foremost. Generally they are fine with children but strangers are cautiously treated. Known visitors are usually happily greeted.
Keep him away from other dogs which are raring for a fight because an attacker will always come off worse.

EXERCISE
In a well fenced and large enough area of land, this dog can happily look after its own exercise demands. Take it with you to the beach, woods, or open countryside occasionally for a change of scene.
In principle it only requires an average level of exercise.

SPECIAL REMARKS
The Tosa Inu or Japanese Tosa is banned as a dangerous breed in Great Britain. For other countries, it is completely unsuitable for beginners.
They should never be placed in a kennel because they like to spend the day close to their handler.

Tosa Inu

Swiss cattle-drivers

Appenzell Mountain Dog

Appenzell Mountain Dog or Appenzeller Sennenhund

COUNTRY OF ORIGIN
Switzerland.

APTITUDE
Previously cattle-protector and driver, tracking, and watchdog. Nowadays mainly a watchdog and family pet.

SIZE
The ideal shoulder-height for dogs is 52 - 56cm (20$^1/_2$ - 22in) for dogs and 50 - 54cm (19$^1/_2$ - 21$^1/_2$in) for bitches. A variation of 2cm ($^1/_2$in) taller is permitted for both sexes.

COAT
The coat is straight-haired with a thick under-wool. The basic colour is black or brown with symmetrical rust-coloured and white markings.

CARE REQUIRED
The fine coat of the Appenzell Mountain Dog requires little attention. Remove loose and dead hairs from time to time with a rubber brush.

CHARACTER
The Appenzeller is a tough, sober, brave, intelligent, and lively dog which makes a good watchdog with a natural keenness. They like to bark.

TRAINING
The Appenzell Mountain Dog responds best to an equable manner of training that is consistent in approach.
Try to ensure that it makes acquaintance as positively as possible with all kinds of situations, people and other animals. This dog learns quite quickly, in part because it is so bright but also because it really wants to have something to do.
This dog does not belong in a kennel although it likes to be out of doors, but only when with its handler. Agility skill trials and fly-ball are suitable sports for this breed.

SOCIAL BEHAVIOUR
The Appenzell Mountain Dog generally gets along with other dogs and its mixing with livestock and household animals will also present few problems if the dog has become used to them when younger. They are rather unsure of strangers but greet family friends effusively. A healthy and well brought up Appenzeller Sennenhund is fine with children.
It is loyal to the whole family but tends to bond closely with one person.

EXERCISE
A dog such as this does not belong in a busy urban environment or suburban estate. It likes to be out of doors and is closely bonded with its territory.

The dog's herding instincts prevent it from running off. Living on a farm, it will get sufficient exercise. In all other circumstances you must take it on really long walks and if you can also find replacement work for it the dog will be completely happy.

Head of an Appenzell Mountain Dog

Bernese Mountain Dog or Berner Sennenhund

COUNTRY OF ORIGIN
Switzerland.

APTITUDE
Previously a cattle-driver, tracking dog, and watchdog among other uses, now a watchdog and family pet.

SIZE
The shoulder-height is 64 - 70cm ($25^1/_2$- $27^1/_2$in) for dogs and 58 - 66cm ($22^1/_2$ - 26in) for bitches.

COAT
The coat is medium-length and straight to slightly curly and has a thick under-layer. The colour is always chiefly black with rust and white markings.

CARE REQUIRED
In those places where the hair readily tangles (hindquarters, neck, the leg sockets, and behind the ears), it must be regularly groomed with brush and comb. When necessary trim any excessive hair growth between the pads of the feet.

CHARACTER
The Bernese Mountain Dog is an equable, vigi-

lant, and friendly dog which is not easily led a-stray by bribes and is very loyal to its handler and family. It is also attentive, calm, intelligent, and seldom barks.

TRAINING
The Bernese Mountain Dog requires an equable, consistent, and very loving approach to being brought up. This dog is a quick learner and an eager pupil which is very responsive to your voice. Never let a growing dog run up and down stairs and avoid them being overtaxed physically. The animal needs all its energy to build strong bones, joints, and to put on weight.

SOCIAL BEHAVIOUR
Bernese Mountain Dogs are normally wonderful with children and will also protect them. Provided they have met cats and other household animals as young dogs, they will always behave properly in their presence. They are good watchdogs but they will never jump up and down and pace your garden fence barking. Unknown visitors will be announced with full-throated barking and then carefully watched. They will stand ready to defend you if required to. Some of them can be rather dominant towards their own kind.

EXERCISE
With this dog you will have to take it out regularly because it is very fond of exercise. When

possible let it run and play off the lead. Make sure that a young dog gets sufficient rest and sleep. Do not take it on long and tiring walks during the growing stage. They do not run off because of their strong territorial instincts.

SPECIAL REMARKS
Given the popularity of this breed in some countries it is advisable to obtain a puppy only through help from a breed society.

Bernese Mountain Dog

Entelbuch Mountain Dog or Entelbucher Sennenhund

COUNTRY OF ORIGIN
Switzerland.

APTITUDE
Formerly a cattle-driver and estate dog among other duties, nowadays a watchdog and family pet.

SIZE
The shoulder-height is 44 - 50cm ($17^1/_2$ - $19^1/_2$in) for dogs and 42 - 48cm ($16^1/_2$ - $18^1/_2$in) for bitches. Examples of the breed 2cm ($^1/_2$in) higher than these standards are accepted.

COAT
The coat is straight-haired with a thick woolly under-layer. The colour is predominantly black with white and rust-coloured markings.

CARE REQUIRED
During moulting use a special comb with a double row of metal teeth to groom the under-layer of the coat. At other times little attention is required.

CHARACTER
This is a lively, temperamental, equable, and brave dog which will not easily be led astray by bribes and makes a good watchdog. It is also high-spirited, intelligent, and keen to learn.

TRAINING
The Entelbuch Mountain Dog responds best to an equable, caring handler who has a firm hand but is consistent at all times. Make sure that this dog, which learns very quickly, has plenty of positive experiences of other animals, people, and situations during its social training. This breed is not suitable for banishing to a kennel - even though the dog likes to be out of doors - but only when it can be with its handler.

SOCIAL BEHAVIOUR
The family comes as priority number one with this breed in common with all the Swiss Sennenhunds. The Entelbuch Mountain Dog will warn you when there is trouble. They tend to be rather uncertain with strangers and will certainly announce their presence. Mostly they are good with children and rarely cause problems with household animals and livestock.

EXERCISE
This Sennenhund needs lots of exercise and to be kept busy. Do not expect it to adapt to the circumstances because it will become moody and uncertain if you limit it to three short outings around the houses. They have a fairly strong territorial instinct so that they are not likely to run away. They are suitable for sports such as fly-ball, and agility skills.

Entelbuch Mountain Dog

Greater Swiss Mountain Dog

Greater Swiss Mountain Dog

COUNTRY OF ORIGIN
Switzerland.

APTITUDE
Formerly a cattle driver among other duties, today a watchdog and family pet.

SIZE
The shoulder-height is 65 - 72cm
($25^1/_2$ - $28^1/_2$in) for dogs and 60 - 68cm
($23^1/_2$ - 27in) for bitches.

COAT
The coat is straight-haired with a thick woolly under-layer. The colour is always black with rust-coloured and white markings.

CARE REQUIRED
The Greater Swiss Mountain Dog requires little grooming. An occasional session with a rubber brush to remove dead and loose hairs is adequate.

CHARACTER
This breed is intelligent, friendly, keen to its work, watchful, reliable, not easily led astray by bribes, and protective.
Its other points are that it is equable, sociable, and obedient. The dogs only bark when necessary.

TRAINING
Even though this breed bonds closely with the family of which they form a part, they are not a suitable breed for everyone. The Greater Swiss Mountain Dog has a very strong character and calls out for a handler who is equally strong.

It must get the chance of growing up in a well-balanced environment and have a clear understanding of what is permitted and what is not, and be able to build a close bond with his family. Make sure that you are always consistent with it. A severe approach will only ruin the dog's nature.
Watch and control it carefully during the growing stage so that all its energy can be used for building healthy bones and muscles. For the same reason do not scrimp with its food.

SOCIAL BEHAVIOUR
This breed gets on well with dogs and other household animals. Under your care it will make a marvellous friend for your children too, but do not forget that it will protect your children against their friends if it thinks they are being pestered by them.

They make excellent watchdogs which will protect you and your family together with all your possessions against wrongdoers. They are not suited to living in a kennel.

EXERCISE
This breed is a diligent worker which means, if you consider its intelligence, that it can make a multi-faceted and reliable working dog for you. In Switzerland it is used as a tracking dog among other roles. This dog has the potential to shine at obedience training and in various other areas of dog sporting activities. When it happens that a week passes in which you are unable to do anything with this dog, it will accept it easily and not misbehave.

SPECIAL REMARKS
This beautiful, imposing dog requires plenty of living space. It will not be happy in a flat or small house without a garden.

Greater Swiss Mountain Dog, study of the head

3. Terriers

Long-legged Terriers

Airedale Terrier

COUNTRY OF ORIGIN
England.

APTITUDE
Originally used for hunting otters and other animals, now mainly a family pet.

SIZE
The shoulder height is 58 - 61cm (22$^1/_2$ - 24in) for dogs and 56 - 58cm (22 - 22$^1/_2$in) for bitches.

COAT
The hard wire-haired coat is smooth. The most common colour is tan with a grey-black "saddle."

CARE REQUIRED
The Airedale Terrier requires little grooming under normal circumstances. The hair should be plucked about twice per year, but for dogs that are to be shown much more intensive grooming is needed.
When necessary, trim excess hair between the pads of the feet.

CHARACTER
The Airedale is tough on itself, loyal to its own people, but stubborn, tends to be playful, watchful, active, intelligent, and resolute. An Airedale does not often bark.

TRAINING
The Airedale Terrier is intelligent enough to perceive quickly what is required of it. Try to ring the changes in its training, because if consistently given the same instructions it is liable to become stubborn.
It is best to make the exercises a challenge. With the right handler, Airedale Terriers can do well in various dog sports including defence dog trials.

SOCIAL BEHAVIOUR
In general, Airedale Terriers get on well with cats and other household animals, and they are very patient with children. They can be rather

Staffordshire Bull Terrier

Airedale Terrier

dominant towards other dogs, but this greatly depends upon their training and the individual dog.

EXERCISE
The Airedale Terrier has an average demand for exercise and will be happy with three circuits of the neighbourhood a day plus playing in the garden. Most of them love to play with a ball, swim, or retrieve objects, and once fully grown will happily run alongside a cycle.

Bedlington Terrier

COUNTRY OF ORIGIN
England.

APTITUDE
In the past the Bedlington Terrier was used to destroy vermin and for hunting hares and foxes, among other smaller animals. Today they are chiefly family pets.

SIZE
The shoulder-height is approximately 41cm (16$^1/_2$in) with a permissible 2.5cm (1in) higher and lower latitude .

COAT
The Bedlington Terrier used to be called a wolf in sheep's clothing. Its coat grows in curly short whirls, which stand out from the body. They

can be plain blue, blue with brown, liver, or sandy-coloured. The most common colour is blue. Puppies are born black or brown.

CARE REQUIRED
This dog needs to visit a dog-trimming parlour at least once a year for its coat to be kept in order. In addition to this it requires regular grooming with brush and comb. It does not moult. Keep the inside of the ears free of hair by removing them yourself or get a trimming parlour to do it for you.

Bedlingtons should not be washed too often or the coat will become lank, which is not considered appropriate for the breed. Dogs which are to be shown require greater levels of grooming.

CHARACTER
The Bedlington Terrier is brave and tenacious, intelligent, peaceful indoors and equable, loving with children, playful, barks little, is loyal, cheerful and has a mind of its own. They tend

Blue Bedlington Terrier

Head of a liver-coloured Bedlington Terrier

to bond closely with one member of the family.

TRAINING
Bedlingtons are intelligent and they grasp things quickly, although they can be a bit stubborn. They react well to your voice, but the occasional corrective measure may be required.

SOCIAL BEHAVIOUR
This breed usually gets on well with children. They need to learn to like cats and also other household animals when they are young.
Generally they can get on with other dogs but keep them away from dominant dogs, because once challenged they are terrifying fighters!

EXERCISE
The Bedlington Terrier can run fast and jump high and it loves doing both. Letting it run beside your cycle is an ideal way for it to burn off energy.

SPECIAL REMARKS
This breed can cope perfectly well with life in a flat or maisonette, provided it gets sufficient outdoor exercise.

Border Terrier

COUNTRY OF ORIGIN
England.

APTITUDE
Hunting dog and family pet.

SIZE
The shoulder-height is approximately 35cm (13$^{1}/_{2}$in).
For dogs the weight is permitted to be 5.9 - 7.1kg (13 - 15$^{1}/_{2}$lb); the weight for bitches is between 5.1 - 6.4kg (11$^{1}/_{2}$ - 14lb).

COAT
The hard coat is thick with a dense under-layer. The recognized colours are red, wheaten, and grey with grey markings.

CARE REQUIRED
Groom them thoroughly at least once a week. Depending upon the condition of the coat, the Border Terrier's coat may need plucking occasionally but must never be trimmed!
Plucking by hand removes old and excess hair.

CHARACTER
The Border Terrier is a tenacious, brave,

Border Terrier

EXERCISE

It has been said of the Border Terrier that it can hold a horse under control. Whether this true is perhaps questionable. It is true that they love to run and play out of doors. A Border Terrier restricted to three short outings per day and spending the rest of his time indoors will adapt to this life but at the expense of some of its zest for life. Border Terriers are suitable for sports like fly-ball and agility skills.

Fox Terrier (Smooth)/
Fox Terrier (Wire)

equable, stubborn, lively dog which is sportive and untiring. This breed can take a blow and is not sensitive to pain. It is loyal to its handler, patient with children, and adaptable.

COUNTRY OF ORIGIN
England.

TRAINING
Training is relatively easy because the Border Terrier learns so quickly.

APTITUDE
Formerly a vermin destroyer and hunting dog for foxes and badgers. Today the Fox Terrier is a family pet.

SOCIAL BEHAVIOUR
It gets on well with children. If you want it to get on with other dogs, cats, and other household animals, then it is essential to introduce them when it is young.

SIZE
The Fox Terrier weighs 7 - 8kg ($15^1/_2$ - $17^1/_2$lb). The shoulder-height may not exceed 39cm ($15^1/_2$in) for dogs. Bitches may be slightly smaller.

Fox Terrier (Wire)

Fox Terrier (smooth)

young how to get on with cats and your other household animals so that it will not chase them later. Fox Terriers are ever alert and will go to the attack if there is danger, but they are not unfriendly towards strangers.

EXERCISE
These dogs are bursting with energy and like to be constantly active. It is certain to be keen on activities like agility skills and fly-ball.
If you are sportive, then one of the two types of Fox Terrier is the dog for you.

Young Fox Terrier (smooth)

COAT
There are two types of Fox Terrier: the smooth-haired and the wire-haired. The Smooth has a dense coat of sleek short hairs which may not be thin anywhere on the body. The Wire has a rough coat that is thick and hard and should be neither curly nor soft.

The Wire is required to have hair embellishments around the muzzle and eyes, and longer hair around the feet. The overriding colour for both is white with markings of tan and/or black considered desirable.

CARE REQUIRED
The coat of the Wire generally requires plucking with the fingers several times each year. In addition to this the dog should be groomed several times a week with brush and comb. For showing even greater levels of grooming will be required. The Smooth can be adequately taken care of with a weekly brushing.
Use a rubber brush during moulting to remove dead and loose hairs.

CHARACTER
The Fox Terrier is a very intelligent and cunning, hardy, lively, and cheerful dog which is watchful, alert, brave, resolute, and self-confident.

TRAINING
Fox Terriers learn quite quickly. They can be rather stubborn - but that is inherent with all Terriers. Make certain you remain consistent in your training.

SOCIAL BEHAVIOUR
This breed usually gets on well with children. Some Fox Terriers can be rather dominant towards their own kind. Teach the dog when

Glen of Imaal Terrier

COUNTRY OF ORIGIN
Ireland.

APTITUDE
This Terrier was once used for a number of purposes, including hunting badgers and destroying vermin. Today it is mainly a family pet.

SIZE
The shoulder-height may be no greater than 35.5cm (14in). In spite of its short height this is a robust dog.

COAT
The Glen of Imaal Terrier has a medium-length, hard and coarse-haired outer coat, and a soft dense under-layer.
The colours range from dark grey (considered blue) with highlights, through brindle, to wheaten.

CARE REQUIRED

If your Glen of Imaal Terrier is a pet, hand-plucking its coat about twice a year will be sufficient grooming; coats of show dogs require more attention. Clip excess hair between the pads of its feet and also remove it from the ear passages.

CHARACTER

This breed is equable, affectionate, brave, and very demanding of themselves, loyal, intelligent but late developers; they can be stubborn, are playful, lively, and boisterous.
They are usually calm indoors and they rarely bark.

TRAINING

The training of this breed need not be difficult. They are keen to learn, but they can be dominant and stubborn. Remain consistent at all times in your approach and intermix play with training routines.

SOCIAL BEHAVIOUR

Glen of Imaal Terriers get on well with children. Some of the dogs of this breed can be rather dominant towards other dogs, but provided they have had positive experiences of cats and other household animals when growing up, they can happily mix with them.
Visitors you wish to see will be cheerfully welcomed, while unwelcome ones will get a less friendly reception. They will bark if they detect danger.

EXERCISE

This breed will adapt its exercise needs to the family situation.

Irish Terrier

COUNTRY OF ORIGIN

Ireland.

APTITUDE

Hunting dog, watchdog, and family pet.

SIZE

The shoulder-height is 46 - 50cm (18 - 19$^1/_2$in) and the weight should be about 14kg (31lb).

COAT

The outer-coat is very hard, while the under-layer is both softer and finer. The accepted colours are golden-yellow, wheaten, and light red. Small white markings on the chest are permissible.

CARE REQUIRED

The Irish Terrier's grooming depends upon the condition of its coat and whether you wish to show the dog, but in any event requires hand-plucking the hairs at least twice a year. Trim excessive hair between the pads of the feet and keep the ears clean.

CHARACTER

The Irish Terrier is a dog of character which is loyal, protective, vigilant, playful, has a sense of humour, is intelligent, tends to be over-courageous, sensitive, active, and bonds very strongly with its family. In the Country of origin it is tellingly dubbed "dare devil."

TRAINING

This breed requires a confident handler who can train it in a very consistent and tactful way.

Irish Terrier

Head of an Irish Terrier

When in a good mood it can learn anything, but try to ensure that there is plenty of variety in the training routine.

SOCIAL BEHAVIOUR
This character of a dog tends to be rather eager to fight when in the presence of other dogs. Teach it when young not to chase cats. It is naturally friendly with people and adores children and is very tolerant of them.
The bitches are generally calmer than the dogs.

The Irish Terrier becomes very dependent upon its family and regards it as a punishment to be left alone for a long time.
It will defend its territory and that of its family against wrongdoers but is not really mistrustful of strangers.

EXERCISE
The Irish Terrier requires a lot of exercise so take it out regularly. They enjoy playing with a ball in the garden or romping in open countryside.
People say that they love riding in cars and want to be taken everywhere with you.

Irish Soft-coated Wheaten Terriër

Soft-coated Wheaten Terrier

COUNTRY OF ORIGIN
Ireland.

APTITUDE
Hunting dog and family pet.

SIZE
The shoulder-height is 46 - 48cm (18 - 18$\frac{1}{2}$in) and the weight in the region of 15kg (33lb).

Soft-coated Wheaten Terrier with puppy

COAT
The coat is very soft and silken with a light wave or curl. The colour is a range of tints from light wheaten to reddish gold. The attractive and distinctive adult coat can take two years to grow. The coat of the Soft-coated Wheaten Terrier must not be woolly.

CARE REQUIRED
This breed is normally trimmed to a set style, leaving the hair around the face, feet, neck, chest, and belly longer than elsewhere.

The dogs do not moult in spring and autumn but loose hairs should be combed out of the coat from time to time. Well-groomed examples shed very little hair in the house.

CHARACTER
This breed is cheerful and extrovert, active and playful, intelligent and eager to learn, and they bond extremely closely with their family. The dogs are also slightly independent, self-confident, and seldom bark.

TRAINING
In common with all other dogs, the Soft-coated Wheaten Terrier needs to be taught what it may and what may not do. Because they are very intelligent, they will generally grasp quickly what is required of them.

They have a straight-forward nature and need to be similarly handled.

SOCIAL BEHAVIOUR
Soft-coated Wheaten Terriers are usually very loving with children and get on reasonably well

with other dogs. Provided they are socialized when young, they will also normally cause no difficulties with cats.

EXERCISE
Wheatens are active dogs which can be very calm indoors provided they get sufficient opportunities out of doors to burn off their energy. They are ideally suited to a number of sporting activities such as agility skills and fly-ball.

Make sure the training has plenty of variety and is a challenge for them because they will quickly lose their enthusiasm if the exercises are too easy-going.

Kerry Blue Terrier

Kerry Blue Terrier

COUNTRY OF ORIGIN
Ireland.

APTITUDE
Watchdog and family pet.

SIZE
The shoulder-height is 45 - 48cm ($17^1/_2$ - $18^1/_2$in). The weight is between 14 - 18kg (31 - $39^1/_2$lb).

COAT
The Kerry Blue has a soft, thick and abundantly curly coat without an under-layer. The colour is light to dark blue. Puppies are born black and it can take up to a year and a half before the coat changes colour to blue.

CARE REQUIRED
The Kerry Blue Terrier needs to be trimmed with scissors and trimmer. In addition to this,

they need grooming occasionally with brush and comb. Dogs for showing will require greater levels of grooming. An advantage of the Kerry Blue is that he does not lose hairs.

CHARACTER
These dogs are intelligent and have a very good memory, they are lively and boisterous, self-confident, vigilant and brave, and they bond very closely with their handler. In addition they can be stubborn, they are hardy, have a mind of their own, and are ever-ready to fight their own kind. They rarely bark. The Kerry Blue can be wilful.

TRAINING
Because this dog is active, self-confident, and stubborn, it needs a handler who is confident of his ability and leadership. They are not therefore suitable for beginners. It may want to attack other dogs in the street and this must not be tolerated - even though it is a natural character trait of the breed. The Kerry Blue certainly has an aptitude for sports like fly-ball and agility training but if you decide to involve the dog, it is important that it relishes the challenge. If lessons or drills are too monotonous for the Kerry Blue, its stubbornness is likely to surface.

Kerry Blue Terriers

This Terrier is loving with children and very attached to its handler and family. Try to make it confident with cats and other household animals when very young so that it will not pester them when older.

Some of them very much enjoy the company of other dogs, while others prefer to go through life as an "only dog." This does not solely depend upon the early social training but is largely dependent upon the individual dog.

Exercise

The Kerry Blue is a sportive dog which likes to accompany its handler on long walks. It will accept the occasional week passing without such a good outing without grumbling.

Special remarks

The Kerry Blue Terrier is something special. Its coat is meant to look unkempt. If you want a dog which is not everybody's friend and which is also fairly unusual, provided you are confident in yourself, can be consistent, value a dog that has a nature all of his own, then the Kerry Blue will be a good choice.

Lakeland Terrier

Lakeland Terrier

Country of origin

England.

Aptitude

Hunting dog (for foxes and other small prey), and family pet.

Size

The shoulder-height may not exceed 37cm (141/2in).The weight is about of 7kg (151/2lb).

Coat

The coat is thick, hard, and sheds water. It can be black and tan, blue and tan, red-grey, red, wheaten, liver, blue, or black in colour.

Care required

The Lakeland Terrier needs its coat to be plucked two or three times each year, meaning the removal of the old hair by pulling it out by hand. Remove loose hairs also from the ear passages and trim excess hair between the pads of the feet.

he coats of show dogs will require more intensive grooming.

Character

This is a sportive, intelligent and affectionate dog which is a good watchdog, self-confident and loving with children, and also lively and cheerful.

Training

This sportive dog learns quite easily. Because of this make sure that the training is full of variety and offers the dog a challenge; in this way it will quickly pick up your intentions.

Social behaviour

Lakelands get on well with children but also with other dogs - not common among Terriers. They can be uncertain of strangers but this does not usually become extreme. Teach them when they are young to get on with cats and other household animals, so that they will not chase them later.

Lakeland Terrier

EXERCISE
A Lakeland Terrier can be kept in a flat but it must get adequate exercise.

They need to run and play off the lead at regular intervals. They are certainly suitable for various sporting activities such as fly-ball and agility skills.

Head of a Manchester Terrier

Manchester Terrier

COUNTRY OF ORIGIN
England.

APTITUDE
Rat-catcher and family pet.

SIZE
The ideal height is 40 - 41cm ($15^1/_2$ - $16^1/_2$in) for dogs and 38cm (15in) for bitches.

COAT
The coat is short, sleek, and shiny. The most usual colour is black and tan.

CARE REQUIRED
The Manchester Terrier does not require much grooming. During the moulting period the dead and loose hairs can be simply removed with a rubber brush.

Afterwards, use a chamois-leather to make the coat shiny. Keep the ear passages clean and the claws short.

CHARACTER
This is a high-spirited, very intelligent and cunning dog which is eager to learn, lively and sportive, alert and vigilant, barks normally only when there is danger, and bonds very closely with its handler.

TRAINING
This dog likes to please its handler and learns quite quickly. They can be outstanding in activities like agility skills and fly-ball, but they also do well in obedience trials.

SOCIAL BEHAVIOUR
Some of the dogs can be rather dominant towards their own kind but they get on well with children. It is advisable to get them used to cats and other household animals quite early on.
Manchester Terriers make exceptional watchdogs because in spite of their size they do not hesitate to go into action when necessary. They are also first-rate rat- and mole-catchers.

EXERCISE
The Manchester Terrier demands plenty of exercise. In addition to the normal daily walks, let it run and play off the lead regularly. They can run very fast and keep the speed up for a long time. It is therefore ideal to exercise alongside a cycle, provided that the exercise is built up gradually.

Manchester Terrier

Parson Jack Russell Terrier

COUNTRY OF ORIGIN
England.

APTITUDE
Hunting dog and family pet.

SIZE
The ideal shoulder-height is 35cm ($13^1/_2$in) for dogs and 33cm (13in) for bitches.

Smooth-haired Parson Jack Russell

COAT
There are smooth-haired and rough-haired Parson Jack Russell Terriers. Both types of coat should be wiry, dense, and thick. They are usually predominantly white with tan, lemon, black, or triple-coloured markings - preferably restricted to the head and root of the tail.

CARE REQUIRED
The Parson Jack Russell Terrier is easy to care for. During moulting you should remove loose hairs every day with a rubber brush. The rough-haired type requires its coat to be plucked occasionally.

CHARACTER
This is a very active, intelligent and cunning dog that is vigilant, bold and enterprising, hard upon itself, brave (sometimes foolhardy), has plenty of self-confidence - verging on dominance - and is quite independent.

Rough-haired Parson Jack Russell

TRAINING
These dogs can learn very quickly but have the tendency to try to have their own way in everything.
Do not let yourself be won over by their mischievous charm; they know perfectly well how to try to win you over. Remain consistent at all times!

SOCIAL BEHAVIOUR
Generally this breed produces uncomplicated and socially acceptable dogs. They get on well with other household pets and love to play with children. When their social training has been good, they can also get on with the household cat but they frequently cannot resist the urge to chase a cat which runs away from them - they are still hunting dogs! Somewhat dominant dogs can often be foolhardy in the presence of larger dogs. Visiting strangers will always be announced.

EXERCISE
This breed has enormous reserves of energy and you must do your best to find ways to burn this off. They get no pleasure at all out of three short circuits of the neighbourhood.
The Parson Jack Russell Terrier needs to run about and frolic every day and they love to dig. They will feel absolutely at home on a farm where they can also be useful in dealing with vermin. They are ideally suited for activities such as agility skills and fly-ball.

Welsh Terrier

COUNTRY OF ORIGIN
Wales.

APTITUDE
Hunting dog and family pet.

SIZE
The weight is about 9kg (20lb) and the shoulder height should not exceed 39cm (15^1/$_2$in).

COAT
The coat is wire-haired, hard and very thick. They are usually red-brown with black.

CARE REQUIRED
The Welsh Terrier will need to have its coat plucked two or three times a year or even more often - depending upon the condition of the coat. It also requires grooming with brush and comb a number of times each week.

Welsh Terrier

Those dogs that are to be shown will require even greater levels of attention. The longer hairs at the feet, on the belly, and particularly around the face, give the Welsh Terrier its typical appearance.

CHARACTER
The Welsh Terrier is a vigilant, active, cheerful and uncomplicated dog, which is affectionate, intelligent, can be dominant towards other dogs, is brave, and obedient.

It bonds very closely with its handler and family although reserved with strangers.

TRAINING
The Welsh Terrier is bright enough to understand quickly what you want of it but is also cunning enough to try to divert you from your intentions.

Give them constant variety in their training and remain consistent towards them.

SOCIAL BEHAVIOUR
The Welsh Terrier can be rather reserved with people it does not know. Generally it is patient with children - and can withstand a bit of rough play. Make sure it becomes confident with cats and other animals of the house when young. This will prevent the dog from chasing them when it grows up.

EXERCISE
The Welsh Terrier is untiring; it is always ready to play with a ball and to run and gambol off the lead in the open countryside, which it loves to do.

Yet if you occasionally find it impossible one time to give the dog this pleasure, it will accept matters without fuss.

Short-legged Terriers

Australian Terrier

COUNTRY OF ORIGIN
Australia.

APTITUDE
Hunting dog and family pet.

SIZE
The shoulder-height is about 25cm (9^1/$_2$in) and the weight is in the region of 5.5 - 6.5kg (12 - 14^1/$_2$lb).

Welsh Terrier

Head of an Australian Terrier

COAT

The hair is straight, hard, and of medium length. The breed has a blue back and deep shades of tan on legs and muzzle.

The locks of hair over the eyes may be blue or silver, but sandy or red is also accepted.

CARE REQUIRED

The Australian Terrier's coat requires plucking about every three months. Groom with brush and comb between these times about once a week and ensure that no hair is growing inside the ear passages.

Because the breed standard prefers a hard coat, it is not a good idea to wash this Terrier too often, which will make the hair lank. An Australian Terrier in good condition loses very little hair.

CHARACTER

The Australian Terrier is vigilant and alert, brave, lively, self-confident, and is very adaptable, intelligent, playful, independent, and a bit stubborn. They are excellent vermin destroyers and like to bark.

Australian Terrier

TRAINING

The training of the Australian Terrier needs to be strict because this self-confident freebooter will sometimes only follow its own ideas. They learn quite quickly.

SOCIAL BEHAVIOUR

Provided children do not tease it, this breed gets along fine with them.

Strangers on the other hand will not be readily accepted yet the breed is not excessively suspicious.

Teach the dogs when young to live with cats so that they too can live together without major conflict.

EXERCISE

The adaptability of the Australian Terrier is phenomenal but it is most happy when able to romp and play.

Cairn Terriers

Cairn Terrier

COUNTRY OF ORIGIN
Scotland.

APTITUDE
Vermin destroyer, hunting dog, and family pet.

SIZE
The shoulder-height is 28 - 31cm (11 - 12$^1/_2$ in) tall, but this must be in proportion to the weight, which can vary from 6 - 7.5kg (13$^1/_2$ - 16$^1/_2$ lb).

COAT
The Cairn Terrier - like the West Highland Terrier - has a double-layered coat, of which the topcoat is hard and abundant, and the undercoat is soft and short. The hair may not curl. Permitted colours are grey, wheaten, cream-red, or almost black. Darker markings on the ears and muzzle are highly regarded. Cairns may not be white or totally black.

CARE REQUIRED
The coat needs regular grooming with a brush and comb. About twice per year - depending upon the condition of the hair - the dead hairs need to be plucked out by hand. This can be done by a trimming salon, but it is good to learn how to do it yourself.

From time to time remove excess hair from the ear passages. A Cairn Terrier should have a rough appearance (described by some breed experts as looking like a road-sweeper's broom), and is therefore not excessively groomed for showing. For showing, any excessive hair around the feet, ears, and tail is removed.

CHARACTER

This is an intelligent, brave, cheerful, lively, playful and extrovert dog which is hard upon itself, uncomplicated, affectionate, eager to learn, alert and vigilant.

TRAINING

Teach this dog early to get on with cats and other household pets, so that it will not chase them when older. Puppies can take a game of pulling on a rope quite seriously. You must decide when the game is to end by giving it the command "drop it." The antics of puppies are often the cause of laughter but do not forget that the strokes the dog might pull as a puppy will be less amusing when it is grown up. The Cairn needs loving but also strict and consistent training.

SOCIAL BEHAVIOUR

The Cairn Terrier makes a first-class friend for children; it can tolerate rough play and has a well-developed sense of humour. They can also get on reasonably well with other dogs, although some dogs of this breed will stand their ground. They go into action when they detect danger.

EXERCISE

This breed is bursting with energy and must get ample opportunity to run and play. It is an ideal dog for a sportive family. It likes to be taken for a walk in the woods or in open countryside where it can run free, but make sure before you do so that the dog will return to you when you call - the hunting instinct is so strong that they can take off.

Cairn Terrier

Cesky Terrier or Bohemian Terrier

Cesky Terrier or Bohemian Terrier

COUNTRY OF ORIGIN

Czech Republic or Slovakia.

APTITUDE

Hunting dog and family pet.

SIZE

The shoulder-height is 27 -35cm ($10^1/_2$ - $13^1/_2$in) and the weight is 6 - 9kg ($13^1/_2$ - 20lb).

COAT

The coat consists of thick shiny hair. The most usual colour is blue-grey in different shade variations; light coffee brown is rarer. Both colours are permitted, with and without white markings. The Cesky does not moult.

CARE REQUIRED

The Cesky should be trimmed regularly, leaving the hair long on the stomach, and legs, and also around the face (moustache, beard, and eyebrows).

If the dog is a pet, it will need to be trimmed about four times a year; dogs for shows require more frequent grooming. The longer hair needs to be brushed or combed twice a week or more, depending on the condition of the coat, to prevent tangles.

lip the excess hair between the pads of the feet and remove loose hairs in the ear passages.

CHARACTER

The Cesky is a good-humoured dog which is affectionate, very adaptable, stalwart and hardy, sportive but also calm, and it is intelligent and sociable.

TRAINING

The training of this breed is not very deman-

ding. It is important to let the puppy meet with various people and different animals in positive circumstances and to experience a variety of situations to enable it to grow up to be an equable adult.

SOCIAL BEHAVIOUR
This sociable dog gets on well with its own kind and with other household animals. In addition, it is always loving with children.
They can be somewhat cautious with strangers.

EXERCISE
The Cesky Terrier has an average demand for exercise. This dog likes to frolic and play but it also enjoys walks through a wood or across open countryside.

SPECIAL REMARKS
Cesky Terriers are always born black. The coat lightens in colour later - in some cases not until the dog is older than two years.

Dandie Dinmont Terrier

COUNTRY OF ORIGIN
Scotland.

APTITUDE
Hunting dog and family pet.

Dandie Dinmont Terrier

SIZE
The shoulder height is approximately 23cm (9in) and the weight 7 - 11kg (15½ - 24lb).

COAT
This Terrier has a double-layered coat: the undercoat is soft, the topcoat is hard. Dandie Dinmonts colours are "pepper" which runs from almost black to a light silver-grey) and "mustard" (a reddish brown to pale beige).

CARE REQUIRED
It needs to be brushed regularly and must also be taken to a trimming salon to have the dead hair plucked out once or twice each year.
Dogs that are to be shown will require additional grooming.

CHARACTER
This is a high-spirited yet calm dog which will be devoted to its handler and family, is equable, intelligent, vigilant and tenacious, but also sensitive.

TRAINING
The training of this dog is fortunately not difficult, providing you make allowance for the fact that it can be stubborn.

SOCIAL BEHAVIOUR
This is a very sociable breed of dog that usually leaves other dogs alone and acts perfectly with cats and other household animals, provided it has met them when young.
hey are normally very loving with children and visitors should also cause no problem.

EXERCISE
The Dandie Dinmont Terrier has an average exercise demand and will adapt to the family circumstances.

Norwich Terrier

Dandie Dinmont Terriers

Norfolk and Norwich Terriers

Norfolk Terrier

COUNTRY OF ORIGIN
England.

APTITUDE
Much used previously as a true terrier (a dog which hunts animals underground), today mainly a family pet.

SIZE
The shoulder-height of both breeds is about 25cm (9$^1/_2$in) and both weigh about 4kg (8$^1/_2$lb).

Norwich Terriers

COAT
These breeds have hard wire-haired coats. The hair on the head and ears is shorter than at the neck, belly, and shoulders. It comes in a variety of shades of red, but also in straw-yellow, black with rust-brown, and grey. A small amount of white is permissible although not preferred.

CARE REQUIRED.
Brush and comb the coat regularly and pluck out the old hair. This is a job that you can do yourself or leave to a professional dog trimming salon. This is usually needed about twice per year, depending upon the condition of the coat. Excess hair between the pads of the feet must also be trimmed.

CHARACTER
These are cheerful, lively, and intelligent dogs which are friendly, brave and bold, cunning, enterprising, straight forward, playful, and can be wilful.

TRAINING
Both Norwich and Norfolk Terriers learn quite quickly. Make sure you are real consistent with them because they are Terriers with a will of their own.

SOCIAL BEHAVIOUR
For a Terrier, these are fairly easy dogs in their relationship with other dogs. Children too are seldom a problem. Visitors will be initially announced by loud barking but then all will be calm.

EXERCISE
These dogs adapt to the circumstances. They will be denied their natural instincts if they are not given the opportunity to dig.

SPECIAL REMARKS
The difference between a Norwich and a Norfolk Terrier is that the former have erect ears while the latter have drooping ears.

Scottish Terrier

COUNTRY OF ORIGIN
Scotland.

APTITUDE
Hunting dog, for foxes and rabbits and other small prey, and family pet.

SIZE
The shoulder-height is 25 - 28cm (9$^1/_2$ - 11in) and the weight 8.5 - 10.5kg (18$^1/_2$- 23lb).

COAT
The coat is hard and wire-haired. The Scottish Terrier or Scottie as commonly known is bred as plain black, broken black with highlights, and wheaten.

CARE REQUIRED
The coat needs to be hand-plucked by an expert about twice per year; the chest, legs, and head are usually clipped. Between the plucking sessions the hair should be regularly brushed and combed. Remove any food remnants from the beard and moustache regularly. Show dogs require more intensive grooming.

CHARACTER
The Scottie is straight forward and sober, becomes very attached to its family, is vigilant, noble, sportive, and sometimes has a mind of its own. It loves to dig.

TRAINING
For the right handler, who is consistent, this aristocrat of a dog is easy to train. Remember though that for all its loyalty to you, this is an independent dog. Training needs to be founded on mutual respect for each other.

SOCIAL BEHAVIOUR
The natural inclination of a Scottie is to get on well with other household animals and its own kind. Provided children do not treat this dog as a toy and leave it alone in its domain, they will get along together. Much depends upon the puppy's social training.

EXERCISE
The Scottie will adapt its exercise demands to the circumstances.

Sealyham Terrier

COUNTRY OF ORIGIN
Wales.

APTITUDE
Hunting dog and companion.

SIZE
The ideal shoulder-height is 31cm (12^1/$_2$in). Dogs weigh about 9kg (20lb) and bitches are slighter lighter.

COAT
The long, hard, wire-haired outer-layer of the coat covers a weather-resistant under-layer. The colours are entirely white, or white with lemon, brown, blue, or badger-coloured markings on the head and/or ears.

CARE REQUIRED
Comb the coat thoroughly on a regular basis and take the dog twice each year to a salon for a trim. With less common breeds like the Sealyham Terrier it is necessary to find a salon where it can be expertly clipped out.

Sealyham Terrier

CHARACTER

This is an equable dog which is brave, tough on itself, very active out of doors but calm indoors. The dog has a loud bark but uses it only when danger is sensed, it remains playful into old age, and can have a mind of its own. Sealyham Terriers are very loyal.

TRAINING

The Sealyham Terrier is generally an intelligent dog which learns easily, but it can try to undermine your authority from time to time. In such circumstances it is appropriate to correct it but make sure you are always consistent with the dog.

SOCIAL BEHAVIOUR

The Sealyham gets on reasonably well with other dogs. For such behaviour with cats and other animals, it needs to be introduced to them when young. Provided it has had positive contact with children when a puppy, it will get along with them when grown up. With visitors it can be friendly or cautious - much depends upon the early social training.

EXERCISE

This breed has average demands for exercise and usually adapts to the circumstances. That does not take away the fact that a Sealyham Terrier likes to get out of its basket for a good long walk in the woods.

They usually love to root around in the ground - bear this in mind if you have a neatly laid out garden. Most Sealyhams like to ride with you in the car.

Skye Terrier

COUNTRY OF ORIGIN

Scotland.

APTITUDE

Historically used to hunt the fox, badger, and otter. Today they are principally family pets.

SIZE

The shoulder-height is a mere 25 - 26cm ($9^1/_2$ - $10^1/_2$in) for dogs, while the length between the

Skye Terriers

nose and the tip of the tail can be more than 100cm (39½in). The bitches are slightly smaller.

COAT
The Skye Terrier has a double-layered coat. The topcoat is long, hard and straight, without curls, while the undercoat is short, thick, and woolly. They can be black or grey, but roe-deer brown and blonde with dark markings on the ears, muzzle, and tail, are also possible.

CARE REQUIRED
The Skye Terrier requires little grooming, even though the coat would appear to suggest otherwise. A good brushing once a week is sufficient to keep it in good condition. The hair should fall into a parting from the centre of the back. Remove loose hairs and dirt from the ear passages and it is also advisable to trim excess hair between the pads of the feet.

Skye Terrier

CHARACTER
This is an affectionate dog which is calm, noble, makes a good watchdog, and is full of character.
The Skye Terrier is a little reserved with strangers and very loyal to its own family. Some of them have the tendency to become one-person's-dogs.

TRAINING
The training needs to be done with mutual respect, with you being fair and consistent, but also giving the dog room for its own initiative.

SOCIAL BEHAVIOUR
Most of the dogs from this breed get on with their own kind and with other household animals, although this has much to do with their early social training. They also get along fine with children but they do not like being teased.

Some dogs are rather dominant towards other dogs.

EXERCISE
Give the Skye Terrier lots of exercise. It loves to accompany you for long walks (on the lead) in woodland or open countryside. If you do not feel like a walk one day, or even if this happens frequently, the dog will adapt without misbehaving.

SPECIAL REMARKS
Skye Terriers can live to be quite old - fourteen or fifteen is not unusual.
There is a variety with drooping ears, but these are very rare.

West Highland White Terrier

COUNTRY OF ORIGIN
Scotland.

APTITUDE
Family pet.

SIZE
The shoulder-height is about 28cm (11in) and the weight about 7.5kg (16½lb).

COAT
The West Highland Terrier or Westie as it is commonly called has a double-layered coat: the topcoat is rough and hard, without curls whilst the undercoat is soft and short.
This breed is always white with darker eyes and darker pigmentation on the pads of the feet, nails, jowls, and nose.

West Highland White Terrier

CARE REQUIRED
The Westie is required to have a hard coat so, to avoid the coat becoming lank, it must not be too frequently washed. When the dog gets dirty playing outdoors, it is best to let the hair dry and then to brush the dirt out.
Its coat should be plucked by hand two or three times each year. The coats of dogs which are to be shown will require more grooming.

CHARACTER
This is a lively, playful, intrepid, vigilant and alert dog which is cheerful, loyal to its handler, is an extrovert, cunning and ingenious but also stubborn, resolute and independent. The Westie is brim-extremely self-confident and not easily impressed.

TRAINING
The straight forward and cheerful character of this dog must not be a passport for it to get away with whatever it likes.

Occasionally it may need to be corrected. Westies can be rather persistently naughty, so remain consistent and do not let yourself soften.

SOCIAL BEHAVIOUR
Westies generally get on well with their own kind and make excellent playmates for children - because they can withstand rough play. Teach them when young to tolerate cats or they will chase them when they are older. Some of this breed can be rather dominant with other dogs, but this depends greatly upon their early social training.

EXERCISE
Westies are mad about playing with a ball, romping and frolicking. They need lots of exercise so do not deny them it.
They enjoy digging and some of them like to wander off so make sure your garden is very well fenced.

Terriers of the Bulldog type

American Staffordshire Bull Terrier

COUNTRY OF ORIGIN
United States of America.

APTITUDE
Watchdog and family pet.

SIZE
The preferred shoulder-height is 45.7 - 48.4cm (18 - 19in) for dogs and 43.2 - 45.7 (17 - 18in) for bitches. The correct relationship between height and weight is more important than these specific heights.

COAT
The coat is short and shiny. Any colour is permitted, although black and tan, liver, plain white, or more than 80 per cent white are less preferred. The most prevalent colours are broken red and beige with highlights, both with and without white patches.

American Staffordshire Bull Terrier

CARE REQUIRED
Remove the dead and loose hairs from time to time with a rubber brush.

CHARACTER
This is a brave dog which is loyal to its family, tenacious, tough on itself, will make a good

American Staffordshire Bull Terrier

watchdog, is boisterous with tremendous stamina, and dominant.

TRAINING
The American Staffordshire is not suitable for people with little experience of dogs. Teach it when young not to pull on the lead because they are amazingly strong when fully grown. This breed can learn a great deal if well trained with a consistent approach. There are various examples of them succeeding in obedience trials.

SOCIAL BEHAVIOUR
The dogs of this breed can make good family dogs provided the family is always consistent towards it and can cope with a boisterous dog. Enthusiasts for these dogs claim that they are loving with children.

This dog will protect house and home and accept cats and other household animals provided it has become acquainted with them when young. Some examples of the breed can be rather eager to fight with other dogs.

EXERCISE
Ensure the American Staffordshire Bull Terrier gets plenty of exercise. They like running alongside a cycle and playing ball games; they also enjoy retrieving things.

Bull Terrier

COUNTRY OF ORIGIN
England.

APTITUDE
Family pet.

SIZE
There is not a standard size; the most important point is for the build to create an impression of a substantial dog.

Bull Terrier

COAT
The short-haired coat can be plain white, white with markings on the head and broken-colouring with highlights. Red, broken black, fawn, and triple-coloured (black and tan with a little white) are all accepted. With non-white animals, one colour must predominate.

CARE REQUIRED
A minimum of grooming is required for a Bull

Terrier. Brushing the coat with a rubber brush to remove dead and loose hairs is considered adequate to keep it in good condition. In addition, you should regularly clean the ears. The dogs need a soft place to lie down.

CHARACTER
They are hard on themselves (almost without any sensitivity to pain), affectionate, stubborn and with a mind of their own, lively and boisterous, loving with children, spontaneous, and cheerful. Some Bull Terriers are rather keen to fight other dogs.

TRAINING
Take your puppy to a good obedience training course. When fully grown, this dog is very strong for its size and it would be very difficult to train. The Bull Terrier is intelligent and learns relatively quickly, but it is also stubborn, with a mind of its own. The potential owner needs plenty of patience but must also be consistent towards the dog, and possess understanding and be able to express affection.

SOCIAL BEHAVIOUR
This breed usually gets on well with children and provided they have social training when young, will not present difficulties with cats or other household animals later. Some Bull Terriers are rather dominant towards other dogs but this depends on the inherent nature of the particular dog and the manner in which its

Bull Terrier

social and other training was carried out. If you already have a dog in your house, never choose a Bull Terrier dog as companion. It may take years before it happens, but there will be a confrontation between them.

EXERCISE
When they get enough exercise, Bull Terriers will be calm indoors. Cycling with the dog is an excellent way to exercise them, but not before they are fully-grown, and not for too long at one session.

Good exercise for this breed includes going for walks and running and playing off the lead.

Staffordshire Bull Terrier

Staffordshire Bull Terrier

COUNTRY OF ORIGIN
England.

APTITUDE
Family pet.

SIZE
The shoulder-height should be 35 - 41cm ($13^1/_2$ - $16^1/_2$in) and the weight 11-17kg ($24 - 37^1/_2$lb).

COAT
The coat is short and smooth. Staffordshires can be black, red, soft brown, white, or blue with any mixture that does not include white. Black and tan and liver are not popular.

CARE REQUIRED
The Staffordshire Bull Terrier requires little grooming.Remove the loose and dead hairs occasionally with a rubber brush to keep the coat in optimum condition.

CHARACTER
This breed is loving with children, obedient, brave, affectionate, has a sense of humour, is intelligent, tenacious, possesses a tremendous stamina, and is boisterous.

Staffordshire Bull Terrier

The Staffordshire learns fairly quickly but can be stubborn. Teach this dog early that it must let go when you have had enough with rope-pulling games.

Remain consistent throughout, but also loving towards it. Introduce the young dog to other household animals.

SOCIAL BEHAVIOUR

These dogs normally get on well with children and they can take rough play without a fuss. Provided they have been properly introduced to cats and other household animals when young, there should not be any problems with such animals. Most Staffordshires (and particularly the dogs) do not like the company of other dogs when they are adult - and they will make this quite obvious.

EXERCISE

When they get sufficient exercise, they are very peaceful in the house.

Most of them love to romp, play with a ball, and retrieve things.

SPECIAL REMARKS

The Staffordshire Bull Terrier has many of the characteristics of a larger dog and is therefore a suitable choice for people who would like one but do not have sufficient space.

Dwarf and Toy Terriers

Silky Terrier

COUNTRY OF ORIGIN
Australia.

APTITUDE
Rat-catcher and family pet.

SIZE
The shoulder-height is about 23cm (9in) for dogs; bitches are generally a little smaller.

Silky Terrier

COAT

The coat is long, smooth, shiny and silky, without an under-layer. The most common colour is light to dark blue-grey (in various shades) with brown, although steel-blue is the most sought-after colour. Silky Terriers are all born black.

Head of a Silky Terrier

CARE REQUIRED

In order to keep the coat in top condition, it is necessary to groom it daily with brush and comb for a quarter of an hour. An occasional bath is acceptable. Check the teeth for tartar. The Silky seldom moults.

CHARACTER

This is a lively, cheerful dog which is eager to learn, full of energy, intelligent, affectionate, loyal, docile, and in spite of its small size, is vigilant and protective. The Silky Terrier likes to be close to its handler.

TRAINING

The training of the Silky Terrier is happily very straight forward because they learn quite quickly.

SOCIAL BEHAVIOUR

Normally they are very loving with children.

Let them get used to cats when they are young or they will chase them when they are older. Visitors are usually announced by barking.

EXERCISE

They adapt their exercise requirements to the family circumstances.

Yorkshire Terrier

Yorkshire Terrier

COUNTRY OF ORIGIN

England.

APTITUDE

Historically a rat-catcher but nowadays usually a family pet.

WEIGHT

The weight is about 2 - 3kg ($4^{1}/_{2}$ - $6^{1}/_{2}$lb).

COAT

This breed has very long silky hair, coloured

golden-brown with steel-grey. As puppies the grey hairs are black.

CARE REQUIRED
The Yorkshire Terrier requires intensive daily grooming with brush and comb. If you do not have the time or the inclination to do this, have the coat trimmed by a salon. The hair is normally kept out of the eyes with a rubber band or a ribbon tied in a bow. The coat of show dogs is usually protected to keep its condition, by rolling it up with curling papers. Check the ears regularly and remove loose hairs from the ear passages.

CHARACTER
This is a lively, intelligent, sometime too-brave dog, which is loving, vigilant, and it becomes attached to its family.
Yorkshire Terriers are very alert and bark whenever they sense danger

TRAINING
The Yorkshire Terrier is a fairly quick-learning pupil. Provided you are consistent in your approach and ensure the lessons are positive, enjoyable and varied, it will soon learn to obey.

SOCIAL BEHAVIOUR
Provided children do not treat them as a toy and do not invade their territory, these dogs will not cause any problems with them.
Some of this breed can be rather foolhardy in their courage towards other dogs but they can get along fine with cats and other household animals. Strangers will always be "announced."

EXERCISE
This breed adapts its exercise needs to the family circumstances and the dogs can readily be kept in a flat.

SPECIAL REMARKS
The beautiful long hair of this breed is much admired at dog shows but to keep such a coat in good condition requires considerable work. Most Yorkshire Terriers which are kept as pets go through life with shorter clipped oats.

Although this is strongly abhorrent to the breed specialist, this is better than an unkempt coat with tangles which hurt and disturb the dog.

Yorkshire Terriër

4. Dachshunds

Dachshund (smooth-haired)

COUNTRY OF ORIGIN
Germany.

APTITUDE
Family pet but also a hunting dog for above and below ground (they are fanatical hunters of badgers, rabbits, roe deer, wild boar, and foxes).

SIZE
Dachshunds are divided into three size groups. The largest are the Standard, with a chest girth upwards from 35cm (13^1/$_2$in).
The Standard should have a maximum weight of 9kg (20lb). The Miniature Dachshund has a chest girth of 30 - 35cm (11^1/$_2$ - 13^1/$_2$in), and the smallest sort, the Kaninchen or "little rabbit" is recognized by a chest girth smaller than 30cm (11^1/$_2$in).

COAT
The coat consists of short smooth-hairs and is most frequently reddish-brown or black and tan but occasionally chocolate brown and dogs with almost tiger-like markings.

CARE REQUIRED
The coat of the Smooth-haired Dachshund needs little attention. It is sufficient to remove dead and loose hairs with a rubber brush from time to time. Keep the ear passages clean and the claws short. Most Dachshunds are dainty feeders but take care not to give them too much to eat because a fat Dachshund is an unhealthy one.

CHARACTER
The Dachshund is brave, dominant, has a mind of its own, is cunning, vigilant, resourceful, lively, is tenacious, and curious, and has a sense of humour. The Smooth-haired almost literally attaches itself to its own people, except when the hunting instinct rears its head.
A Dachshund needs to be introduced to all types of situation when young for its positive development.

Red Long-haired Standard Dachshund

TRAINING
The Smooth-haired is dominant and has a mind of its own as already noted above. Hence it has to be consistently trained. With the right approach and much patience it is possible to teach him quite a bit, though it will never slavishly follow your commands.

Dachshunds can sulk terribly if they feel they have been unfairly punished and they are very determined when they want something which you do not agree with. It is a very sensible move to take a Dachshund to a good puppy training course.

SOCIAL BEHAVIOUR
The family comes first with a Dachshund and they have little time for strangers. This is shown by a rather reserved manner to people the dog does not know.
If they are introduced early to children so that they have positive experiences with them, the Smooth-haired will not cause any problems with children.

They usually get on reasonably well with other dogs, although some of them can be somewhat over-courageous in their approach to larger dogs. Because of its passion for hunting, this breed is not a suitable playmate for other small household animals. Let it have happy meetings with cats when young to prevent later problems.

Red smooth-haired Standard Dachshund

EXERCISE
Give this breed plenty of exercise to keep it fit. If it is allowed to run free, off the lead, there is a high chance that its hunting instincts will cause it to run off.

If you wish to hunt with your Dachshund, contact the breed association. Dachshunds are strong healthy dogs which can live quite long but avoid their back becoming injured through excessive strain from constantly running up and down stairs and similar activities.

SPECIAL REMARKS
The Smooth-haired Dachshund is the original strain of this family of dogs. The Wire-haired and Long-haired Dachshunds were attained by crossing the Smooth-haired with other breeds.

Dachshund (Long-haired)

COUNTRY OF ORIGIN
Germany.

APTITUDE
Family pet but also a hunting dog - above and below ground (for badgers, rabbits, roe deer, wild boar, and foxes).

SIZE
See Smooth-haired Dachshund.

COAT
The Long-haired Dachshund is most often seen with a plain deep chestnut coat, in reddish-brown, and black and tan.

CARE REQUIRED
This Dachshund is happy with an occasional grooming, giving those places where tangles can form special attention. If necessary clip excess hair growth between the pads of the feet. Keep the claws short.

CHARACTER
This Dachshund is brave, has a mind of its own, is vigilant, intelligent, with a good sense of humour, lively, sociable, and playful. The Long-haired variety has a gentler nature than its

Black and tan Standard Long-haired Dachshund

Smooth-haired family member. It has been suggested that this is due to the crossing with Spaniels and Irish Setters (to achieve the long hair).

TRAINING
Long-haired Dachshunds are easier to train than Smooth-haired ones but because it too has a mind of its own, the training needs to be patient and you will constantly need to feel your way with this dog.

SOCIAL BEHAVIOUR
The family is number one with this Dachshund too, though they are friendlier towards strangers than the Smooth-haired.
They get on well with children provided their first youthful experiences with them were positive ones.

They usually get along with other dogs but the contact with other animals can be problematical - they remain hunting dogs. Cats will be tolerated provided they have learned to live with them early but do not expect any affection in the relationship.

EXERCISE
The Long-haired Dachshund needs fairly substantial exercise so take it for regular long walks.

Dachshund (Wire-haired)

COUNTRY OF ORIGIN
Germany.

APTITUDE
Family pet but also a hunting dog - above and below ground (for badgers, rabbits, roe deer, wild boar, and foxes).

SIZE
See the Smooth-haired Dachshund.

COAT
The coat consists of wire-hairs which lie flat and should be as hard as possible, with a dense under-layer. The hair on the head and ears should be very short and there should be a definite beard and moustache.

The colour is almost always that indeterminate mix of natural colours often found in wild animals; black and tan occurs less frequently. Sporadically dogs with a red or chocolate coat may be encountered.

CARE REQUIRED
The Wire-haired Dachshund needs to have its coat plucked about twice per year, depending on the condition of the coat. The hair on the top of the head should be kept short. Trim excess hair which may grow between the pads of the feet.

CHARACTER
This is a brave, dominant dog with a sense of humour and a mind of its own, which is cunning, vigilant, resourceful, lively, tenacious, and curious. It is essential to introduce the Wire-haired Dachshund to all manner of situations early in its life to encourage its development.

TRAINING
See Smooth-haired Dachshund.

SOCIAL BEHAVIOUR
See Smooth-haired Dachshund.

EXERCISE
See Smooth-haired Dachshund.

Wire-haired Standard Dachshund

Wire- and Smooth-haired Miniature Dachshunds

5. Spitz and other primitive breeds

Arctic breeds and sledge dogs

Alaskan Malamute

COUNTRY OF ORIGIN
North America (Alaska).

APTITUDE
Sledge dog and family pet.

SIZE
The shoulder-height is about 64cm (25$^1/_2$in) for dogs and about 58cm (22$^1/_2$in) for bitches.

COAT
The Alaskan Malamute has a thick, coarse outer-coat with a greasy and woolly under-coat. The normal colours are wolf-grey, or black with white - always with white on the stomach and a white face or top of the head. Other colours are permitted but white is the only plain colour which is accepted.

CARE REQUIRED
This breed's coat does not need much in the way of grooming. During moulting it is best to use a coarse comb with a double row of teeth to remove loose and dead hairs.

CHARACTER
This is an affectionate dog which is intelligent, friendly, loyal, and noble, but can have a mind of its own and be dominant and certainly never slavishly following your whims.The Alaskan Malamute learns quite quickly and has tremendous stamina.

TRAINING
Despite its friendly nature, this dog needs a firm hand in its training. The Malamute therefore calls for a handler with plenty of confidence who can understand the character of this dog. With such a handler they can learn a great deal - even including agility skills, although it will be outperformed in competition by one of the sheepdog breeds.

Japanese Spitz

Alaskan Malamute

SOCIAL BEHAVIOUR
Alaskan Malamutes generally get on well with children - they are actually friendly with everyone - which makes them quite unsuitable as watchdogs.

With other dogs of the same sex as themselves, they can display dominant behaviour - but this is more the exception than the rule. Cats are not really suitable companions in the same house unless you have accustomed the dog to cats when it was young. In this case there should be no problem.

EXERCISE
Exercise is probably the most important aspect in an Alaskan Malamute's upbringing. This breed needs copious amounts of exercise and if you know that you cannot face, say, an hour each day of hard exercise with the dog, it is best to avoid this breed. In many countries there are sledge dog organizations which arrange competitions - with a wheeled cart in place of a sledge where there is no snow.

Malamutes are happy whether they are indoors or out of doors but they do not like to be alone. Keep this dog on the lead whenever it is taken out unless you have it firmly under your control because it is liable to run off.

Alaskan Malamute

Greenland Dog

Head of an Alaskan Malamute

Greenland Dog

COUNTRY OF ORIGIN
Scandinavia.

APTITUDE
Sledge dog.

SIZE
The shoulder-height is a minimum of 60cm
(23$^1/_2$in) for dogs and 55cm (21$^1/_2$in) for
bitches. There is no maximum height.

COAT
The Greenland Dog has a double-layered coat:
the under-layer is soft and thick, the outer-layer
protects well against the weather.
All colours are accepted with the exception of
albino.

CARE REQUIRED
This breed does not need much attention to its
coat. During moulting, when the under-layer
of the coat is shed, the best way to remove loose
hairs is to use a comb with a double row of
metal teeth.

CHARACTER
This breed is independent, equable, dominant,
tough on itself, and has a mind of its own. The
Greenland Dog rarely barks but howls quite a
lot.
This is definitely not a family pet. They have an
amazing amount of energy with tremendous
stamina.

TRAINING
Training this dog is not particularly easy due to
its rather independent nature, with a mind of its
own.
This is a sledge dog, not a family pet, which
can cover enormous distances and will do so
given half a chance, staying away for days at a
time - so that a good fence is essential. Pulling
a sledge is when it is most in its element so this
breed is ideal for someone wanting a dog for
this very purpose.

SOCIAL BEHAVIOUR

This breed cannot stand being left on its own. If you decide on it, you should get two dogs. They are perfectly happy in an outdoor kennel. They do not usually get on well with either cats or other household animals. Friends and strangers alike will be exuberantly greeted, probably with howling.

Consequently they are not suitable as watchdogs in spite of their size.

EXERCISE

It must already be obvious that the Greenland Dog needs a great deal of exercise. The best form for them is pulling a sledge or wheeled cart.

If you know that you will be unable to provide this dog with such exercise, it is better to take the choice for another breed.

They are too strong to be exercised running alongside a cycle. Avoid much activity with them in warmer weather and do not let the dog work above a temperature of 15°C (59°F).

Samoyed

Samoyed

COUNTRY OF ORIGIN
Western Siberia.

APTITUDE
Herding-dog, watchdog, sledge dog, hunting dog, and family pet.

SIZE
The shoulder-height is 57cm (22$1/_2$in) for dogs and 53cm (20$1/_2$in) for bitches. Variance of 3cm (1$1/_2$in) above and below these heights is permitted.

COAT
The protective topcoat is wiry and erect, while the undercoat is short and dense. The coat is white, cream, or white with light brown.

CARE REQUIRED
Do not brush the Samoyed too much because this can harm the under-layer of its coat. If too many hairs are shed in your home, use a comb

with a double row of metal teeth to remove the loose hairs from the undercoat.

CHARACTER

The Samoyed is a dog of contradictions. It is friendly and cheerful, intelligent and reasonably obedient, yet never follows your orders slavishly and can be extremely stubborn. It is sensitive and gentle-natured but dominant and vigilant, affectionate but not obtrusively so.

The Samoyed loves to wander, has considerable stamina, and remains playful into old age. They love to hear themselves and can be very noisy.

TRAINING

Training the Samoyed is no easy task and needs to begin very early. Make sure there is plenty of variety in the drills. Constantly practising the same command can have an adverse effect on this breed, its stubbornness taking over. Teach it when very young that it must come to you when you call and arrange for as many positive encounters with cats and other household animals as possible. Your authority should be clearly seen but with a friendly touch. Screaming and shouting at it and hitting it will lose you any respect it may have had.

SOCIAL BEHAVIOUR

These dogs are gentle-natured and patient with children but can be rather dominant towards their own kind. Do not forget that the Samoyed is a hunting dog which enjoys chasing something if it gets the chance.

Social training with cats and other pets is therefore very important! The dog is reasonably vigilant.

EXERCISE

The Samoyed needs lots of exercise. Once it is fully grown, take it on really long walks or get it to run alongside a cycle to keep it in good condition.

Because they naturally like to wander, it is advisable to make sure your garden is properly enclosed with a fence.

Siberian Husky

COUNTRY OF ORIGIN
Alaska.

APTITUDE
Sledge dog.

Siberian Husky

SIZE
The shoulder-height is 53 - 60cm (20$^1/_2$ - 23$^1/_2$in) for dogs and 51 - 56cm (20 - 22in) for bitches.

COAT
The Husky has a double-layered, medium-length coat. Every colour and combination are accepted. With this breed even partially blue eyes are permissible.

CARE REQUIRED
An occasional brushing and combing, particularly during moulting, is adequate for this breed. The coat is usually more handsome when the Husky is kept in an outdoor kennel.

CHARACTER
This breed is independent with a mind of its own, is very intelligent, full of energy, cheerful, loves to wander, and is very fond of its handler and family.
Because they are friendly with everyone, they are not ideal watchdogs.

TRAINING
Most Huskies do not fill the role of family pet very well, although perhaps a very sportive family might be better suited.

The Husky is a sledge dog in heart and soul. To teach the Husky anything will require a careful approach and being very consistent towards it. The other requirements are considerable patience and an understanding of the character of Arctic dogs.

A Husky will only obey a command in which it sees any point. If you consider to acquire a Husky, it is sensible to contact a specialist on Arctic dogs and/or the breed society before doing so.

SOCIAL BEHAVIOUR
Siberian Huskies generally get along with their own kind but the contact with other household animals needs careful handling and training. Cats and jerboa or other pet rodents are not really suitable companions to share a home with this dog

Fortunately children are not a problem. This breed finds it hard to be left on its own so it is advisable to have more than one Husky.

EXERCISE
This breed needs considerable exercise and there can be no concession in this requirement. Should you wish to get involved in the sport of dog-sledging, then there is no better choice than the Husky. This breed is world-famous for its speed. If you cannot or do not wish to run a Husky before a sledge at least twice per week, then an alternative is essential such as cycling with the dog for at least an hour a day.

Lonely Huskies that are locked up with too little exercise will howl and become destructive. This is not the fault of the dog but of an owner who has made a wrong choice of dog. Take a Husky out on a lead and fence your garden or it is likely to run off.

Siberian Husky

SPECIAL REMARKS
Siberian Huskies will usually be happy to share an outdoor kennel with one or more other dogs. The thick coat protects it against rain and cold. Rather more protection is necessary for these dogs from high temperatures, so never work them in the summer.

Scandinavian Arctic dogs

Finnish Spitz

COUNTRY OF ORIGIN
Finland.

APTITUDE
Hunting dog for birds, estate dog, and family pet.

SIZE
The shoulder-height is 53 - 60cm

$(20^1/_2$ - $23^1/_2$in) for dogs and 51 -56cm (20 - 22in) for bitches.

COAT
The coat consists of thick, erect, medium-length hair with a thick under-layer of straight hair. The colour may be red-brown or a yellowish red and small white markings are permissible.Puppies are born much darker and acquire their reddish coat later.

CARE REQUIRED
The Finnish Spitz has a self-cleaning coat in common with the other Arctic dogs. Regular grooming with brush and comb is however still necessary. The coat of this breed does not have the customary smell usually associated with dog hair.

CHARACTER
This breed is lively and curious, though not overwhelmingly so. It is a watchdog that only barks when necessary. They are delightful with children, homely and sociable, very loyal to their own family but do not follow their handler's orders slavishly.

TRAINING
Those looking for a dog that always obeys should look elsewhere than the Finnish Spitz but with ample patience and understanding, together with a consistent manner, it is possible to achieve the basic level of training with these dogs.

Finnish Spitz

SOCIAL BEHAVIOUR
Finnish Spitz usuallu do not cause problems in the intercourse with other dogs. They get along fine with children. Visitors will always be announced. But that is all, it is no defender.

EXERCISE
This dog likes to be out of doors but will not be very happy on its own in a kennel. With some companions of its own kind it will be quite happy. This is a very suitable dog to live in the country but they are plenty of examples of this breed living successfully in towns. The answer is plenty of exercise.
Afterwards it is content to spend the evening at its handler's feet.

Elkhound with Elk

Elkhound or Jämthund

COUNTRY OF ORIGIN
Sweden.

APTITUDE
Hunting dog for large game.

SIZE
The shoulder-height is 60 - 65cm $(23^1/_2$ - $25^1/_2$in) for dogs and 55 - 60cm $(21^1/_2$ - $23^1/_2$in) for bitches.

COAT
The Elkhound has a cream-coloured thick undercoat with thick, densely packed covering hair. The colour of the outer-coat is dark or light grey and there should be cream-coloured

patches on the nose, cheeks, throat, stomach, front of the chest, legs, and underside of the tail.

CARE REQUIRED
The coat hardly needs any grooming. During moulting is best to use a comb with a double row of metal teeth to remove loose hairs from the under-layer of the coat. In common with other Arctic dogs, the hair of the Elkhound does not have the typical dog smell.

Elkhound

CHARACTER
This breed is equable, straight forward, intelligent and cunning, has a sense of humour, is sensitive to nuances in the voice, and is physically demanding of itself.

TRAINING
This dog needs a calm handler who exudes a natural authority. An equable and consistent manner of approach to their training is essential.

SOCIAL BEHAVIOUR
The Elkhound gets on with other dogs even though its bark can have a frightening effect upon them.
They are rather reserved with strangers and yet they are no watchdogs. Children and Elkhounds together do not usually cause any problems and the same applies to any animals present in and around the house.

EXERCISE
The Elkhound is a hunting dog through and through and is still used for this purpose to this day in its native country. Its task is to track large wild animals independently and bring them down.

To do this, it searches large areas of terrain. This dog is really unsuitable as a pet in a busy urban environment. If it is allowed off the lead, the chance is that its hunting instincts will cause it to run away, with all the consequences that could follow.

In wild countryside, the Elkhound will normally be constantly on the move. It verges on cruelty to animals to enclose such a dog and limit it to three short walks each day. From this it is clear that the Elkhound is only suitable for the few people who are able to hunt with it.

Head of an Elkhound

Karelian Bear Dog

COUNTRY OF ORIGIN
Finland.

APTITUDE
Hunting dog for large wild game.

SIZE
The shoulder-height is 54 - 60cm ($21^{1}/_{2}$ - $23^{1}/_{2}$in) for dogs and 49 - 55cm ($19^{1}/_{2}$ - $21^{1}/_{2}$in) for bitches. The ideal height is 57 - 58cm ($22^{1}/_{2}$ - $22^{1}/_{2}$in) for dogs and 51 - 53cm (20 - $20^{1}/_{2}$in) for bitches.

COAT
The short-haired coat consists of straight and stiff hairs while the under-layer is soft and dense. The Karelian Bear Dog is white with black. Black speckles in the white are a fault.

CARE REQUIRED
The coat of these dogs requires little attention. Use a special metal comb during the moult for the easy removal of loose hairs from the under-coat.

Karelian Bear Dog

CHARACTER
This dog is very loyal to its own family and makes a good household companion which is dominant but also sensitive, independent, intelligent, cunning, tough on itself, is energetic, and has a sense of humour.

They can often be rather anti-social towards other dogs.

TRAINING
This dog needs a handler who exudes natural authority. Their training should be very consistent, with both a firm hand and affection. This is certainly not a breed for inexperienced people.

SOCIAL BEHAVIOUR
With regard to other dogs Karelian Bear Dogs display dominant behaviour and do not go out

Head of a Karelian Bear Dog

of their way to avoid a fight. They are affectionate towards people making them quite unsuitable as watchdogs. Both welcome and unwelcome visitors will be announced but that is an end to it. Those who are well known will get an enthusiastic welcome, and strangers may be treated with some reserve, even perhaps non-acceptance. The Karelian Bear Dog can live with other household animals if the training is properly handled.

EXERCISE
This breed can be kept in an outdoor kennel. Take account of the need for the Karelian Bear Dog to be able to stretch its legs for at least an hour per day. Provided you have them well under control and can keep them so, it is possible to exercise them running alongside a cycle. If it gets too little exercise or becomes bored, there is a chance it will take this out on your furniture.

Make sure that your garden is well fenced because Karelian Bear Dogs have a tendency to go hunting.

SPECIAL REMARKS
In common with most Arctic dogs, the Karelian Bear Dog does not have the usual smell of dog hair. It also requires relatively little food to keep it in good condition.

Lundehund

Lundehund

COUNTRY OF ORIGIN
Norway.

APTITUDE
The Lundehund was specially used to catch puffins and bring them to their handler. Such

139

nests were often found high up in rocky crevices on cliffs.

SIZE

The shoulder-height is 35 - 38cm (13$\frac{1}{2}$ - 15in) for dogs and 32 - 35cm (12$\frac{1}{2}$ - 13$\frac{1}{2}$in) for bitches. Dogs should weigh about 7kg (15$\frac{1}{2}$lb) and bitches 6kg (13$\frac{1}{2}$lb).

COAT

The Lundehund has a short coat of reddish brown to drab red hairs which have slightly black tips. There is a soft undercoat.

CARE REQUIRED

The coat of this breed does not require much attention. During the moult it is best to remove the loose hairs with a strong comb.

They do however need special care with their diet because they lack an enzyme that is necessary for the digestion of food. Seek specialist advice.

CHARACTER

These dogs have a mind of their own and a sense of humour, they are cheerful, mischievous, intelligent and cunning, and also dominant. They rarely bark.

TRAINING

The training needs to have as much variety as possible. Repeating the same exercise will bore this dog and causes the undermining of your authority. Make sure that you are always consistent with it.

EXERCISE

This breed does not require much exercise. It is sufficient to keep it in physically fit to take it for a walk three times a day together with some time to play in the garden.

SPECIAL REMARKS

Experts cannot agree whether this breed is a part of the domesticated dog family (Canis familiares). It is possible that the breed forms part of the primitive wild dog family (Canis ferus) because it possesses a number of features unknown in any other domesticated breed.

This dog can quite literally close its ears - not just to orders it does not like but, more practically, when creeping through rocky crevices, in order to prevent dirt getting in.
This protects the dog's exceptional hearing ability. In addition to this, they have six toes and eight pads on each foot, compared with five toes and six pads with other dogs (see photograph p 141).

Lundehunds are the only breed of dog to possess - like humans - collar bones so that they can spread the front legs out to the side. Finally they can bend their head right back over themselves - which is useful for crawling through narrow rock crevices. No other breed shares this feature with them.

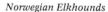

Norwegian Elkhounds

The feet of a Lundehund has six toes

Norwegian Elkhound

Norwegian Elkhound

COUNTRY OF ORIGIN
Norway.

APTITUDE
Hunting dog for large wild game.

SIZE
The shoulder-height is ideally 52cm (20$^1/_2$in) for dogs and 49cm (19$^1/_2$in) for bitches. Variance of 2cm ($^1/_2$in) is permitted.

COAT
The Elkhound has a thick, woolly, cream-coloured under coat and a hard, dense, and longer outer coat.
This outer coat comes in various shades of grey, with black markings behind the ears and around the muzzle. There are also black Elkhounds, which are recognized as a separate breed. The black Elkhounds are permitted to have white markings.

CARE REQUIRED
The coat of an Elkhound requires little grooming. An ideal way to remove loose hairs during moulting is to use a wooden comb with a double row of metal teeth. In common with other Arctic dogs, they do not have the usual smell of dog hair. The coat is both water- and dirt-resistant.

CHARACTER
The Elkhound is tough on itself, straight forward, equable, friendly, and gentle-natured. However quiet it may be indoors, it will be a bundle of energy outside.

TRAINING
Like other Arctic dogs, the Norwegian Elkhound has a mind of its own and is fairly independent. It is important to be firm with them but show them your affection as well and make sure you are fair with them.
You can upset this dog for a long time by punishing it unfairly - and it will let you know how it feels.

SOCIAL BEHAVIOUR
The Norwegian Elkhound is somewhat reserved with strangers but will greet family friends it knows with enthusiasm. They can be dominant towards their own kind but this is rather the exception than the rule.

They usually get on with each other and reasonably well with children too provided they do not pester the dogs. They will announce the presence of visitors but that is all.

Head of a Norwegian Elkhound

EXERCISE

Exercise of an hour a day is the minimum to keep this dog happy.

Take it out with you cycling or let it have a really good run in the woods but do not forget that if it gets the scent of wild game, it will be quite deaf to your calls.

Norbottenspets

Norbottenspets

COUNTRY OF ORIGIN
Sweden

APTITUDE
Hunting dog.

SIZE
The shoulder-height is about 45cm (17^1/$_2$in) for dogs and 42cm (16^1/$_2$in) for bitches.

COAT
The very short coat is dense, protecting the soft undercoat. Every colour is permitted but the ideal colour is white with yellow or reddish brown patches.

CARE REQUIRED
Little grooming is needed for the coat of this breed. An occasional brushing, particularly during moulting, is sufficient to keep it in good condition.

CHARACTER
This is an alert dog which is independent, extremely active, friendly, likes to bark, is intelligent and cunning, and has a mind of its own. The Norbottenspets has considerable stamina, is very energetic and likes to wander.

TRAINING

The very individual nature of this dog means that its handler needs considerable patience, power of persuasion, and an insight into the character of the dog to be able to achieve the most basic levels of training.

SOCIAL BEHAVIOUR

This dog gets on well with other dogs. Visits by strangers will be announced but that is all. They are friendly with everyone. Animals which were already present in the household will be unquestionably accepted and there will be no problems worth mentioning in their attitude to children - although they will not accept everything a child might do to it.

EXERCISE

The Norbottenspets is very energetic and it requires considerable exercise. Despite its small size, it can happily run alongside a cycle provided this is built up gradually. When running free off the lead, they are quite deaf to your calls - their hunting instincts are stronger than the bond with their handler. If you live surrounded by open countryside, this need not be a problem but for those living in more built-up areas an accident is not out of the question so make sure your garden is well fenced. Norbottenspets are usually very strong dogs.

West Siberian Laika

West Siberian Laika

COUNTRY OF ORIGIN
Western Siberia.

APTITUDE
Hunting dog, sledge dog, and family pet.

SIZE
The shoulder-height is 55 - 62cm

$(21^1/_2 - 24^1/_2\text{in})$ for dogs and 51 - 58cm (20 - $22^1/_2\text{in})$ for bitches.

COAT
The coat consists of straight, rough covering hair with masses of hair in the undercoat. Permitted colours are white, salt and pepper, grey, any shade of red, black and multi-coloured.

CARE REQUIRED
The coat of the West Siberian Laika does not needs much attention.
During moulting, which is normally of short duration but very heavy, the loose hairs are best removed using a comb with a double row of metal teeth.

CHARACTER
This is a friendly dog which is intelligent, eager to learn, uncomplicated and honest, equable and sober.

TRAINING
The West Siberian Laika is not difficult to train. They learn commands quickly and like to work. Both agility skills and obedience training will be easily absorbed.

SOCIAL BEHAVIOUR
This very original and healthy breed usually gets on well with its own kind and is very patient and loving with children. The West Siberian Laika is a true friend to humans. They will go into action if strangers visit but will not pursue the warning aggression.

EXERCISE
The West Siberian Laika has an average demand for exercise but this does not mean it should be condemned to three brief trots around the corner a day.

Scandinavian Spitz guard and watchdog

Finnish Lapphund

COUNTRY OF ORIGIN
Finland.

APTITUDE
Sheepdog, estate dog, and watchdog.

SIZE
The shoulder-height is 46 - 52cm $(18 - 20^1/_2\text{in})$ for dogs and 40 - 46cm $(15^1/_2 - 18\text{in})$ for bitches.

COAT
The Finnish Lapphund has an abundant coat. The outer layer is long and coarse, the undercoat is soft, thick, and dense. Every colour is permitted provided the main colour predominates.

Finnish Lapphund

Finnish Lapphund

CARE REQUIRED
The wire brush used for German Shepherds is ideal to remove the loose hairs from the thick undercoat of this breed during moulting.

CHARACTER
This is a friendly, intelligent and sociable dog which wants to work for its handler, is very active, energetic. Tough on itself, and affectionate.

TRAINING
The Finnish Lapphund is intelligent and keen to learn and therefore makes an excellent pupil. It can compete on level terms with the best in dog sports such as fly-ball and agility skills trials.

SOCIAL BEHAVIOUR

This dog is naturally very sociable. It gets on extremely well with children and in normal circumstances can take a great deal from them. It also gets on well with other household animals and dogs.

The Finnish Lapphund is alert in the sense that it will warn you of visitors but it is too gentle-natured to defend your property.

EXERCISE

This breeds needs fairly substantial exercise and running alongside a cycle is one of the possibilities, but it will also really enjoy long walks through woods. Its sheepdog instincts will keep it close to you and prevent it from wandering off.

Iceland Dog

COUNTRY OF ORIGIN

Iceland.

Iceland Dog puppies

APTITUDE

Sheepdog and family pet.

SIZE

The shoulder-height is 42 - 48cm ($16^1/_2$ - $18^1/_2$in) for dogs and 38 - 44cm (15 - $17^1/_2$in) for bitches. The dog weighs about 14kg (31lb).

Iceland Dog

COAT

The Iceland Dog has a double-layered coat of soft, sleek hairs. The predominant colours are white with pink markings and light roc-deer brown with black tips to the hairs.

A few dogs turn up that are black with white markings.

CARE REQUIRED

The coat of the Iceland Dog does not require much attention. Comb out the loose hairs of the undercoat during the moult.

CHARACTER

This is a high-spirited and friendly dog which is sociable, equable, intelligent and eager to learn, affectionate, attentive and vigilant, that is hard on itself, brave, and can be stubborn. It likes to bark.

TRAINING

The training of the Iceland Dog is not usually difficult. The breed learns quickly and is intelligent. Handle them always with utmost consistency and in a friendly manner, trying to bring as much variety as possible into the exercises. Bear in mind that the dog must see the purpose of the command.

They do quite well at both fly-ball and agility skills trials.

SOCIAL BEHAVIOUR

This delightful family dog needs quite a lot of exercise to keep it happy. Take it regularly for longer walks, giving it the chance to run and play off the lead.

These dogs like to be part of the family and regard being left on their own as severe punishment.

EXERCISE

This nice family dog needs quite some exercise to feel happy. Take it on long walks regularly and let it run and play freely. This breed bonds strongly to the family. If they are left alone major parts of the day, this will be felt as a severe punishment.

Norwegian Buhund

COUNTRY OF ORIGIN

Norway.

APTITUDE

Farm estate dog and sheep-herder. Bu in Norwegian means farm or homestead.

Norwegian Buhund

SIZE

The shoulder-height is 43 - 47cm (17 - 18$^{1}/_{2}$in) for dogs and 41 - 45cm (16$^{1}/_{2}$ - 17$^{1}/_{2}$in) for bitches.

The weight is 14 - 18kg (31 - 39$^{1}/_{2}$lb) for dogs and 12 - 16kg (26$^{1}/_{2}$ - 35$^{1}/_{2}$lb) for bitches.

COAT

The Buhund has a soft, woolly thick undercoat with an abundant thick topcoat. The colour should be wheaten or biscuit, although black with a little white is also known.

CARE REQUIRED

It is not difficult to keep the coat in good condition. Loose hairs can be removed from the undercoat during moulting with a wooden comb that has a double row of metal teeth.

CHARACTER

This dog is vigilant, cheerful, active and untiring, intelligent, attentive and affectionate. It also likes to bark.

Norwegian Buhunds are normally quite calm indoors.

TRAINING

The Norwegian Buhund likes to be taught, is intelligent, and also learns very quickly. It requires a firm hand in its training which should be as varied in nature as possible to retain its interest.

They like to be busy, enjoy retrieving, and with the right approach to training can shine in various dog sports.

SOCIAL BEHAVIOUR

The are generally very good with children and get on fine with other dogs and animals of the household.

It will pervasively warn you of any strange visitors but that is all - it is no defender.

EXERCISE

The Norwegian Buhund is an energetic dog with considerable stamina. One of its favourite pastimes is retrieving objects. Let it run free off the lead regularly without fear of it running away - its shepherding instincts will prevent it from roaming. It will follow you perfectly on a cycle.

Norwegian Buhund

Västgötaspets

COUNTRY OF ORIGIN

Sweden.

APTITUDE

Livestock herder, watchdog, and family pet.

SIZE

The ideal shoulder-height is 33cm (13in) for dogs and 31cm (12$^1/_2$in) for bitches.

COAT

The coat consists of smooth-laying yet coarse wiry hairs with a soft, woolly undercoat. The colour is steel grey with darker outer hairs or slightly reddish yellow with lighter patches. Streaked, spotted, grey-brown, and yellow-brown are also permissible but not preferred. Small white markings are also acceptable but they must never cover more than a third of the total coat.

Västgötaspets

CARE REQUIRED

Regular brushing and combing will keep the coat in good condition. Of course the ear passages should be kept clean and the claws kept short.

CHARACTER

This dog is vigilant, alert, active, eager to learn, intelligent, and both affectionate and very loyal.

TRAINING

This dog is not difficult to train because it understands quickly what is expected of it.

SOCIAL BEHAVIOUR
The Västgötaspets can get along well with children and it enjoys playing with them. It will always protect them from strangers who try to get close to them.

This is a characteristic of herding dogs. They generally get along with other dogs but tend to be rather reserved towards strangers.

EXERCISE
The Västgötaspets is a working dog that needs plenty of exercise. Given its size, it can of course be kept in a flat but it is essential to give it ample opportunities to burn off its energy.

Nothing will make this dog happier than to train it for agility skills trials, or some similar activity, which will provide it with a constant stream of new challenges.

Swedish Lapphund

COUNTRY OF ORIGIN
Sweden.

APTITUDE
Sheepdog.

SIZE
The ideal shoulder height is 48cm (18^1/$_2$in) for dogs and 43cm (17in) for bitches. A difference of 3cm (1^1/$_2$in) is permitted.

COAT
The Swedish Lapphund has a thick woolly topcoat, the hairs of which should be erect, and a dense curly undercoat of fine hairs.

The colours are brown, black, and a combination of the two. For the show ring, plain colours are preferred. White markings occur in some dogs but are considered a fault.

CARE REQUIRED
During moulting when the hairs begin to fall out of the thick undercoat, the best way to deal with them is to use one of the special combs designed for grooming German Shepherds.

CHARACTER
This is an intelligent, sociable and friendly dog which is similar in nature to the Finnish Lapp-hund, meaning that it loves children, is very tolerant of them, and it is keen to learn, affectionate, lively, and not squeamish about pain.

TRAINING
This dog learn quickly and easily, so that you can consider involving both of you in agility skills and obedience training or perhaps flyball.
Handled properly, this breed can compete at the highest levels.

SOCIAL BEHAVIOUR
A Swedish Lapphund from good breeding lines gets on well with other dogs and as already mentioned is very tolerant of children. You will be warned of strangers but that is all because this dog is friendly with everyone.

EXERCISE
This breed has tremendous stamina and likes to be kept busy. They love to be taken for walks and will always stay close to you.

SPECIAL REMARKS
This breed looks physically very similar to the Finnish Lapphund.

European Spitz

Pomeranian

COUNTRY OF ORIGIN
Germany.

APTITUDE
Companion and pet.

SIZE
The shoulder-height of the smaller Pomeranians is 18 - 22cm (7 - 8½in) and 23 - 28cm (9 - 11in) for the larger ones.

COAT
These dogs have long, erect hairs and a thick undercoat.
The colours are plain white, orange, black, brown, or grey.

Small Pomeranian

CARE REQUIRED
The coat should be well combed with a coarse comb every three weeks and then lightly brushed.
If you use too fine a comb or groom the dog frequently, you run the risk of damaging the undercoat.

CHARACTER
This is a lively dog, which is boisterous, can be too brave, is intelligent, eager to learn, very loyal to its handler and family, vigilant, energetic, has a delightful nature and does not cling to its handler.

TRAINING
Teach this dog early that it may bark a couple of times when the doorbell rings or there are visitors but then to keep quiet. Be very consistent about this!
Pomeranians are generally fairly easy to train because they are so intelligent and eager to learn.

SOCIAL BEHAVIOUR
Too much attention from children can make these dogs rather nervous. They usually get along with other dogs and household animals without problem.

Some of them think they are much larger and do not hesitate to attack much bigger dogs. You need to protect them from themselves.

Both breeds are happy with short walks and like to play in the garden but they can walk a distance without becoming tired.

Keeshond

COUNTRY OF ORIGIN
Germany.

APTITUDE
Vermin destroyer, watchdog, and family pet.

SIZE
The ideal shoulder-height for Keeshonds is 46cm (18in) with deviations of 4cm (1^1/$_2$in) accepted.

A slightly larger related variety is known in The Netherlands, where most Keeshonds come from, as the Wolfkeeshond. The ideal shoulder-height for this 'Wolf Spitz' is 50cm (19^1/$_2$in) with deviations of 5cm (2in) accepted.

CHARACTER
These dogs are boisterous, loyal to their handler, vigilant, not easily led astray by bribes, intelligent, and eager to learn.

TRAINING
These dogs quickly know what is expected of them.
Training them is therefore fairly easy. Keeshonds are often successful in dog sports such as agility skills trials.

SOCIAL BEHAVIOUR
Keeshonds are naturally good with other dogs and children but they need to be introduced when young to cats.
Strangers approaching will always be noted by barking.

EXERCISE
The Keeshond has an average need for exercise and will usually adapt to family circumstances.

Wolf-grey Keeshond

Medium-sized Keeshond

COAT
These dogs have a thick undercoat with longer covering hair.
They are wolf-grey, plain black, brown, or white.

CARE REQUIRED
During moulting the coat needs to be brushed and combed regularly to remove the dead hair.

At other times there should be a minimum of combing to avoid damaging the undercoat.

Smaller Keeshond

COUNTRY OF ORIGIN
Germany.

APTITUDE
Vermin destroyer and family pet.

SIZE
The ideal shoulder-height if 32cm (12^1/$_2$in) but heights of 29 - 36cm (11^1/$_2$ - 14^1/$_2$in) are acceptable.

COAT
This dog has a thick undercoat with longer erect covering hair.
The Smaller Keeshond can be plain white, black, brown, orange, or wolf-grey.

CARE REQUIRED
During moulting it will be necessary to groom regularly with a coarse comb and with a brush to remove dead hairs.

At other times this must not be done too often to avoid damaging the undercoat.

CHARACTER
This breed is boisterous, loyal to its handler and family, vigilant, not very easily led astray by bribes, intelligent and can bark a lot.

TRAINING
The Smaller Keeshond quickly grasps what is intended. This makes training it fairly easy. When your dog proves to be one of those that likes to bark, it is advisable to train it not to.

SOCIAL BEHAVIOUR
These dogs get on well with their own kind and with children. Let them make acquaintance of cats early in their lives. Strangers will always be announced by barking.

EXERCISE
This breed has an average need for exercise and will normally adapt to the family circumstances.

Primitive Asian Spitz breeds

Japanese Akita

COUNTRY OF ORIGIN
Japan.

APTITUDE
Vermin destroyer and family pet.

SIZE
The ideal shoulder-height is 67cm (26^1/$_2$in) for dogs and 61cm (24in) for bitches. Variations of 3cm (1^1/$_2$in) will be accepted.

COAT
The dog has straight, coarse covering hair with a soft dense undercoat. Permitted colours with the Japanese breed society are red, white, and streaked. A dark face is regarded in Japan as a fault.

In some countries such as the USA spotted and speckled dogs with a black face are permitted at shows. In such countries these coats are much favoured.

Smaller Keeshond

Japanese Akita

Japanese Akita

CARE REQUIRED
This breed is easy to care for. About twice per year they have a brief heavy moulting when a good comb with a double set of metal teeth should be used.

CHARACTER
These are equable, thoughtful, intelligent, and friendly dogs which are reasonably obedient, imperturbable, have a strong hunting instinct, are good watchdogs without barking too much, but they can also be independent and rather dominant. They will become friends, never slaves.

TRAINING
With a confident handler who is consistent in his approach, the Japanese Akita can learn a great deal. They do best if the drills are not constantly repeated.

They are not a suitable breed for beginners unless you follow advice very closely.

SOCIAL BEHAVIOUR
Most Japanese Akitas have no time for other dogs and prefer not to have any other dog for company. They virtually all tend to extreme dominancy with other dogs, especially ones of their own sex.
They need to become acquainted with cats and other animals early on to prevent later pro-

blems. They usually get on reasonably well with children, provided the children do not invade the dog's own territory. They could never be considered a playmate for them. Strangers will get a rather reserved reception from this dog.

EXERCISE
Japanese Akitas have considerable stamina but if you miss a long walk one day, they will accept it without a fuss.

Never forget that they have strong hunting instincts so that if they are permitted to run free, there is a strong possibility they will take off.

SPECIAL REMARKS
The Akita is highly revered in Japan as almost a national icon.

Chow Chow (Short-haired)

COUNTRY OF ORIGIN
China.

APTITUDE
The Chow Chow had various roles in the past, including hunting dog and as an item on Chinese menus. Today it is a vigilant family pet.

SIZE
The shoulder-height is 48 - 56cm (18$^{1}/_{2}$ - 22in) for dogs and 46 - 51cm (18 - 20in) for bitches.

COAT
The coat is short-haired as indicated in the name. The most common colours are plain red, black, blue, and cream. The Chow Chow has a blue tongue and blue pigmentation.

Short-haired Chow Chow

CARE REQUIRED

The care of the Short-haired Chow Chow is much less than that of the longer-haired variety. In spite of this, it must still be groomed regularly with thorough brushing, especially during moulting.

CHARACTER

This is an attentive dog with a mind of its own, that is peaceful and noble, independent, reasonably active, dominant, vigilant, brave, quite demanding of itself, and full of character.

TRAINING

The Short-haired Chow Chow calls for a handler who is calm, equable, and exudes natural authority. It is asserted that the shorter-haired variety is more active and learns faster than the longer-haired family member.

SOCIAL BEHAVIOUR

Most Chow Chows are fairly dominant towards other dogs. In contrast, they are quite good with children. Provided they are acquainted with cats and other household animals early in their lives, problems can be prevented. In the company of strangers they are rather reserved.

EXERCISE

This breed does not require a great deal of exercise but likes to be out of doors. Find it a cool place to lie in summer where it can withdraw to the shade because they do not like hot weather.

Chow Chow

Head of a Chow Chow

Chow Chow (Long-haired)

COUNTRY OF ORIGIN
China.

APTITUDE
The Chow Chow had various roles in the past, including hunting dog and as an item on Chinese menus. Today it is a vigilant family pet.

SIZE
The shoulder-height is 48 - 56cm (18$^1/_2$ - 22in) for dogs and 46 - 51cm (18 - 20in) for bitches.

COAT
The coat consists of long erect hairs and the colours that are most common are plain red, black, blue, and cream. Chow Chows have a blue tongue and blue pigmentation.

CARE REQUIRED
The Chow Chow needs regular thorough brushing, especially in those places where tangles may form. Get the young dog used to this ritual so that grooming does not become a battle of wills when it is fully grown and stronger.

CHARACTER
This breed has a mind of its own but is calm and noble, independent, dominant, vigilant, brave, demanding of itself, and full of character.

TRAINING
The future owner of this breed needs to be a calm person who is naturally equable and exudes authority.
With such a handler, the Chow Chow can develop well. Do not expect great obedience from

Eurasian

them - they are born stubborn and with a mind of their own. The dogs can learn because they are certainly not stupid but they must see the point of your command.
It is important to be consistent at all times with them.

SOCIAL BEHAVIOUR
The majority of Chow Chows are dominant towards other dogs. In contrast, they are usually good with children.
They need to be introduced when young to cats and your other household animals to prevent problems. The Chow Chow is somewhat reserved in the company of strangers.

EXERCISE
This breed does not need a great deal of exercise but does like to be out of doors. Make sure that they have a cool place to which they can withdraw because they do not like hot weather.

Eurasian

COUNTRY OF ORIGIN
Germany.

APTITUDE
Family pet.

SIZE
The shoulder-height is 52 - 60cm (20$^1/_2$ - 23$^1/_2$in) for dogs and 48 - 56cm (18$^1/_2$ - 22in) for bitches. The ideal height is 56cm (22in) for dogs and 52cm (20$^1/_2$in) for bitches.
The optimum weight for dogs is 26kg (57lb) and 22kg (48$^1/_2$lb) for bitches.

COAT
The outer coat is of medium-length stiff hair which has a ruffled appearance. The undercoat is thick and woolly. Every combination of colours is permitted except white, white patches, or liver.

CARE REQUIRED
The Eurasian does not need much grooming. It is indeed recommended to avoid regular grooming which might loosen too much of the woolly under-layer.
During moulting a comb with a double row of metal teeth should be used to remove dead and loose hairs.

Japanese Spitz

COUNTRY OF ORIGIN
Japan.

APTITUDE
Family pet.

SIZE
The shoulder-height is 30cm (11^1/$_2$in) for dogs
and slightly less for bitches.

COAT
The long-haired coat, which has a thick under-
layer, is always white.

CARE REQUIRED
Do not groom the Japanese Spitz with brush
and comb too often to avoid damaging the
undercoat.
During moulting use a comb with a double row
of metal teeth to remove loose hairs from the
under-layer.

CHARACTER
This is a high-spirited, intelligent and playful
dog which is vigilant and obedient.

TRAINING
The Japanese Spitz is not difficult to train although it is important for the handler always to
be consistent. They learn quickly and derive
much pleasure from spots such as agility skills
trials and fly-ball.

SOCIAL BEHAVIOUR
In general this dog is good with children. The
majority of them tend to be rather reserved

CHARACTER
This is a calm, equable dog which is alert,
friendly, can have a mind of its own but is reasonably obedient, that is intelligent, and very
loyal to its family. The Eurasian does not bark
much.

TRAINING
This breed is not difficult to train although the
handler needs to be consistent to have adequate authority. Eurasians are not a suitable
breed to live in a kennel.

SOCIAL BEHAVIOUR
This breed gets on very well with children but
is rather reserved towards strangers. Contact
with other dogs does not normally cause any
problems.
Get them used to other animals when they are
still young.

EXERCISE
This breed needs fairly substantial amounts of
exercise. An hour per day walking with the dog
is a minimum.
Additionally, the dog loves to run around and
play off the lead.

towards strangers. The company of other dogs and other household pets does not usually lead to problems.

EXERCISE
To keep the dog healthy in body and soul, take it for three walks every day and also let it regularly run and play off the lead.

Japanese Spitz

Shiba Inus

Shiba Inu

COUNTRY OF ORIGIN
Japan.

APTITUDE
Hunting dog and family pet.

SIZE
The shoulder-height standard is 39.5cm (15$^1/_2$in) for dogs and 36.5cm (14$^1/_2$in) for bitches. Variations of 1.5cm ($^1/_2$in) are permitted.

COAT
The Shiba Inu has a short straight-haired coat with a soft undercoat. Red, red highlighted with white, white, black, black and tan, and salt and pepper are the most common colours.

CARE REQUIRED
The coat of the Shiba Inu does not require much attention. Remove dead hairs from time to time to keep the coat in good condition, using a coarse comb with a double row of metal teeth.

Shiba Inu

CHARACTER
This is a lively, equable dog which barks little and bonds closely with its handler yet is independent.
It is also curious, cheerful and vigilant. It is natural for a Shiba Inu to keep itself clean and it is therefore easily house-trained.

TRAINING
The training of this dog is not such a problem, provided you make allowance for it having a

155

mind of its own and being naturally independent. Vary the exercises with play so that the dog will enjoy itself.

SOCIAL BEHAVIOUR
The Shiba Inu normally gets on with dogs and other animals. It is a bit reserved with strangers but children do not usually cause any problems with them.

EXERCISE
This undemanding dog will adapt to your circumstances but should it ever be necessary, it can walk for hours on end.

Primitive Spitz breeds

Basenji

COUNTRY OF ORIGIN
Africa.

APTITUDE
Hunting dog and companion.

SIZE
The ideal shoulder-height is 43cm (17in) for dogs and 40cm (15^1/$_2$in) for bitches.

Head of a Basenji

COAT
The coat is short-haired, dense and fine. Basenjis are usually red with white, but black with white, and black with tan and white (triple-coloured) are also permitted.
Not every country accepts those dogs having blends of colours with highlights.

CARE REQUIRED
Groom occasionally with a coarse rubber brush or with a rubber glove. These dogs naturally keep themselves very clean.

CHARACTER
This remarkable breed acts in many ways like a cat. They clean themselves by licking their coat, do not bark, instead emitting a kind of yodel. They are independent dogs with minds of their own yet bond very closely with their handler and family and need to be in their company. The majority detest rain and cannot stand the cold or draughts.

TRAINING
If the quest is for a perfectly obedient family dog, then look elsewhere than this breed. Basenjis are independent and headstrong dogs which are not easy to train. Much is demanded of the trainer including considerable cunning to get this breed to listen and respond with the odd corrective measure.

Head of a Basenji

Basenji

Pharaoh Hound

COUNTRY OF ORIGIN
Malta.

APTITUDE
Hunting dog (by sight, hearing, and scent), and family pet.

SIZE
The ideal shoulder-height is 56cm (22in) for dogs and 53cm (20^1/$_2$in) for bitches.

COAT
These dogs have a short, shiny coat in colours ranging from light to dark reddish-brown. A white tip to the tail is a desirable feature, and white markings on the chest, feet, and even a small white blaze are all permissible.

CARE REQUIRED
The Pharaoh Hound needs little grooming. It is

Pharaoh Hound

However it is not sensible to attempt to create the ideal obedient dog with this breed because in doing so you will harm the natural character of the dog.

SOCIAL BEHAVIOUR
To a degree these dogs can be trusted with children, provided the children do not invade the dog's own domain, but they can never be considered real playmates for children. They are naturally reserved towards strangers and have a natural instinct to protect their handler. Contact with other dogs is usually no problem.

Do not forget that the origin of the Basenji is as a hunting dog for wild game so it is advisable to familiarize them with cats and other animals early on.

EXERCISE
This breed will adapt to the circumstances so that it can live in a flat, provided it is taken out for regular walks.

SPECIAL REMARKS
The bitches of this breed normally come into season only once per year.

only necessary to remove dead and loose hairs with a rubber brush.

CHARACTER

This is a reasonably independent dog which is playful, brave, equable, not intrusive, affectionate, and loyal to its handler and family. It is also peaceful in the house, friendly, intelligent, and reasonably obedient.
The Pharaoh Hound has considerable stamina and deeply rooted hunting instincts.

TRAINING

Training should not be too difficult. The handler needs to understand the dog's character and to be consistent in approach.

SOCIAL BEHAVIOUR

Dogs of this breed can be rather dominant towards other males. They tend to get on with children but treat strangers with reserve. Cats and other animals do not make ideal household companions for this breed because they will be regarded as prey.
However with the right approach and very early social training, they can be taught to live with the household cat.

EXERCISE

The Pharaoh Hound needs lots of exercise. Set aside an hour each day to cycle with the dog. Coursing is an alternative if you do not wish to hunt with the dog.

These dogs can keep on running if they spy or scent wild game because they never lose their instinct to hunt alone.
To prevent this, you will need a sound high fence around your garden because they can jump very high.

SPECIAL REMARKS

The Pharaoh Hound is often considered to be a bit of a Greyhound because it hunts by sight, sound, and scent.

Primitive Spitz-type hunting breeds

Cirneco dell' Etna

COUNTRY OF ORIGIN

Sicily.

APTITUDE

Hunting dog and family pet.

SIZE
Dogs 46-50cm(18 1/2-19 1/2in), bitches (16 1/2-18 1/2in).

COAT
This Sicilian dog has a short-haired coat. All shades of red are permissible and one white marking is accepted, although this is fairly rare.

CARE REQUIRED
This breed's coat does not require much attention. The sheen on the coat can be kept in good condition by occasionally running a rubber glove over it. Check at frequent intervals that the ear passages are clean and keep the claws short.

CHARACTER
This is a friendly, affectionate, active dog which is intelligent and very loyal to its handler and the family and is also vigilant.
The majority of this breed likes to be heard and also demands plenty of attention.

TRAINING
The Cirneco dell' Etna is a relatively easy dog to train but the handler needs to be very consistent.

SOCIAL BEHAVIOUR
This breed tends to be rather reserved with other dogs but generally gets on with its own breed.

Head of a Cirneco dell' Etna

There will be no problems with your own cat but strange cats will be chased. They are loving and patient with children. They mark the arrival of strangers but that is all.

EXERCISE
Because this breed needs lots of exercise it is necessary to set aside an hour every day for this purpose.

Running alongside a cycle or coursing are ideal forms of exercise for them.

SPECIAL REMARKS
The Cirneco dell' Etna is considered a bit of a greyhound, because it hunts by sight and sound as well as by nose. Only let them run free off the lead if you are absolutely certain there is no wild game nearby or its hunting instincts will rear their head and it will go on a solitary poaching foray.

They can jump extremely high so your garden needs a good high fence. They like to be near you and are quite unsuitable for kennel life.

Ibizan Hound

Ibizan Hound

COUNTRY OF ORIGIN
The Balearic Islands.

APTITUDE
Hunting dog (by sight, sound, and scent), and family pet.

SIZE
The shoulder-height is 66 - 72cm (26 - 28$^{1}/_{2}$in) for dogs and 60 - 67cm (23$^{1}/_{2}$ - 26$^{1}/_{2}$in) for bitches.

Head of an Ibizan Hound

COAT
The Ibizan Hound has short-haired, long-haired, and rough-haired varieties. The most usual is the short-haired; the long-haired is very rare. The rough-haired has a longer coat of rough hair that is softer textured than the other two varieties.
Predominant colours are various shades of red, white, or a combination of them.

CARE REQUIRED
The short-haired version can be groomed occasionally with a rubber brush. The rough-haired ones do not need hand-plucking and can also be groomed by an occasional brushing.

CHARACTER
This is a calm and affectionate dog which is very loyal to its family, and reasonably independent, vigilant, alert, intelligent, and keen to learn.

It is also fairly obedient, has tremendous stamina, is energetic, brave, and equable. The Ibezan Hound has a strongly developed hunting instinct.

TRAINING
This breed likes to learn and does so quickly. Provided they have been properly trained, they can participate in various types of dog sports. They are very sensitive to the voice of their handler and a friendly request achieves more than a gruff command.

SOCIAL BEHAVIOUR
These dogs get on well with children but hold back watchfully with strangers. Once they decide the stranger means no harm, they thaw very quickly.

The dogs of this breed can be rather dominant towards other males. Provided their social training introduced them to your cat when they were young, there will be no problems.

EXERCISE
Despite the enormous ability to adapt of this breed - it can even be kept in a flat - it still needs a great deal of exercise. They can run alongside a cycle but not before the dog is fully grown!

They may want to investigate something which attracts their interest, because they remain very much hunting dogs. To prevent this, you will need a good fence of at least 2m (6ft 7in) high: they can even apparently climb over fences. The majority enjoy retrieving for you, and coursing is an ideal sport for them.

SPECIAL REMARKS
Given their character, these dogs do not belong in a kennel.

They are considered half Greyhound because they hunt by sight, scent, and sound.

Thai Ridgeback Dog

Thai Ridgeback Dog

COUNTRY OF ORIGIN
Thailand.

APTITUDE
Hunting dog and watchdog.

Size
The shoulder-height is 53 - 61cm ($20^{1}/_{2}$ - 24in) for dogs and 48 - 56cm ($18^{1}/_{2}$ - 22in) for bitches.

Coat
The coat is very short-haired and soft, with a definite ridge of hair along the back (the pile of which grows in the opposite direction to the rest of the hair). They can be blue, silver, chestnut, or black.

Care required
This Ridgeback requires little grooming. Brushing occasionally will keep the coat in good condition.

Character
This is a vigilant, intelligent dog which has a mind of its own, with considerable stamina, that is lively and active, but reserved in the company of strangers.

Training
The training of the Thai Ridgeback calls for a soft touch but with a very consistent approach.

Social behaviour
The company of other household animals does not cause any problems provided the dog grows up with them. They are rather reserved towards strangers.

Exercise
This Thai breed needs quite a lot of exercise. Running alongside a cycle or regular long walks are certainly necessary to keep the dog fit. They have been known to complete various training courses successfully.

Special remarks
The Thai Ridgeback Dog is quite rare outside Thailand.

Thai Ridgeback Dog

6. Hounds

Hounds

Basset Artésien Normand

COUNTRY OF ORIGIN
France.

APTITUDE
Hound and family pet.

SIZE
The shoulder-height is 30 -36cm (11$^{1}/_{2}$in) for both dogs and bitches.

COAT
The short-haired coat is dense. Only three-coloured examples or ones with a white and orange coat are permitted. White feet are preferred.

CARE REQUIRED
Run a rubber brush over the dog occasionally to remove loose hairs. Keep the ears clean using a recognized brand of ear cleaner for this purpose - never cotton buds, which will push any dirt further into the ear.
Keep the claws short by filing them whenever necessary.

CHARACTER
This is a sociable, companionable and friendly dog which is gentle-natured, independent, and possesses a good scenting nose.

The Basset Artésian Normand has a deep bark which it lets be heard from time to time. This is usually not a problem if they are kept indoors.

TRAINING
Even though this Basset has a mind of its own, they can be well trained with patience, love, and perseverance. Make sure you are consistent with them.

SOCIAL BEHAVIOUR
In France these dogs live in packs so they can happily get on with other dogs. Provided they have early social training with cats and other animals, they will get along with these too.

Petit Bleu de Gascogne

Basset Artésian Normand

Basset Artésian Normand

However loudly visitors are announced, they can still count on a warm welcome.

EXERCISE
Take this Basset regularly for longish walks but take care: if it comes across the scent of wild animals, it will be off - in common with most of the dogs in this group.
Should this happen, lay an item of clothing or other item bearing your scent where the dog disappeared. The odds are that you will find it at this spot within a few hours or not later than the next morning.

Petit Bleu de Gascogne

COUNTRY OF ORIGIN
France.

APTITUDE
Hound and family pet.

SIZE
The shoulder-height is 34 - 40cm
($13^1/_2$ - $15^1/_2$in).

COAT
The short-haired and very dense coat has a white ground speckled with black, and with black patches, or a large black area with tan markings.

CARE REQUIRED
These dogs do not require much grooming. Groom them occasionally with a rubber brush to remove loose hairs. The ears must be carefully looked after though. Check regularly that they are clean and keep the ear passages clean with a good quality proprietary ear cleaner. Keep the claws short by filing them.

Basset Bleu de Gascogne

CHARACTER
These are friendly, sociable dogs with a sense of humour that are gentle-natured, independent, and have a good nose. The Basset Bleu de Gascogne has a loud bark which is music to a huntsman's ears.

This is rather less valued in a household pet, but fortunately it does not usually become a real problem. They welcome both welcome and unwelcome visitors.

TRAINING
This dog is born with somewhat of a mind of its own. That does not mean they cannot be trained.
Provided training is not forced too quickly and you take its character into account, this French dog can become a fine companion in the house.

SOCIAL BEHAVIOUR
These dogs live in packs in France so that they can happily get along with other dogs. Children and visitors will also present no problems. Let them get used to cats and other animals when young so that they will share their company without difficulty.

EXERCISE
Take this dog for regular long walks but beware: once they catch a hint of wild game, they will take off after it.

Basset Fauve de Bretagne

COUNTRY OF ORIGIN
France.

APTITUDE
Hound for hunting wild game, and a family pet.

SIZE
The shoulder-height is 32 - 38cm ($12^1/_2$ - 15in) with a variation of 2cm ($^1/_2$in) taller or shorter permitted.

COAT
The coat consists of hard dense hairs which are almost short. Golden or darker shades of pink are most common. Small white patches are considered a fault.

CARE REQUIRED
Remove excess hair in the ear passage and keep the claws short.

Comb the hair regularly and have it plucked about twice per year (depending upon the condition of the coat). It is possible to do this yourself. The coat must never be trimmed.

CHARACTER
This is a cheerful dog that has a little bit of a mind of its own. It is intelligent, friendly, brave, active, and has a good scenting nose.

TRAINING
The Basset Fauve de Bretagne is a hound through and through.
To prevent it from using its skills during a walk in the woods, teach it at a young age that it must come to you on command.

SOCIAL BEHAVIOUR
This dog gets along well with children and other dogs and animals.

In common with most other dogs, it needs to be introduced when young to cats and the other of household pets.

EXERCISE
The dogs of this breed have an average need for exercise.
Let them romp and play regularly. In countries like France, they are kept in packs to hunt rabbits.

Basset Fauve de Bretagne

Basset Griffon Vendéen (Grand and Petit)

COUNTRY OF ORIGIN
France.

APTITUDE
Hound (pack hound for hunting wild game) and family pet.

Small(Petit) Basset Griffon Vendéen

Small (Petit) Basset Griffon Vendéen puppy

SIZE
The shoulder-height of the smaller or Petit Basset Griffon is 34 - 38cm ($13^1/_2$ - 15in) and 38 - 42cm (15 - $16^1/_2$in) for the larger or Grand Basset Griffon.

COAT
The rough-haired coat is hard, not very long, and although not curly, has an open unkempt look. They are either single-coloured, two-coloured, or three-coloured.

The single colour is grey-white or hare-colouring; the two colours are white with either grey, red, orange, or black patches; and the combination of three colours are either white-black-red, or white or hare-grey with a greyish white and red. Single-coloured drab red is not preferred.

CARE REQUIRED
The coat requires regular grooming with brush and comb. Keep the ears, and especially the ear passages, clean. File claws that become too long

and clip any hair that becomes too long between the pads of the feet to prevent tangles between the toes which could trap thorns or such like. About once a year pluck the loose and dead hair out by hand.

If you wish to show the dog, the neck should be emphasized by removing more hair from this area. The breed standard requires the Petit Bassett Griffin to have small ears and a tail which is accentuated by clipping excessive hair.

CHARACTER

These are high-spirited, lively, sociable, loving and sensitive dogs, that are clever, with a bit of a mind of their own, but they are quite straightforward.

TRAINING

As these dogs have something of a mind of their own there is little point cherishing the idea of turning one of them into the perfect dog. With the right approach, and with patience it is possible to train it to an extent.

SOCIAL BEHAVIOUR

Dogs, pets, children, and visitors are all accepted without problem as if the dog's motto were "the more the merrier."

EXERCISE

Because these hounds need substantial amounts of exercise, it is necessary to take them for long walks regularly.

In France they are hunted in packs. The larger Grand Bassett Griffon is used to hunt for hares and roe deer, while the smaller Petit is used for rabbit hunts.

They usually adapt well to becoming family pets.

Grand Basset Griffon Vendéen

Two-coloured Basset Hound dog

Basset Hound

COUNTRY OF ORIGIN
England.

APTITUDE
Hound and family pet.

SIZE
The shoulder-height is 33 - 38cm (13 - 15in).
They are heavy dogs for their size.

COAT
Bassets have a dense short-haired coat which is
smooth. The most usual colour combination is
brown, black, and white. Other colours include
red and white but almost any hound-colouring
is permissible.

CARE REQUIRED
There is little to the grooming of a Basset
Hound. Remove dead and loose hairs during
moulting with a rubber glove. Keep the ears
clean by attending to them about once a week,
inside and out.
Keep the claws short and when necessary clean
the folds of skin.

Do not give Bassets too many little tit-bits
because they have a tendency to become fat. For
dogs with drooping eye-lids it is advisable to
administer eye-drops occasionally. They grow
very rapidly when young and you must ensure
they have a good nutritious and ample diet
during this period.

CHARACTER
The Basset Hound has a mind of its own but
is lovable, sociable, calm, playful and patient,
it enjoys companionship, has a sense of humour
and a real personality which can be influenced

positively by its handler. They have a very good
scenting nose.

TRAINING
These dogs have a mind of their own so they do
not exactly jump to your command. A consistent approach with much patience can work
wonders though.

Never exhaust a young Basset by taking on too
long a walk. Young dogs need all their energy
to develop a strong body.

SOCIAL BEHAVIOUR
These dogs make superb playmates for children
and fortunately get along fine with their own
kind and with other animals. They are friendly
towards strangers but if they sense danger, you
will certainly hear their loud barking.
They do not like to be left on their own. If you
know that it will be necessary to leave it alone
quite often, it is far better to have two Basset
Hounds.

EXERCISE
This breed does not require much exercise and
will be quite content with three trots around the
block each day provided they can also play in
the garden.

Make sure your garden is adequately fenced
because the majority of them love to explore.

Basset Hound, bitch

Beagle

COUNTRY OF ORIGIN
England.

APTITUDE
Hound and family pet.

SIZE
The shoulder-height is 33 - 41cm (13 - 16^1/$_2$in)
and the dog weighs about 15kg (33lb).

COAT
The coat is short and weather-protective. The
three-coloured Beagle is the most usual - that is
a white ground, a brown head and back, with
a black saddle but any recognized hound colourings are permissible. Liver-coloured Beagles
are not acceptable.

CARE REQUIRED
Brush the coat daily to remove dead and loose
hairs. In common with other breeds with han-
ging ears, the ears should be regularly checked
to ensure they are clean.

CHARACTER
This is a lively, cheerful, sociable, brave, and
intelligent dog with a mind of its own, that is
resolute, and vigilant. They have the tendency
to follow their nose.

TRAINING
The Beagle is not the most obedient of dog
breeds. It is both an independent hunting dog
and will make a highly suitable pet for your
home.
It is sensible to take your Beagle to an obedience class.

SOCIAL BEHAVIOUR
Beagles normally tend to get on well with other
dogs and children but even strangers will get a
friendly greeting.
Get them used to cats and other household animals when they are young.

EXERCISE
This breed needs quite a bit of exercise. A well-
fenced garden will prevent your Beagle taking
itself for a walk.
Take it yourself for long walks regularly but do
not allow it to trot around freely off the lead
until you are certain that you have the dog well
under control or you run the risk of disappear-
ing it in search of wild game.

SPECIAL REMARKS
For sportive people this is an ideal family pet
but it is less suitable for life in a flat. They like
to be out of doors and can happily live in an
outdoor kennel with other dogs.

Bloodhound

COUNTRY OF ORIGIN
Belgium.

APTITUDE
Hound or tracking dog, and family pet.

SIZE
The shoulder-height is 63 - 69cm
(24^1/$_2$ - 27^1/$_2$in) for dogs and 58 - 63cm
(22^1/$_2$ - 24^1/$_2$in) for bitches.

COAT
The Bloodhound has a short smooth-haired
coat. The most usual colours are black and red,

liver and red, and plain red. A small amount of white on the chest, feet, and tip of the tail is permissible.

CARE REQUIRED
There is little to the grooming of a Bloodhound. Brush them from time to time to remove loose and dead hairs. More attention is necessary for the ears. Check them for dirt to prevent infections and it does no harm to wash them (for example after the ears dropped in the feeding bowl).
The majority of dogs of this breed have drooping eye-lids. If necessary administer eye-drops containing vitamin A.

CHARACTER
The dogs of this breed are gentle-natured and affectionate, boisterous when young, friendly, tenacious, independent, do not keep barking but have a very loud bark, and they possess a very good scenting nose.
Once their interest is aroused by something, it is difficult to get their attention for anything else.

Bloodhound

Bloodhound

TRAINING
The new owner of a Bloodhound will need to have plenty of patience and to possess tact for training to succeed. The most important consideration is to be consistent - they know full well how successfully they can get around you with a pathetic look and make use of it to get their own way.

Do not expect too much by way of obedience from this dog - they are naturally gentle-natured animals that have minds of their own rather than following your orders. Do not over-tire them with long walks, for example, until fully grown.
The Bloodhound is a big dog that grows rapidly and needs all its energy for developing strong bones, joints and muscles.

SOCIAL BEHAVIOUR
The Bloodhound usually gets on well with children. Make sure they do not pester the dog because these dogs are so good-natured that they will lie there and meekly let children clamber all over it.
Both wanted and unwanted visitors will be greeted as if the Bloodhound thinks "the more the merrier." They can live in harmony with other dogs and household pets.

EXERCISE
This breed has a phenomenal level of stamina and can walk for hours on end. If you have one as a pet, you will have to do a fair bit of hiking quite regularly.
They are primarily tracking dogs which when they encounter an interesting scent want to find its source. Make sure that your garden is well fenced. Consider hunting with this hound or having it trained as a search dog.
They are resistant to cold and can be kept in a kennel provided they get sufficient exercise and attention.

Long-legged French Bassets

Short-legged hounds such as the Basset Bleu de Gascogne, the Basset Fauve de Bretagne, and the Bassets Griffon Vendéen makes them ideal household pets and they are kept as such in many countries. The long-legged French Bassets are in contrast almost only kept in kennels in packs for hunting.
In this category are included breeds such as the Poitevin, Billy (Grand), Anglo Français de Petit

Petit Bleu de Gascogne

Because they hunt together without orders from their owner, they have developed as very independent dogs which are brave and very sociable. This group of dogs is rarely seen outside of France.

Because of their loud voices (which they like to use), these are less suitable dogs for keeping in a home as a pet than the short-legged Bassets or the French Pointing Bassets.

An exception to this is the Petit Bleu de Gascogne, which with the right training can make a reasonably good family pet.

Porcelaine

Porcelaine

Anglo Français de Petite Vénerie

Vénerie, Briquet Griffon Vendéen, long-legged Griffons, Petit and Grand Blue de Gascogne, and Porcelaine. All these breeds hunt large wild game in packs, letting the hunters know where the quarry is by their loud cries. Such dogs have deeply rooted hunting instincts and a good nose.

It is obvious that these dogs, which live in packs, are able to get on with other dogs, but they are also friendly to children, if somewhat boisterous in their presence.

Swiss hunting dogs

This category includes dogs such as the Niederlaufhund and the Laufhund. There are eight types in all: the Berner, the Luzerner, Schweizer, and Jura Niederlaufhunds; and the same group of Laufhunds. The Jura is often known in English as a Jura Hound.

Head of a Jura Hound

The difference between the two groups is their size. In every other respect, they are identical. The Niederlaufhunds have a shoulder-height of 33 - 41cm (13 - 16$^1/_2$in) with an ideal height of 36 - 38cm (14$^1/_2$ - 15in).

The Laufhunds have a shoulder-height greater than 40cm (15$^1/_2$in). In addition, they have different colours: the Berner is white with black, the Jura is either light brown or brown with a black saddle, the Luzerner is blue or mottled grey, and the Schweizer is white or yellowish-brown. These Swiss hounds are specially bred as pack dogs for hunting wild game. When they find the trace of a wild animal, they give chase, baying as they go so that the hunters know where they are.

Generally speaking such dogs make fine household pets provided you involve them in some activity, such as drag-hunting or other activity which fulfills their natural instincts. In Switzerland the Jura and Luzerner Hounds are often kept as single dogs for such activities.

All of the dogs in these breeds like the company of other dogs and can be difficult if on their own.

Deutsche Bracke

Deutsche Bracke or Steinbracke

COUNTRY OF ORIGIN
Germany

APTITUDE
Harrier and family pet.

SIZE
The shoulder-height is 40 - 53cm (15$^1/_2$ - 20$^1/_2$in).

COAT
The smooth-coat is hard to the touch. The colours usually range from red to yellow with a

black saddle, or a black mantle with a white blaze, collar, chest, and more white markings on the feet and tip of the tail. The undercoat is light-coloured. There is supposed to be a flesh-coloured patch on the nose as this is one of the breed points.

CARE REQUIRED
The Deutsche Bracke does not require much grooming. Run a rubber brush over the coat occasionally to remove dead and loose hairs. Check the ear passages regularly to ensure they are clean and remember that this breed is supposed to have fairly long claws.

CHARACTER
This is a friendly, sociable, affectionate, sensitive, shy, yet curious dog which has great reserves of stamina, that is reasonably obedient although independent-minded, and is vigilant. They have a good scenting nose and make excellent hunting dogs.

TRAINING
Training this breed is not too difficult. They grasp quickly what is required of them but they must never be drilled since this ruins their friendly nature. With patience, love, and understanding, plus a consistent approach, the handler can achieve a lot.

Pair of Deutsche Brackes

SOCIAL BEHAVIOUR
These are sociable dogs which will rarely cause any problems in the company of other dogs. They are also fine with children. One of these dogs will certainly warn you of any strangers visiting.
Introduce them when young to cats and other household animals. They hold their ground with strangers.

EXERCISE
The breed is ideally suited for drag-hunting or as a harrier for hunting hares, rabbits, and foxes. Most of them like to swim. If you do not intend to hunt with them, make sure you find some other means of fulfilling their exercise needs. In common with other hounds, they are likely to forget everything in the interest of chasing an exciting scent, so do not let them run around off the lead.

Otterhounds

Otterhounds

COUNTRY OF ORIGIN
Great Britain.

APTITUDE
Hound and family pet.

SIZE
The shoulder-height is about 67cm (26$^1/_2$in) for dogs and 63cm (24$^1/_2$in) for bitches.

COAT
The coat is rough and weather-resistant. All recognized hound colours are permitted, including plain grey, blue, red, wheaten, sandy, black and tan, and blue and tan.

CARE REQUIRED
The Otterhound must not be clipped because it is supposed to look natural; therefore brush it as little as possible.

CHARACTER
These dogs are friendly, cheerful, boisterous, intelligent, independent, affectionate, equable, but have a mind of their own. They are calm dogs indoors if they have had sufficient exercise.

TRAINING
The Otterhound is not exactly the most obedient dog you could wish for but that does not prevent you from being able to succeed with basic training.

The best results are achieved with a soft but consistent hand. Enthusiasts for the Otterhound call this "training with an iron fist in a velvet glove." They have a good scenting nose, are ideally suited to drag-hunting or searching.

SOCIAL BEHAVIOUR
The Otterhound is a friend to all - other dogs, the family pets, children, and people in general.

EXERCISE
They need plenty of exercise yet because they have a tendency to forget everything in the chase after an exciting scent, you should only allow them to run free off the lead where they can be controlled and it is safe. Make sure your garden is well fenced.

SPECIAL REMARKS
Otterhounds can be kept indoors or outside in a kennel.

Dalmatian

COUNTRY OF ORIGIN
Croatia.

APTITUDE
Family pets. Dalmatians used to be bred as carriage dogs, to be decorative when running ahead of the coach and to act as watchdogs in the stables.

SIZE
The shoulder-height is 56 - 61cm (22 - 24in) for dogs and 54 - 59cm ($21^{1}/_{2}$ - $23^{1}/_{2}$in) for bitches.

COAT
The coat is always short-haired. The most attractive coat does not have the spots overlapping each other.
The ideal size for the spots is a diameter of 2 - 3cm ($^{1}/_{2}$ - $1^{1}/_{2}$in). There are white with black-spotted Dalmatians and the ones with liver-coloured spots.

CARE REQUIRED
The Dalmatian sheds very little hair in your home. Remove loose hairs daily by grooming with a rubber glove during moulting.

CHARACTER
This is a high-spirited dog with lots of stamina that is friendly, affectionate, intelligent, vigilant, curious, equable, and sociable.

TRAINING
This is not a difficult dog to train. Praise excessively when it does something well and it will quickly understand your intentions. They can turn a deaf ear to commands they do not like.

Dalmatian

In such cases hold your ground and do not soften.

SOCIAL BEHAVIOUR
These are excellent playmates for children, although they can be too boisterous for smaller children. With other dogs and household pets, there is also generally no difficulty. With visitors, they either act very vigilantly or rather half-heartedly, depending on the character of the individual dog.

EXERCISE
The Dalmatian will adapt to your family circumstances but you do it an injustice if you limit this dog to three little outings per day. Running alongside a cycle, swimming, playing, and running free through woods and in open countryside will all be good for this dog.
Avoid over-exercising them before they are fully grown.

SPECIAL REMARKS
It is extremely difficult to breed good show dogs. Dalmatians are born white and acquire their spots later. Some puppies are born deaf and it is really advisable to get your puppy from a really reliable breeder.

Dalmatian puppy

7. Pointers

Continental European Pointers

Bracco Italiano

COUNTRY OF ORIGIN
Italy.

APTITUDE
Field sports dog and family pet.

SIZE
The shoulder-height is 58 - 67cm
($22^1/_2$ - $26^1/_2$in) or dogs and 55 - 62cm
($21^1/_2$ - $24^1/_2$in) for bitches.

COAT
The Bracco Italiano has a coat of short, dense, and shiny hair.
Permitted colours are white; white with large or small patches of orange, amber, or chestnut; and white with light orange or chestnut-brown mottling.

CARE REQUIRED
The coat of this dog does not require much attention. During the moult you can remove dead and loose hairs by grooming with a rubber brush. Keep its ear passages clean.

CHARACTER
This is an equable and compliant dog which is intelligent, has a sense of humour, is thoughtful, gentle-natured, calm in the house, affectionate, and sensitive.
They do not grow up mentally until they are two and a half to three years old. They are used as all-round field sports dogs for game birds.

TRAINING
They need to be training with a consistent but gentle approach. They are very sensitive to and react strongly to the sound of your voice.
Praise them if they do well. When trained in the right way, they pick things up quickly. Too tough an approach has an adverse effect.

It will achieve nothing except for the dog to lose its respect for you. Avoid over-taxing them physically during early growth. In particular limit going up and down stairs and steps.

Drentse Patrijshond

Bracco Italiano

Bracco Italiano

SOCIAL BEHAVIOUR
Bracco Italianos get along well with other dogs and do not usually cause any difficulties with other household animals.

They become close friends with children. They will always go into action at the hint of danger.

EXERCISE
It is important for this breed to get sufficient freedom of movement for exercise. The ideal solution is to own a large garden and to be honest they are not dogs to be kept in a flat. They love to swim and retrieve and once they are physically mature (at about $1^1/_2$ years), they can begin controlled exercise running alongside a cycle. As hunting dogs, they are considered sound workers with an outstanding scenting ability.

Cesky Fousek

Cesky Fousek

COUNTRY OF ORIGIN
Czech Republic and Slovakia.

APTITUDE
Field sports dog and family pet.

SIZE
The shoulder-height is 60 - 66cm ($23^1/_2$ - 26in) for dogs and 58 - 62cm ($22^1/_2$ - $24^1/_2$in) for bitches.

COAT
The coat is rough-haired and the most usual colour is a brown roan (with or without patches), but plain brown with a white chest is also possible.

CARE REQUIRED
The condition of the coat determines how often the Cesky Fousek needs to have its hair hand-plucked: never, once a year, or more times each year. The beard, moustache, and eyebrows are left alone during this process.
Between plucking sessions, brush the coat occasionally and clip any excess hair between the pads of the feet. Check for any hair growth in the ear passages and remove it.

CHARACTER
This is a friendly, intelligent, and gentle-natured dog which is affectionate, tractable, obedient, and vigilant. Indoors they are calm; out of doors they are very active and tough on themselves. The Cesky Fousek is an all-round field sports dog but is a specialist pointer (they stand unmoving facing their prey as the wind carries the scent of wild game to them).

TRAINING
Because they are quick and eager pupils, the training of this breed is not particularly difficult. Make sure though that there is plenty of variety because when made to do the same all the time they will protest.

SOCIAL BEHAVIOUR
Cesky Fouseks get on fine with other dogs and your other household animals, although their hunting instincts can cause problems with cats, for example.
They are fine with children provided they are not pestered in their own domain.

EXERCISE
These through-and-through hunting dogs need lots of exercise to get rid of their energy. If you are unable to hunt with the dog or do not wish to do so, then is essential to trot them alongside a cycle regularly and to let them run and play off the lead.
This will keep this dog mentally as well as physically fit.

Drentse Patrijshond

Drentse Patrijshond

COUNTRY OF ORIGIN
The Netherlands.

APTITUDE
Field sports dog and family pet.

SIZE
The shoulder-height is 55 - 63cm ($21^1/_2$ - $24^1/_2$in). Provided the dog is attractive and well-proportioned in its build, a variance of 1cm ($1/_2$in) taller or shorter will be accepted.

COAT
The Drentse Patrijshond has a dense coat of medium-length hair. The colours are white with

brown or orange patches, which can include tan markings or mottling. A brown mantle is permissible but not preferred.

CARE REQUIRED
Brush them once per week and give particular attention using a special 'German Shepherd' comb to the parts of the coat with longer hairs. The ear passages need checking from time to time to ensure they are clean and excess hair between the pads of the feet should be trimmed.

CHARACTER
These are attentive, intelligent, curious, and vigilant dogs, which are affectionate, gentle-natured, obedient, and equable. They do not take well to life in a kennel. They normally bark only when they sense danger.

TRAINING
Train these dogs with a consistent but gentle hand. The Drentse Patrijshond makes an easy pupil because it quickly grasp what is expected of it.

SOCIAL BEHAVIOUR
This breed gets on extremely well with children and does not cause any problems with other dogs or household animals.
They are vigilant but not badly behaved towards strangers.

EXERCISE
They do not need a great deal of exercise for their size. Let them swim or run beside a cycle; playing games in which they retrieve things or going for long walks will make them happy. If a week passes when you have less time for such activities, they will not misbehave, provided they feel part of the family.

Drentse Patrijshonds

Wire-haired German Pointer

German Pointer (Wire-haired)

COUNTRY OF ORIGIN
Germany.

APTITUDE
Field sports dog and family pet.

SIZE
The shoulder-height is 60 - 67cm ($23^1/_2$ - $26^1/_2$in) for dogs and 56 - 62cm (22 - $24^1/_2$in) for bitches.

COAT
The rough, wire-haired coat is close and dense, with a dense undercoat. The colours are brown roan, brown with or without white, and white with a brown head and brown markings.
A black roan is also permissible.

CARE REQUIRED
The hairs of the coat should be as hard as possible but must not look untidy. The hairs need to be hand-plucked occasionally - how often depends on the condition of the coat. Between such plucking sessions, brush thoroughly about once per week.
This is a good chance to check the ear passages to ensure they are clean.

CHARACTER
This is an affectionate, active, and intelligent dog which is loyal to its own family, and is eager to learn, equable, vigilant, has a good nose, and can be dominant.

TRAINING
Wire-haired German Pointers learn quickly, though they need a handler who is consistent in approach. In common with the short-haired variety, they like to be occupied and they enjoy working for their handler.

They are outstanding all-round field sports dogs.
The Wire-haired is more dominant than the short-haired type.

SOCIAL BEHAVIOUR
This breed usually gets along well with other dogs and household animals. They are normally patient with children.
They are friendly with those they know but can be vigilant if necessary.

EXERCISE
The Wire-haired German Pointer is best-suited to a sportive family. It gets no pleasure out of three little trots around the corner each day and needs plenty of exercise.
Most of them love swimming and retrieving. When they get enough exercise and things to keep them busy, they will be calm indoors.

Short-haired German Pointer

German Pointer (Short-haired)

COUNTRY OF ORIGIN
Germany.

APTITUDE
Field sports dog and family pet.

SIZE
The shoulder-height is 62 - 66cm ($24^1/_2$ - 26in) for dogs and 58 - 63cm ($22^1/_2$ - $24^1/_2$in) for bitches.

COAT
The short-haired coat is recognized in brown (with and without white markings), dark brown roan, light brown roan, and white with brown markings on the head or with brown patches or spots.

There are also black coats with the same combinations of markings as the brown varieties. Yellow markings are also permissible.

CARE REQUIRED
This breed does not need much attention to its coat. An occasional brushing will keep the hair in good condition. Check from time to time to ensure that the ears are clean.

CHARACTER
These dogs are tractable, intelligent and eager to learn, loyal, active, spontaneous, brave, vigilant, playful, friendly, and have a good scenting nose.

TRAINING
Because they are intelligent and eager to learn, Short-haired German Pointers are not difficult to train provided their handler is consistent in approach. They like to be busy and they enjoy working for their handler. They are outstanding all-round field sports dogs.

SOCIAL BEHAVIOUR
German Pointers generally get on well with their own kind, other animals, and with children. Although they tend to be friendly with everyone, they can be vigilant.

EXERCISE
The Short-haired German Pointer is best-suited to a sportive family. Bear in mind that this is a hunting dog that likes to be kept busy and it cannot and will not adapt to an easy-going life.

Head of a Long-haired German Pointer

Most of them like to swim and retrieve. If you arc unable to hunt with the dog, you will need to take it for regular long walks and give it the chance to run and play off the lead. When they get enough exercise and things to keep them busy, they will be calm when indoors.

Long-haired German Pointer

Long-haired German Pointer

German Pointer (Long-haired)

COUNTRY OF ORIGIN
Germany.

APTITUDE
Field sports dog and family pet.

SIZE
The shoulder-height is 63 - 66cm (24^1/$_2$- 26in) for dogs and 60 - 63cm (23^1/$_2$ - 24^1/$_2$in) for bitches.

COAT
The long-haired coat can be plain brown, but also brown with a white band or white with a brown head and brown markings.

CARE REQUIRED
This breed does not need much attention to its coat. Brush the hair regularly and trim any excess hair between the pads of the feet.

Occasionally it is necessary to pluck old (brown) hair. It is simple to recognize this because it will be lighter than the rest of the coat.

CHARACTER
These dogs are affectionate, lively, loyal to their family, gentle-natured and equable, intelligent and eager to learn, and have a good scenting nose.

TRAINING
These dogs can learn and want to, making their training much easier. This makes them an ideal choice for those without much experience They are outstanding all-round field sports dogs.

SOCIAL BEHAVIOUR
This German Pointer is very sociable and gets on well with dogs and other animals. Most of them are very loving with children.

EXERCISE
This breed is first and foremost a hunting dog which likes to swim and search. There is no greater pleasure you can give this dog than to take it on a hike through the countryside. They belong with a sportive family which likes to be out of doors.
When the Long-haired German Pointer gets sufficient exercise, it is quite calm when indoors.

SPECIAL REMARKS
The Long-haired German Pointer is highly regarded by field sports people who find it a very reliable working dog. They also make first-class family pets provided they are kept active and get enough exercise.

Epagneul Bleu de Picardie

COUNTRY OF ORIGIN
France.

APTITUDE
Formerly mainly a field sports dog, today a family pet.

SIZE
The shoulder-height is 57 - 60cm ($22^1/_2$ - $23^1/_2$in) for dogs and slightly less for bitches.

COAT
The medium-length hair forms a smooth or lightly waved coat.
The black and white colours are so intermingled that the appearance is of a blue coat.

CARE REQUIRED
This breed does not need much attention to its coat. An occasional brushing, particularly in the areas where the coat is thickest, is sufficient to keep it in good condition.

Check the ear passages regularly to ensure they are clean.

CHARACTER
These dogs are gentle-natured, sociable, intelligent and obedient, pliable, loyal, friendly, affectionate, and they have a good scenting nose.

TRAINING
These dogs learn quickly and easily. They react well to the voice and no firm correction should be necessary.
Because they like to please their handler, they are an ideal choice for those without much experience of dogs.

SOCIAL BEHAVIOUR
This breed is very adaptable and gets on well with dogs and other animals. They are generally very loving and patient with children. They are certainly vigilant and will always announce the presence of strangers - and, if necessary, will protect the people close to it.

This former field sports dog can be very happy in its role as family pet but that does not mean it will be content with three little circuits of the neighbourhood each day. Take it on hikes regularly and give it the chance to run about and to play. They are normally mad keen on water and love to retrieve.

Epagneul Bleu de Picardie

Epagneul Breton

Epagneul Breton

COUNTRY OF ORIGIN
France.

APTITUDE
Field sports dog and family pet.

SIZE
The shoulder-height is 48 - 50cm ($18^1/_2$ - $19^1/_2$in) for dogs and 47 - 49cm ($18^1/_2$ - $19^1/_2$in) for bitches.
They weigh about 15kg (33lb).

COAT
The coat consists of lightly or strongly waved fine hairs. The breed colours are white and orange, white and chestnut, white and black, three-coloured, or a roan of one of these colours.
The most common colour is white with reddish brown.

CARE REQUIRED
This breed does not need much attention to its coat. An occasional brushing, particularly in the areas where the coat is thickest, is sufficient to keep it in good condition. Check the ear passages regularly to ensure they are clean.

CHARACTER
These are lively, intelligent dogs that love to retrieve but which can have a mind of their own, they rarely bark, are gentle-natured, affectionate, and obedient. These outstanding and un-tiring field sports dogs are highly thought of by French hunters.

TRAINING
Epagneul Bretons are easily trained because they are intelligent, learn quickly, and are obedient. Bear in mind that they are sensitive to hard words and any undercurrents of unrest in the home.

SOCIAL BEHAVIOUR
A well-trained Epagneul Breton is very loving with children, and gets on well with dogs and other animals. They will bark if they sense danger.

EXERCISE
Although this breed fits into the role of family pet extremely well, it remains heart and soul a field sports dog. It will not be content with three little circuits of the neighbourhood each day.
Consider working the dog in the field which will satisfy both its need to work and its exercise requirements. Alternative activities could be agility skills trials or fly-ball. Swimming and retrieving are among this breed's most enjoyed pastimes.

Epagneul Français

COUNTRY OF ORIGIN
France.

APTITUDE
Field sports dog and family pet.

Epagneul Français

SOCIAL BEHAVIOUR
These dogs are friendly with everyone and anything, including other dogs, household animals, and children. They will bark though if they sense danger.

EXERCISE
This through-and-through field sports dog does not belong in front of the hearth all day long. If you are unable or unwilling to work this dog in the field, you must find another form of exercise for them.
They are normally mad keen on water and love to retrieve.

Epagneul Français

Munsterlander (large)

COUNTRY OF ORIGIN
Germany.

APTITUDE
Field sports dog and family pet.

SIZE
The shoulder-height is 60 - 65cm ($23^1/_2$ - $25^1/_2$in) for dogs and 58 - 63cm ($22^1/_2$ - $24^1/_2$in) for bitches.

COAT
The lank long-haired coat may be white with black patches and spots, but black roan is also permitted.

CARE REQUIRED
This breed needs little attention to its coat. Groom it regularly with brush and comb and check the ear passages well to ensure they are clean.

SIZE
The shoulder-height is 55 - 61cm ($21^1/_2$ - 24in) for dogs and 54 - 59cm ($21^1/_2$ - $23^1/_2$in) for bitches.

COAT
The coat consists of medium-length lightly or strongly waved fine hairs. The colour is always white with brown patches, with or without brown spots.

CARE REQUIRED
This breed needs to be groomed with brush and comb about once each week. Check the ear passages regularly to ensure they are clean and trim any excess hair between the pads of the feet.

CHARACTER
These are lovable and affectionate dogs that are obedient, eager to learn, energetic yet calm in the home. The Epagneul Français has considerable stamina, a good scenting nose, and generally barks little.

TRAINING
This dog needs a soft-handed but consistent approach. They like to please their handler so training is not very difficult.

CHARACTER

These are intelligent, lovable and affectionate dogs that are vigilant, brave, eager to work, that can be somewhat dominant. They have a good scenting nose, and bond with their family.

TRAINING

Because they are so bright and keen, these dogs are easily trained. Munsterlanders are know to be fairly dominant, requiring a handler who will take positive control.

SOCIAL BEHAVIOUR

This breed has no problems whatsoever with other dogs and household animals. The majority of them are delightful and patient with children. They tend to be friendly with everyone although they will act as a watchdog when necessary.

EXERCISE

This dog is primarily a field sports dog but that does not mean that it cannot be a family pet. Provided you give them sufficient opportunity for exercise, this dog will feel very content with you. Most of them are mad keen on water and love to retrieve.

Large Munsterlander

Large Munsterlanders

Heidewachtel

Heidewachtel, or small Munsterlander

COUNTRY OF ORIGIN
Germany.

APTITUDE
Field sports dog and family pet.

SIZE
The shoulder-height is 50 - 56cm ($19^1/_2$ - 22in) for dogs and 52 - 56cm ($20^1/_2$ - 22in) for bitches. Variations of 2cm ($^1/_2$in) are permitted.

COAT
The Heidewachtel (or small Munsterlander) has a long-haired coat that is lank or lightly waved. The colour is usually brown with white but brown roan is also permissible.

CARE REQUIRED
Check the ear passages regularly to ensure they are clean and remove any excess hair in the ears, and trim such hair between the pads of the

185

feet. The coat should be groomed with brush and comb about twice a week.

Occasionally light-brown hairs appear on the brown areas of the coat. These hairs should be plucked out.

These dogs are only fully physically mature at three years.

CHARACTER
The Heidewachtel loves to swim, is obedient, intelligent, cunning, gentle-natured, cheerful, and fairly tough on itself.

TRAINING
These fine family pets want to please their handler. Train them with a gentle but consistent approach.

SOCIAL BEHAVIOUR
Dogs of this breed are renowned for getting on well with children. They also mix well with other dogs and household pets without any problem.

EXERCISE
This is primarily a field sports dog with tremendous stamina.

If you are unable to work them in the field, then find alternatives such as agility skills trials or fly-ball - which are both ideal for them.

Take this dog regularly to woods and open countryside and let it retrieve objects out of the water, which it enjoys doing.

Wire-haired Pointing Griffon

Head of a Wire-haired Pointing Griffon

Griffon (Wire-haired Pointing)

COUNTRY OF ORIGIN
France.

APTITUDE
Field sports dog and family pet.

SIZE
The shoulder-height is 55 - 60cm
($21^1/_2$ - $23^1/_2$in) for dogs and 50 - 55cm
($19^1/_2$ - $21^1/_2$in) for bitches.

COAT
The hard and rough-haired coat should never feel woolly. The undercoat is soft and dense. The most popular colours are blue-grey, grey with brown patches, and plain brown (often shot through with grey hairs). White with brown is also permissible.

CARE REQUIRED
The Wire-haired Pointing Griffon should be groomed regularly with brush and comb. Check during grooming that the ear passages are clean and trim excess hair between the pads of the feet.

CHARACTER
These dogs are intelligent and eager to learn, affectionate, sociable and friendly, vigilant and protective, brave, tough on themselves, and have enormous stamina.

TRAINING
Dogs of this breed are not generally difficult to train, although the new owner needs to be consistent with them. The dog is intelligent enough to grasp quickly what is required of it.

SOCIAL BEHAVIOUR
Generally these dogs get on well with children and also cause no problems with other dogs. Provided they are correctly socially trained, they will also put up with cats and your other household animals.
Family friends will be heartily welcomed but persons of evil intention will be stopped in their tracks.

EXERCISE
This through-and-through field sports dog needs lots of exercise to keep it physically and mentally fit. It is a reliable all-round field sports dog but if you do not plan to work this dog in the field, you must take it for long walks regularly.
Once fully grown, it can run alongside a cycle and other favourite activities include retrieving and swimming.

Spinone Italiano

Spinone Italiano

COUNTRY OF ORIGIN
Italy.

APTITUDE
Field sports dog and family pet.

SIZE
The shoulder-height is 60 - 70cm
($23^1/_2$ - $27^1/_2$in) for dogs and 58 - 65cm
($22^1/_2$ - $25^1/_2$in) for bitches. The weight is 28 - 37kg ($61^1/_2$ - $81^1/_2$lb).

COAT
The rough, thick, wire-haired coat lies reasonably flat. The permissible colours are plain white, white with orange markings or flecks, white with brown markings or brown roan - with and without larger brown markings.

Spinone Italiano, study of the head

This breed gets on well with its own kind and with other household animals, and they make outstanding playmates for children.
Both wanted and unwanted visitors are likely to be treated to a warm welcome.

EXERCISE
The Spinone needs lots of exercise and also plenty of space so that it is not suitable for a flat or a home in a densely crowded urban area.

They love to swim and once they are fully grown, will enjoy running alongside a cycle. Consider working them in the field.

Braque de Bourbonnais

CARE REQUIRED
Groom the Spinone occasionally with a coarse comb. Trimming them is strictly against breed society standards. Check that the ear passages are clean and trim excess hair between the pads of the feet.

CHARACTER
These dogs are equable and friendly, very gentle-natured and affectionate, but they can have a mind of their own.
They are mad about water and are all-round field sports dogs which have a very fine scenting nose.

TRAINING
Do not expect miracles from this breed in terms of obedience because they have minds of their own. Despite this, they are gentle-natured and affectionate enough to want to please you provided you do not expect too much. Remember that the Spinone is likely to follow its nose if it picks up an interesting scent. Make sure that your garden is well fenced and never let the dog run off the lead unless closely supervised.

French Braques (Pointers)

Breeds within the group of French Braque or Pointers include the Braque d'Auvergne, the Braque de Bourbonnais, the Braque Saint-Germain, and the Braque Français. These short-haired breeds are principally used for field sports in their country of origin.
Depending upon the specific breed, the shoulder-height is 48 - 68cm ($18^{1}/_{2}$ - $26^{1}/_{2}$in). That they make first-class household pets is unknown by all but a few. Their character is described as friendly, pliable, affectionate, intelligent, and obedient.
These quick-on-the uptake pupils get little benefit from a harsh approach and are more successfully trained with a consistent and loving one. They get on fine with other dogs and are very friendly with children. Introducing them early to cats and other household animals prevents problems.
Generally speaking, all of these breeds need lots of exercise and activity. Work them as sporting dogs in the field which they enjoy

tremendously but do not worry if this is not possible. Provided you make sure that they have plenty of exercise and things to occupy them, they will adapt to home life perfectly.

Braque d'Auvergne

Braque d'Auvergne

Stabyhoun

COUNTRY OF ORIGIN
The Netherlands.

APTITUDE
Field sports dog and family pet.

SIZE
The ideal shoulder-height is 53cm (20 $^1/_2$in) for dogs and 50cm (19$^1/_2$in) for bitches.

COAT
The coat consists of long lank hair. The most usual colour is black and white but black roan, brown and white, and brown roan occur.

CARE REQUIRED
The Stabyhoun requires little grooming. Brush and comb them regularly where tangles can occur, such as the chest, tail, and between its legs. Trim excess hair between the pads of the feet.

CHARACTER
These dogs are affectionate, intelligent and eager to learn, calm, have considerable stamina, are vigilant, and they can somewhat obstinate.

Stabyhoun

This intelligent dog likes to do things for its handler but can have a mind of its own. During training, which must be very consistent in manner, it is essential to bear in mind that the dog reacts strongly to your voice.

It is advisable to take the young dog to a puppy and/or obedience class.

SOCIAL BEHAVIOUR
Dogs of this breed generally get on extremely well with other dogs, other animals, and with children. At the hint of danger, they will warn you with full voice.

EXERCISE
Stabyhouns are by origin working field sports dogs and they need lots of exercise. All of them like to go for long country walks and to have the chance to run and play off the lead. They also love to swim and retrieve things.

Provided they get enough exercise, they will be calm when indoors.

Young Stabyhoun

Vizsla, short-haired and wire-haired

COUNTRY OF ORIGIN
Hungary.

APTITUDE
Hunting dog and family pet.

SIZE
For short-haired Vizslas the shoulder-height is 56 - 61cm (22 - 24in) for dogs and 52 - 57cm ($20^1/_2$ - $22^1/_2$in) for bitches. Variations of up to 4cm ($1^1/_2$in) are permitted provided the dog looks correctly proportioned.

For wire-haired Vizslas the shoulder-height is 58 - 62cm ($22^1/_2$ - $24^1/_2$in) for dogs and 54 - 58cm ($21^1/_2$ - $22^1/_2$in) for bitches. Variations of

Short-haired Vizsla

up to 3cm ($1^1/_2$in) are permitted provided the dog looks correctly proportioned.

COAT
The short-haired Vizsla is plain dark wheaten or dark gold. The wire-haired Vizsla is usually seen in shades of sandy-yellow. A small white patch on the breasts of both types is permissible.

CARE REQUIRED
The short-haired coat requires little grooming. During moulting it is best to remove loose and dead hairs with a rubber brush.

The wire-haired coat needs to be plucked from time to time - the old and dead hairs must be removed by hand. Trim excess hair between the pads of the feet.

CHARACTER
These are equable, affectionate, loyal, and intelligent dogs which are eager to learn, sportive, like to retrieve, have a good scenting nose, and considerable stamina.

TRAINING
Generally these are not difficult dogs to train

because they like to please their handler. It is
important to be consistent with them.

Wire-haired Vizsla

SOCIAL BEHAVIOUR
The Vizsla gets on with its own kind, with other
household animals and with children. They will
bark at the presence of strangers but that is usually all.

EXERCISE
This energetic breed needs lots of exercise and
plenty to keep it occupied for it to feel both
physically and mentally happy.
Consider hunting with them. If you do not want
to do this, let them run and play off the lead at

regular intervals. Most Vizslas like to retrieve and love water.

Weimaraner

Head of a Weimaraner

Weimaraner

COUNTRY OF ORIGIN
Germany.

APTITUDE
Field sports dog and family pet.

SIZE
The ideal shoulder-height is 59 - 70cm (23$^1/_2$ - 27$^1/_2$in) for dogs and 57 - 65cm (22$^1/_2$ - 25$^1/_2$in) for bitches.

COAT
There are two different types of coat: the short-haired and the long-haired, both of which are silver/roe-deer or mouse-coloured.
Small white marks on the chest and feet are permitted.

CARE REQUIRED
The short-haired Weimaraner needs little attention for its coat. Remove dead hairs occasionally with a rubber brush. With the long-haired type it is best to brush the coat followed by combing. Check regularly to ensure that the ears are clean.

CHARACTER
These dogs are friendly, intelligent, keen to work, energetic with considerable stamina, vigilant, and protective. The Weimaraner is a good field sports dog.

TRAINING
Weimaraners are quick to learn and eager to please their handler, and intelligent enough to understand what is required of them. The handler needs to exude confidence because this breed can be somewhat dominant.

Long-haired Weimaraners

SOCIAL BEHAVIOUR

The dogs are usually very friendly with children and if they are properly socially trained when young, they can share companionship with cats and other animals without a problem. They also get on equally well with other dogs.

They are reasonably vigilant but not particularly unfriendly towards strangers. But be assured when necessary this dog will be there for you.

EXERCISE

Consider working this dog at field sports. If you do not wish to do so, it will be necessary to take this dog for regular long walks because three little outings each day are certainly not sufficient. They need lots of exercise and things to occupy them and make them feel content.

If they get sufficient exercise, they will be calm in the house. They like to retrieve and to swim and can happily be kept in an outdoor kennel provided they get enough attention and exercise.

Young long-haired Weimaraner bitch

English Setters

English Setters

Setters and Pointers

English Setter

COUNTRY OF ORIGIN
England.

APTITUDE
Field sports dogs and family pets.

SIZE
The shoulder-height is 65 - 68cm
(25$^1/_2$ - 26$^1/_2$in) for dogs and 61 - 65cm
(24 - 25$^1/_2$in) for bitches.

COAT
The coat is long, silk-like, and wavy. English
Setters colours are blue belton (white with blue-
black), orange belton (white with orange),
lemon belton (white with lemon-yellow), and
liver belton (white with liver). There are also
three-coloured English Setters.

CARE REQUIRED
From time to time the English Setter needs to
have the excessive and old hair clipped or trimmed.

If you intend to show this breed, then considerably more attention is required. For household
pets the coat can be kept in good condition
between trims by clipping excess hair between
the pads of the feet and also under the ears.
This last point is important to let air reach the
ears to prevent infections.

CHARACTER
The English Setter is a friendly, gentle-natured,
sensitive dog that bonds with its family. It is
lively, intelligent, sociable, and cautious.

TRAINING
This breed is not difficult to train but they do
tend to have a mind of their own and this needs
to be taken into account.

They respond best to a consistent and loving
approach. In some cases it is advisable to attend
puppy courses with them.

SOCIAL BEHAVIOUR
These dogs are naturally happy with other dogs
and household animals.

Companionship with children will never lead to
problems. These dogs are friendly to all people
and will greet everyone as a friend.

EXERCISE
The English Setter needs quite a lot of exercise. Take it for regular long walks or let it run
alongside a cycle once it is fully grown.
They have a tendency to wander and you should
make sure you have a good fence.

Gordon Setter

Gordon Setter

COUNTRY OF ORIGIN
Scotland.

APTITUDE
Field sports dog and family pet.

SIZE
The shoulder-height is about 66cm (26in) for
dogs and about 62cm (24$^1/_2$in) for bitches.

Young Irish Setter

manner of situations and experiences with people, animals, and things. Only by doing so will you ensure the well-balanced development of this dog.

In general they get on well with other dogs and with children - because they are a friend to everyone. Good early social training will also ensure they can get along with cats and other household animals. If strangers visit they adopt a wait-and-see attitude.

EXERCISE
This breed needs plenty of exercise. Running beside a cycle is an ideal manner to keep them fit but wait until the dog is fully grown.

A Gordon Setter that gets enough outdoor activity will be calm when indoors. They are apt to roam, so a good fence around your property is not an unnecessary luxury.

Irish Setter

COAT
The coat, which must never be curly, consists of medium-length hair with feathering.
The colour is always black with warm chestnut markings. A small white patch on the chest is permissible.

CARE REQUIRED
Groom this dog regularly and check the ear passages to ensure they are clean. The excess hair beneath the ear should be trimmed to let air reach the inner ear in order to avoid infections. The hair on the outside of the ear should never be clipped - something that is permitted with other Setters.
If you wish to show your dog, grooming will require considerably more attention.

CHARACTER
These are lovable, friendly, sociable, and intelligent dogs that are gentle-natured and sensitive, but they also have a mind of their own.

TRAINING
The training of this dog is certainly not difficult, provided you take account of the fact that it can have a mind of its own.
They call for a handler who is both consistent and loving in approach. It is a good idea to attend a puppy training course.

SOCIAL BEHAVIOUR
It is necessary to introduce the young dog to all

Irish Setter

COUNTRY OF ORIGIN
Ireland.

APTITUDE
Field sports dog and family pet.

SIZE
There are no standard dimensions. The shoulder-height is about 65cm (25^1/$_2$in) but there are many much larger specimens.

COAT
The coat is relatively long and flat, with as few curls or waves as possible. The colour is rich chestnut without a trace of black. Markings such as white on the chest, throat, chin, or feet,

or a small star on the forehead and a white blaze are all undesirable. There is also a red-white Irish Setter which has a predominantly white coat with red markings.

CARE REQUIRED
The Irish Setter should be trimmed occasionally, removing excess hair. To show this breed will require considerably more grooming. For dogs kept solely as pets, the coat can be kept in condition between trims by clipping excess hair between the pads of the feet and underneath the ears.
This latter point is necessary to prevent infections if the ear is not ventilated.

CHARACTER
These are lively, lovable, gentle, cheerful, and playful dogs that have a mind of their own, and bond with their family. Generally Irish Setters do not bark much.

TRAINING
The training of these dogs is generally not difficult.
They are intelligent enough to understand quickly what is expected of them but they do have minds of their own, which calls for a handler who is both consistent and loving in his approach. It can be a good idea in some cases to attend a puppy training course.

SOCIAL BEHAVIOUR
Irish Setters are usually loving so that even unwanted visitors are enthusiastically welcomed.
They do however let you know of the arrival of visitors. With children they are friendly and patient and mix harmoniously with other dogs.

Mixing with other animals in the house will not be a problem if the young dog has got to know them early in its life.

EXERCISE
Because this breed needs plenty of exercise you will need to take it on regular long walks. Letting the dog run beside a cycle is an ideal form of exercise once the dog is fully grown.

Some Irish Setters follow their nose when they come across what they consider to be an interesting scent. In such cases they tend to have a deaf ear to your calls.

Teach the young dog that it must come to you when you order it to do so.

Pointer

COUNTRY OF ORIGIN
England.

APTITUDE
Pointer for game birds and family pet.

SIZE
The shoulder-height is 63 - 69cm (24$\frac{1}{2}$ - 27$\frac{1}{2}$in) for dogs and 61 - 66cm (24 - 26in) for bitches.

COAT
The topcoat is short-haired while the undercoat is short and smooth.
Pointers can have the following colour combinations: white and yellow, white and liver, and white and black. Three-coloured varieties are also permissible.

CARE REQUIRED
The grooming of this breed is simple. All that is required is to use a rubber brush during its moulting to remove dead and loose hairs.

CHARACTER
These are friendly, lovable, affectionate, and equable dogs which are intelligent, and obedient, that make first-class game pointers.
(The dog stands absolutely still pointing towards wild game birds as it catches their scent on the wind.)

TRAINING
The Pointer is a reasonably quick learner because the dog is intelligent enough to understand what you intend.

SOCIAL BEHAVIOUR
This breed get on well with their own kind and with other household animals. They are also generally loving and patient with children and they are friendly towards both known and unknown people.
They will get along fine with cats and other household animals if they have been introduced to them when young.

EXERCISE
Because Pointers are primarily field sports dogs, most owners are people who are involved in these activities.

They need lots of exercise so consider letting them work at field sports. If this is not possible, then it is essential that the dog gets at least half an hour every day to run about.

Head of a Pointer

Pointer working

8. Gundogs and retrievers

Retrievers

Chesapeake Bay Retriever

COUNTRY OF ORIGIN
United States.

APTITUDE
Field sports dog and family pet.

SIZE
The shoulder-height is 58 - 66cm ($22^1/_2$ - 26in) for dogs and 53 - 61cm ($20^1/_2$ - 24in) for bitches. Greater consideration is given in the show ring to correct proportion than to height.

COAT
The Chesapeake's coat is its trade mark; thick and short with a dense woolly undercoat. The coat may be wavy in some places but never curly, and it feels greasy to the touch. The colour is between yellow-brown, and dark brown. The darker colouring is more usual.

CARE REQUIRED
Grooming of this breed is fairly simple. During moulting it is necessary to brush the dog to remove dead and loose hairs, but take care not to harm the texture of the coat.
For this same reason it is not advisable to wash this breed.

CHARACTER
These are friendly, intelligent, and obedient dogs with a mind of their own, that are mad about water, tough on themselves, boisterous, full of energy, and vigilant. The dogs in particular can be rather dominant.

TRAINING
This breed is not recommended for the inexperienced new dog owner. The handler needs to be confident and to exude authority because these dogs like to have their own way.

They are less gentle-natured than, for example the Golden Retriever. A consistent but kind

Golden Retriever

approach is the most successful way and it is recommended to attend an obedience class with this dog. They are usually slow to mature to adulthood.

SOCIAL BEHAVIOUR
This dog will get along perfectly well with a cat that is already present in the house, yet it will chase other cats. The dogs in particular can behave dominantly towards other males, although this much depends upon their social training.

Make sure therefore to take the young dog with you as often as possible and introduce it to other dogs so that it has the chance to grow up equably.
Chesapeake Bay Retrievers get on extremely well with children but are somewhat reserved towards strangers.

EXERCISE
This breed needs lots of exercise. If they do not get it, they tend to become badly behaved through boredom.
Swimming and retrieving are two activities which they revel in - together with field sports. They are most certainly not quick learners!

Chesapeake Bay Retriever

Curly Coated Retriever

Curly Coated Retriever

COUNTRY OF ORIGIN
England.

APTITUDE
Field sports dog and family pet.

SIZE
The shoulder-height is about 68.5cm (27in) for dogs and 63.5cm (25in) for bitches.

COAT
The Curly Coated Retriever has a curly, waterproof coat. The hair on the head and on the legs is short and without curls. They are recognized in two colours: liver and black.

CARE REQUIRED
The coat of this breed should be brushed as little as possible to avoid changing its nature from the breed standard.
Grooming cannot be avoided though during the moult. Afterwards the coat should be soaked with water by letting the dog swim or by sponging it down. This puts the curl back into the coat. If the coat becomes too long, it can be trimmed with scissors.

CHARACTER
This is an intelligent, friendly, boisterous dog which can be dominant, that is active, independent, vigilant, and has a good nose for scents.
The Curly Coated Retriever likes to please its handler and learns commands fairly quickly. In spite of this, it has a mind of its own.
The males are more dominant than the bitches.

TRAINING
This breed is intelligent enough to grasp what is expected of it. Make the training a challenge for this dog and vary the exercises because monotony will cause it to lose interest. It is also important always to be consistent.

SOCIAL BEHAVIOUR
In normal circumstances this breed usually gets on well with dogs and other household animals.
Provided children do not pester them, they are mainly very patient with them. If strangers visit, they will usually look everywhere else but, if needs be, they will stand by you.

EXERCISE
This retriever is first and foremost a working dog which likes to retrieve and to swim. The dog could be trained for field sports but members of this breed have also become well known in other areas of dog sports.
Whichever you choose does not matter so long as the dog gets enough exercise and activity.
A Curly Coated Retriever that does not get enough exercise or work becomes extremely badly behaved.

Head of a Curly Coated Retriever

Flat Coated Retriever

Flat Coated Retrievers

COUNTRY OF ORIGIN
England.

APTITUDE
Field sports dogs and family pets.

SIZE
The shoulder-height is 58 - 61cm (22^1/$_2$ - 24in) for dogs and 55 - 58cm (21^1/$_2$ - 22^1/$_2$in) for bitches.

COAT
The smooth, medium-length hair of the Flat Coated Retriever can be black or liver. Occasionally a blonde example occurs but these are not recognized.

CARE REQUIRED
Groom them twice each week with a brush and comb, especially in those places where tangles occur. Check the ear passages at the same time to ensure they are clean and trim excess hair between the pads of the feet. If necessary the Flat Coated Retriever can be trimmed.

CHARACTER
These are intelligent, friendly, equable dogs that are happy to work for their handler, pliable, loyal, mad about swimming, with tremendous stamina, but they can have minds of their own. Most of them are not particularly vigilant and they rarely bark.

TRAINING
This breed is reasonably easy to train. They learn fairly quickly and are intelligent enough to quickly grasp your instructions. They can be stubborn. Attempt to avoid this by being very consistent in your handling of them.

SOCIAL BEHAVIOUR
Mixing with other dogs and animals never presents difficulties and they make reliable playmates for children provided they do not pester the dog.
Strangers will be announced but that is all to be expected.

EXERCISE
This breed needs lots of exercise and they find it enormous fun to swim and retrieve. If you miss a day in exercising them, they will accept it without a fuss but if this is longer, then expect them to be very badly behaved. This is first and foremost a working dog.

Flat Coated Retrievers

Golden Retriever

COUNTRY OF ORIGIN
England.

APTITUDE
Field sports dog and family pet.

SIZE
The shoulder-height is 56 - 61cm (22 - 24in) for dogs and 51 - 56cm (20 - 22in) for bitches.

COAT
The hair is smooth and wavy with a weather-resistant undercoat. The coat may be golden or cream. A single small white marking on the chest is permissible.

CARE REQUIRED
Groom regularly with brush and comb, trim excess hair between the pads of the feet, and check that the ears are clean at fixed intervals. If necessary, they may be trimmed to create a well-groomed appearance.

CHARACTER
This is a lovable, intelligent, sociable, self-confident, sensitive dog with a good memory, that has great adaptability and is not given to barking very much.

TRAINING
The Golden Retriever learns quickly and remembers what it has learned for the rest of its life. Never treat them harshly because they are very sensitive and you will harm their accommodating nature.
It is sensible to vary the training as much as possible and obedience classes are strongly recommended.

SOCIAL BEHAVIOUR
Dogs of this breed get on fine with other dogs, animals, and children, although the dog might need protection from the children. Most of these dogs become real friends with humans, although some can be very vigilant and cautious with unknown visitors.

EXERCISE
The Golden Retriever will adapt itself to your family but do not forget they need more exercise than the average dog. Once fully grown they can be exercised alongside a cycle. Most of them love to swim, retrieve things, and they draw highest levels of attention when they participate in obedience competitions, fly-ball, and agility skills trials which they also enjoy doing.

SPECIAL REMARKS
The Golden Retriever is a very popular dog. Purchase a puppy only from very reputable breeders.

Labrador Retriever

COUNTRY OF ORIGIN
England.

APTITUDE
Field sports dog, guide dog for the blind, drugs search dogs, and family pet among numerous roles.

SIZE
The shoulder-height is 56 - 57cm (22 - $22^1/_2$in) for dogs and 54 - 56cm ($21^1/_2$ - 22in) for bitches.

COAT
The coat is thick and dense with a weather-resistant undercoat. The Labrador's colours are plain black, yellow, or chocolate brown (liver). A small white marking on the chest is permissible.

CARE REQUIRED
The coat is not difficult to care for. Brush it once a week and give it more attention during moulting.

CHARACTER
This is a friendly, good-natured, intelligent dog that is keen to work, is obedient, sociable, affectionate, pliable, sensible, thoughtful, loyal, with an outstanding good scenting nose. Labradors mature quite late bodily and mentally.

Labrador Retriever

TRAINING
The Labrador Retriever is an intelligent dog that is not difficult to train because it learns quickly and likes to work for its handler. It is a great pity if such a dog can do nothing more than be a pet.

They are excellent field sports and search dogs, but they also excel in obedience competitions. If you partake in any of these activities, you will see how much pleasure it gives this dog.

SOCIAL BEHAVIOUR
This breed usually gets on fine with other dogs and animals. With children they are both patient and good-natured but that is not strange because they are true friends to humans, which does not make them particularly vigilant.

EXERCISE
They will adapt themselves completely to your family but do not forget they need quite a lot of exercise.

Take them for fairly long walks and give them the chance to run and play off the lead. They are crazy about water and retrieving.

Head of a Nova Scotia Duck Tolling Retriever

Nova Scotia Duck Tolling Retriever

COUNTRY OF ORIGIN
Canada.

APTITUDE
Field sports dog and family pet.

SIZE
The shoulder-height is 48 - 51cm (18$^1/_2$ - 20in) for dogs and 45 - 48cm (17$^1/_2$ - 18$^1/_2$in) for bitches.

COAT
The Nova Scotia Duck Tolling Retriever has a double, water-resistant coat of medium-length hair with a softer undercoat.
The colour is between red and orange, usually with a blaze and a white marking on the tip of the tail, the feet, and the chest.

CARE REQUIRED
The coat does not call for much attention. A brushing once a week is sufficient.
During moulting more attention will be required.

CHARACTER
The Toller is a high-spirited, friendly, attentive, and intelligent dog that is obedient, lively, and sociable.

TRAINING
Training does not present much in the way of a problem because these dogs are fast learners which quickly remember new instructions. They also like to work for their handlers.

SOCIAL BEHAVIOUR
These are excellent family pets which get on well with other dogs, and animals, and which are very patient with children.
They bark when they sense danger but that is likely to be all.

EXERCISE
This breed needs quite a lot of exercise and like to swim and retrieve, which are ideal activities for them.

With the right training they can do well in sports like fly-ball, agility skills trials, and obedience competitions.

Springers

American Cocker Spaniel

COUNTRY OF ORIGIN
United States.

APTITUDE
Field sports dog by origin, mainly a family pet today.

SIZE
The shoulder-height is about 38cm (15in) for dogs and 35.5cm (14in) for bitches.

COAT
The hair on the head is short and fine while the body hair is medium length. There should be feathering of silken hair on the ears, chest, belly, and legs.
merican Cocker Spaniels are recognized by this long hair. Almost any colour is accepted, including black, deer red, light beige, black and tan, and multi-coloured.

CARE REQUIRED
The grooming of the coat is very important. With this Spaniel it is necessary to brush and comb the hair every day. Additionally, if you want to keep the dog's appearance according to the breed standard, you will need to take it about every four weeks to a dog-trimming parlour. Of course, the ears should be examined regularly and excess hair between the pads of

the feet, under and inside the ear, should be trimmed.

If you do not have the time for the grooming required or cannot afford the cost of regular visits to a trimming salon, then it is best to avoid this breed.

CHARACTER
These are lovable, gentle, and playful dogs that are intelligent and obedient.

TRAINING
Training the American Cocker Spaniel rarely leads to any problems. Train them with a gentle hand and bear in mind that they are sensitive to the tone of your voice and any upsets within the home.

SOCIAL BEHAVIOUR
Dogs of this breed are very sociable and consequently they get along fine with their own kind and with other household pets.

Because they will meekly accept virtually anything, it is sensible to protect them from children's play which can become too rough.

EXERCISE
This Cocker Spaniel loves to play and frolic. Provided you bear this in mind, there is no reason why they cannot be kept in a flat. A few of the breed are still used to spring birds for the shoot. Most of them are mad keen on swimming and retrieving.

SPECIAL REMARKS
In view of the popularity of this breed, it is advisable to purchase a puppy only from a recognized and reliable breeder.

Clumber Spaniel

COUNTRY OF ORIGIN
England.

APTITUDE
Field sports dog and family pet.

WEIGHT
The weight is about 36kg (79lb) for dogs and 30kg (66lb) for bitches.

Clumber Spaniel

COAT

The Clumber Spaniel has a dense coat of medium-length silken hair. The colour is usually white with lemon markings, although orange markings are also permissible.

CARE REQUIRED

The coat must be groomed regularly with brush and comb and the ear passages should be kept clean. Some of them have trouble with irritation of the ear but there are special lotions which provide relief. Occasionally it will become necessary to trim them back to breed standard, removing the unruly hairs which stick out, leaving the dog looking first class once more. If too much hair grows under the ears, it is best not to wait until the next overall trim to clip this.

CHARACTER

This is a gentle-natured, equable, cheerful, yet noble dog which has a good memory, a considerable stamina, and is calm indoors.

TRAINING

The good memory combined with the fact that it likes to do things for its handler make this a fairly easily taught pupil.

SOCIAL BEHAVIOUR

Clumber Spaniels get on well with other dogs and that is true also for cats and other household animals. They are usually very trustworthy with children but they will avoid strangers - these are not dogs that are friends with everybody.

EXERCISE

The Clumber Spaniel is primarily a field sports dog but it has no difficulty in adapting its exercise needs to the family. Watch the diet carefully if they do not get much exercise.

Clumber Spaniel

English Cocker Spaniel

English Cocker Spaniel

COUNTRY OF ORIGIN

England.

APTITUDE

Field sports dog and family pet.

SIZE

The shoulder-height is about 39 - 41cm (15^1/$_2$ - 16^1/$_2$in) for dogs and 38 - 39cm (15- 15^1/$_2$in) for bitches.
The weight is about 13kg (28^1/$_2$lb).

COAT

The hair is smooth, silken, and medium length. It should never be curly.
The most usual colours are russet brown, liver, black, black and tan, white with black, red, or liver patches (with or without tan markings), blue roan, orange roan, and liver roan (with or without tan markings).

CARE REQUIRED

The coat of Cocker Spaniels tangles easily, so it is necessary to brush and comb them thoroughly regularly. Do not overlook the hair between the front and back legs and the hair on the ears. These should be cleaned regularly and excess hair removed.

The Cocker Spaniel should have excessive hair on the top of the head, beneath the ears, and on the neck plucked out regularly by hand. Depending upon the condition of the coat this should be done - by a dog parlour if necessary - twice to four times each year.

CHARACTER

These are cheerful, lively, gentle and affectionate dogs that are intelligent and pliable.

English Cocker Spaniel

TRAINING

The Cocker Spaniel is a naturally pliable dog which grasps what you want it to do.
Train them with understanding and consistency. Given half a chance by you, the English Cocker Spaniel will lead you a merry dance.

SOCIAL BEHAVIOUR

Dogs of this breed can usually get on well with pets, other dogs, and children.
Make sure the children are not too rough with the dog because they allow themselves to be used as toys.

EXERCISE

This dog is reasonably content with three quick turns around the neighbourhood but do not overlook its need for regular opportunities to run freely in the countryside. Most of them love to swim.

English Springer Spaniel

COUNTRY OF ORIGIN

England.

APTITUDE

Field sports dog and family pet.

SIZE

The shoulder-height is about 51cm (20in).

COAT

The coat is dense, smooth, and water- and dirt-resistant.
The permitted colour combinations are liver with white, and black with white, which can include tan markings.

CARE REQUIRED

The coat of the English Springer Spaniel must be brushed regularly. Remove excess hair from the ear passages and also from beneath the ears so that they are adequately ventilated. Do not forget to trim excess hair between the pads of the feet.
An English Springer Spaniel needs to visit a dog-trimming parlour about twice to four times each year.

CHARACTER

These are gentle, friendly, and sociable dogs that are intelligent and cunning, pliable, obedient, equable, and very active.

TRAINING

The training of this breed is usually trouble-free. They are intelligent and pupils that like to please are eager to learn.

English Springer Spaniel

SOCIAL BEHAVIOUR

Dogs of this breed are renowned for their friendly nature. They live in harmony with other dogs, pets, and children.

EXERCISE

In general terms they adapt effortlessly to the family situation but it is not fair to limit them to three short outings a day. They love to retrieve and swim.

Take them for a long walk regularly and let them have a chance to run and play off the lead. They perform very well in both agility skills trials and obedience competitions.

Field Spaniel

Field Spaniel

COUNTRY OF ORIGIN
England.

APTITUDE
Field sports dog and family pet.

SIZE
The shoulder-height is about 46cm (18in).

COAT
The shiny and water-resistant coat is smooth with waves and has a silken texture. The most usual colours are liver, yellow-brown, mahogany, black, or a roan of one of these colours, sometimes including white or tan markings.

Field Spaniel

CARE REQUIRED
The Field Spaniel usually needs to visit a dog-trimming parlour about four times each year. Dead hairs are removed by hand-plucking and hair on the ears, legs, and neck is also thinned out. Keep the ears clean.

CHARACTER
This breed is gentle, affectionate, intelligent, and just a little bit stubborn, temperamental, and playful, but they are very calm indoors. It is said that they have a tendency to become one-person's-dogs.

TRAINING
These quick-learning pupils react very strongly to your voice. Train them with a kind but consistent manner.
Harsh words and a tough approach will disturb its sensitive nature. They need contact with people and become extremely neurotic if shut away in a kennel.

SOCIAL BEHAVIOUR
These dogs are friendly with everyone. In general they are very patient with children but if the play becomes too much for them, they become withdrawn. Make sure the dog is not pestered by children.
Prevent problems later in the dog's life with other animals by introducing it to them when it is young.

EXERCISE
The Field Spaniel adapts effortlessly to the family situation but they are primarily a working field dog.
This means that it needs lots of exercise and that a sportive family suits it best. Because they have deeply-rooted hunting instincts, it is essential to have a good fence surrounding the property or they are likely to take off after any interesting scent.

209

Kooikerhondje or Dutch duck hunter's dog

COUNTRY OF ORIGIN
The Netherlands.

APTITUDE
Duck hunter's dog, vermin destroyer, and companion.

SIZE
The shoulder-height is 35 - 40cm ($13^1/_2$ - $15^1/_2$in) and the weight is about 10kg (22lb).

COAT
The medium-length hair is lightly waved. The coat is predominantly white with orange patches and black ear tips - which are known as "earrings" within breed circles.

CARE REQUIRED
This breed needs little attention to its coat. Brush the dogs regularly and keep the ears clean.
If necessary, trim excess hair between the pads of the feet.

CHARACTER
This is a cheerful, friendly, and brave dog that is attentive and intelligent, self-confident, and not a friend to all-comers. They seldom bark. They bond closely with their own people and can be a good watchdog if called upon. The Kooikerhondje is so sensitive that it can be rather touchy and it is therefore not a suitable playmate for children.

TRAINING
In common with all breeds, the training of a Kooikerhondje has to be carried out consistently.
They are intelligent and eager to learn - properties which make them an easy dog to train, and they are also sensitive to the intonation of the voice so that a tough approach is absolutely unnecessary. The handler must be firm though because over-leniency will bring out the breed's dominant trait.

SOCIAL BEHAVIOUR
They get on well with dogs and cats provided they meet them when they are young. This breed is not a friend-to-all and they are reserved towards strangers. In contrast, familiar family friends will get an enthusiastic welcome.

EXERCISE
They like to run about and to frolic. Do not sentence them to three short outings a day.

Most of them like to swim and to retrieve. They perform well at obedience and agility skills trials and also shine at fly-ball.

Kooikerhondje

Rhodesian Ridgeback

COUNTRY OF ORIGIN
Zimbabwe.

APTITUDE
Hunting dog (principally for lions), and also watchdog, and family pet.

SIZE
The shoulder-height is 64-69cm (25$^1/_2$ - 27$^1/_2$in) for dogs and 61 - 62cm (24 - 24$^1/_2$in) for bitches.

COAT
The short-haired coat has its characteristic ridge along the back, which is a strip of hair in which the pile is opposite to the rest of the coat, making it appear darker.

The colour is light to reddish wheaten with a dark mask. A small amount of white on the chest is permissible.

CARE
There is little to the grooming of a Ridgeback. Brush them regularly and during the moult use a rubber brush to remove dead hairs.

CHARACTER
These are intelligent, cunning but straightforward dogs that are loyal to the family, have something of a mind of their own, are brave, vigilant, reserved towards strangers, and possess considerable stamina.

TRAINING
They react best to an extremely consistent and equable approach to training. Ridgebacks are intelligent and learn quickly but they are also strong and a bit stubborn.
The handler needs to be confident and to exude natural authority.

Rhodesian Ridgebacks

SOCIAL BEHAVIOUR

Provided this dog meets cats and other pets when it is young, any potential problems will be prevented.

hey are usually kind with children but only so long as they are not pestered by them. They mix satisfactorily with other dogs under most circumstances.

They tend to be rather reserved towards strangers.

EXERCISE

This dog is a hunting dog by origin and it has tremendous stamina - meaning its exercise needs are also substantial.

Let them run beside a cycle and take them for regular long walks.

Rhodesian Ridgeback

Sussex Spaniel

COUNTRY OF ORIGIN
England.

APTITUDE
Field sports dog and family pet.

SIZE
The shoulder-height is about 30cm (11$^1/_2$in) and the weight is 18 - 21kg (39$^1/_2$.- 46$^1/_2$lb). For its height, the Sussex Spaniel is a heavy dog.

COAT
The Sussex Spaniel has soft medium-length hair which forms a smooth coat without curls. The colour is only a golden-glistening shade of liver.

CARE REQUIRED
Groom them regularly with brush and comb

Head of a Sussex Spaniel

and keep the ears clean. Trim excessive hair between the pads on the bottom of the feet but leave the tufts growing between the toes on the upper part of the feet.

If necessary, have the older and lighter hairs removed by plucking. Too much hair under beneath the ears should be trimmed at fixed intervals.

Check when new teeth emerge that they do not push existing teeth aside, resulting in crooked teeth.

CHARACTER
This is a lovable, cunning, and affectionate dog that is cheerful, and likes to bark. They make pleasant household companions. Some of them can be rather jealous and want to keep their handler to themselves.

TRAINING
These quick-learning pupils can have minds of their own. It is therefore important to be consistent with them.

Because they like to bark, it is sensible to teach them when they are young that one bark, for instance when the doorbell rings, is sufficient.

SOCIAL BEHAVIOUR
These are very sociable dogs which usually get on with children, cats, and other dogs.

EXERCISE
The Sussex Spaniel will quickly put on weight if it gets too little exercise. It likes to be out of doors in fields and woods but bear in mind its tendency to follow its nose.

Swimming and retrieving are both activities which it enjoys.

This breed is fairly rare. If it interests you, visit one of the major international dog shows where you will usually find one or more examples.

It is difficult to find a first-class show dog because of the wide diversity within the breed.

Sussex Spaniel

Welsh Springer Spaniel

COUNTRY OF ORIGIN
Wales.

APTITUDE
Field sports dog and family pet.

SIZE
The maximum shoulder-height is 48cm (18^1/$_2$in) for dogs and 46cm (18in) for bitches.

COAT
The coat consists of medium length silken and lank hair.
Curls are not permitted and the colour is always red and white.

CARE REQUIRED
Regularly clip excess hair from the inner ear to prevent infections and also trim too much hair between the pads of the feet. Groom the coat at fixed intervals with brush and comb.

The Welsh Springer needs to visit a dog-trimming parlour about two to four times each year.

CHARACTER
These are gentle, intelligent, sociable, and equable dogs that are pliable and obedient but a little bit stubborn.
The breed is mad about water and has an outstanding sense of smell.

TRAINING
These dogs are not difficult to train although they can have minds of their own. They learn fairly quickly.

Use your voice and praise them a lot but be consistent to achieve the best results. The breed has a strong desire to hunt so that it is advisable to train them to come to your command.

SOCIAL BEHAVIOUR
This breed is generally trouble-free in the company of other dogs and children. That is also usually true of cats and other household animals, but the dog should be introduced to them in a positive way when it is young. They are always friendly with people.

EXERCISE
Provided they get the opportunity to enjoy themselves and run around, they will be perfectly behaved indoors.

Welsh Springer Spaniel

Water dogs

Barbet

COUNTRY OF ORIGIN
France.

APTITUDE
Hunting dog and family pet.

SIZE
The shoulder-height is a minimum of 54cm (21^1/$_2$in) for dogs and 50cm (19^1/$_2$in) for bitches.

COAT
The coat is water-resistant and long, soft, and wavy or curly. Permitted colours are black, white, grey, or chestnut.

CARE REQUIRED
The coat must be regularly and thoroughly groomed with brush and comb to prevent tangles forming which can be difficult to remove.

CHARACTER
These are equable, pliable, and very affectionate dogs, which are loyal, lively, friendly, intelligent, and eager to learn.
They are also tough on themselves and straightforward by nature.

TRAINING
The Barbet learns quickly, and is sensitive to the voice of its handler, whom the dog wants to please. It is also important to be consistent during training because the handler who accepts everything and exudes little authority will eventually not be taken seriously by them.

SOCIAL BEHAVIOUR
They get on well with other dogs and other pets

Head of a Barbet

and usually present no problems in the company of children.
They will certainly warn of danger but do not expect further action.

EXERCISE
These are working dogs by origin which love water and retrieving. They fit in perfectly as a family pet and like doing so.
They should not be shut away in a kennel where they will probably pine. Take them for regular long walks during which they get a chance to enjoy themselves off the lead.

Barbet

Irish Water Spaniel

COUNTRY OF ORIGIN
Ireland.

APTITUDE
Hunting dog and family pet.

SIZE
The shoulder-height is 53 - 59cm (20^1/$_2$ - 23^1/$_2$in) for dogs and 51 - 56cm (20 - 22in) for bitches.

COAT
The oily coat of the Irish Water Spaniel consists of dense, permanent curls which should never be fluffy. The only recognized colour is a dark shade of liver.

CARE REQUIRED
Do not groom them too much to prevent the coat becoming fluffy. After a thorough brushing, the dog should be washed or allowed to swim to put the curl back in the coat.
It is likely that the coat will require trimming from time to time to keep it in accordance with the breed standard.

A major advantage of this coat is that loose hairs are not shed, so that few will be found on the carpet. For showing they require more specialized grooming.

CHARACTER
This character of a dog is lively and cheerful, with considerable stamina and drive, a very good nose, and it is intelligent, cunning, equable, and tough on itself. It can have something of a mind of its own.

TRAINING
Training needs to begin early with these dogs. They learn quickly but require a handler that is consistent. If you let them have their own way too much and are too forgiving in the dog's eyes, then the struggle will eventually be lost and the dog will do as it pleases.

Bring as much variety as possible into training and make sure the dog enjoys it. They can be very bad tempered and cannot be expected to perform consistently.

SOCIAL BEHAVIOUR
This breed usually gets on well with children. There is no problem with the company of cats and other pets provided the dog has been socially trained when young. They will bark to warn of danger but that is all. With strangers, they are rather cautious.

Irish Water Spaniel

EXERCISE
These are hunting dogs with tremendous stamina. They are mad keen on retrieving and water, so let them swim regularly - when the climate permits. They will gladly leave their basket for a good long walk.

Head of an Irish Water Spaniel

Perro de Agua Español

COUNTRY OF ORIGIN
Spain.

APTITUDE
Water dog, herding dog, and family pet.

SIZE
The shoulder-height is 40 - 50cm (15$\frac{1}{2}$ - 19$\frac{1}{2}$in) for dogs and 38 - 45cm (15 - 17$\frac{1}{2}$in) for bitches.

COAT
The curly, woolly, and weather-protective coat should form cords when it becomes longer. The most usual colours are brown, black, white, black and white, or brown and white.

Head of a Perro de Agua Español

CARE REQUIRED
This dog needs little grooming. Unlike the Puli or Komondor which have similar coats, the cords form themselves. It is permissible to cut the cords short.

CHARACTER
This is an active, friendly, and intelligent dog that is eager to learn, playful, sociable, vigilant, and enterprising.

TRAINING
This breed learns new instructions quickly so that training should present no major problems.

SOCIAL BEHAVIOUR
These dogs usually get along with other dogs and with children and other animals without problems.

They need to get to know cats so that the company of them will also cause no difficulties. They will warn of danger but little more.

EXERCISE
This breed has fairly substantial exercise demands. They like to swim, enjoy retrieving, and usually perform well in both obedience competitions and at fly-ball.

Perro de Agua Español

Portuguese Water Dog

COUNTRY OF ORIGIN
Portugal.

APTITUDE
Fisherman's working dog and family pet.

SIZE
The shoulder-height is 50 - 57cm (19$^1/_2$ - 22$^1/_2$in) for dogs, but a height of 54cm (21$^1/_2$in)

is preferred, and 43 - 52cm (17 - 20$^1/_2$in) for bitches, with a preferred height for them of 46cm (18in).

COAT
The coat is dense and wavy, or curly. The most usual colours and combinations are black, brown, white, black and white, and brown and white.

Portuguese Water Dog with wavy coat

CARE REQUIRED
The wavy-coated variety is usually closely clipped at the hindquarters and on the nose but the curly-coated dogs mostly have a working retriever clip (especially in the United States), with which only the tail is close-clipped. Groom them regularly with brush and comb.

CHARACTER
These are high-spirited, friendly, obedient, and sociable dogs, which are keen to work, intelligent, and quick to grasp things. They also have a good nose for scents.

TRAINING
Provided you understand the dog's character, training is not difficult. They like to work hard, are intelligent, and understand quickly. These dogs are sensitive to the intonations in your voice.
Alternate training and play and bear in mind that this extremely intelligent dog will take liberties if you think you can just fit a bit of training in when it suits you. Make sure you are consistent.

SOCIAL BEHAVIOUR
The companionship of dogs and other animals will be accepted without difficulty and with children these dogs are friendship personified.

The Portuguese Water Dog, as its name suggests, loves to swim.

There is no greater pleasure you can give it than to throw sticks or a ball for it to retrieve from water.

They are suitable for agility skills trials and numerous other dog sports.

Wetterhoun

COUNTRY OF ORIGIN
The Netherlands.

APTITUDE
Hunting dog, watchdog, farm dog, and family pet.

SIZE
The Wetterhoun's coat is curly and oily. It must not be woolly. Accepted colours are plain black, or brown, black and white, brown and white, or brown roan.

CARE REQUIRED
Little grooming is required for the Wetterhoun. Comb the coat occasionally and check that the ears are clean.

They can happily live in an outdoor kennel provided they have sufficient contact with you and get their daily exercise.

CHARACTER
This dog is physically very demanding of itself and can be sensitive. It is an intelligent, somewhat independent dog, often with a mind of its own, that is brave, reliable, and very vigilant. The Wetterhoun likes swimming.

TRAINING
This is not a suitable dog for the beginner. They are intelligent and learn quickly but they are independent-minded enough to refuse your commands.
A consistent but kind approach is absolutely essential. Depending upon the individual dog, corrective action may be appropriate.

SOCIAL BEHAVIOUR
For its own people the Wetterhoun is a good-natured and friendly dog - and this includes the children, provided they treat him properly.

For unknown visitors the story is entirely different. In this case it will take up a cautious watch and will protect the home from intruders. Family friends on the other hand will get a hearty welcome. Other dogs and pets will be accepted without a murmur.

EXERCISE
The Wetterhoun needs lots of exercise. The ideal situation for this dog is to have a large piece of land that it can run around on freely and which it will protect vigorously and rid of vermin.

They do not tend to run off because there is no roaming instinct in the breed.

SPECIAL REMARKS
A Wetterhoun will pine away in a flat or living in busy urban areas because they are not suited to such a life.

They are rarely seen outside their country of origin.

Wetterhoun

Head of a brown Wetterhoun

9. Toy and other miniature dogs

Bichons

Bichon Frisé

COUNTRY OF ORIGIN
Belgium/France.

APTITUDE
Family pet.

SIZE
The shoulder-height may not exceed 30cm ($11^1/_2$in) and the weight should be about 4kg ($8^1/_2$lb).

COAT
The silken coat consists of locks spirally formed hairs. There is no undercoat and the colour is always pure white.

CARE REQUIRED
The coat should be combed thoroughly every day and occasionally it will need clipping to prevent it becoming too long. In common with other dogs with such coats, the Bichon Frisé is clipped out to a specific style which can vary from country to country.
To keep the coat white, it will be necessary to wash the dog regularly with a recognized dog shampoo. Check at set intervals that the hairs around the eyes are not causing irritation and use the special lotion for this purpose to remove any "tear" stains.
Clip excess hair between the pads of the feet and remove loose hairs and any dirt from the ear passages.
This breed does not shed hair; dead hairs need to be removed with a brush.

CHARACTER
These dogs bond very closely with their handler, though they can be left alone occasionally, they are also pliable, cheerful, active, playful, intelligent, sociable, and sensitive.

TRAINING
Since these are bright dogs which quickly catch

Maltese

on to what you want them to do, there is no real problem in training them.

SOCIAL BEHAVIOUR
Bichons are naturally sociable dogs which are happiest as the member of a family which takes them everywhere. This sociable trait also means that they are fine in the company of other dogs, pets, and children.

EXERCISE
This breed adapts itself entirely to the family circumstances.

SPECIAL REMARKS
People for whom an unkempt appearance will be difficult to bear, yet who have no time for the intensive grooming required for this breed, are advised to look elsewhere.

Bichon Frisé

Bolognese

COUNTRY OF ORIGIN
Italy.

APTITUDE
Family pet.

SIZE
The shoulder-height is 25 - 30cm ($9^1/_2$ - $11^1/_2$in) and the weight is 2.5 - 4kg ($5^1/_2$ - $8^1/_2$lb).

Bolognese

SOCIAL BEHAVIOUR
The Bolognese gets on well with other dogs, pets, and children. They prize your company highly and it can therefore be very difficult to leave them on their own. They are cautious towards strangers.

EXERCISE
This breed is satisfied with an average level of exercise but that does not mean it will refuse a long walk.

SPECIAL REMARKS
If the intensive grooming required for this breed is beyond your capabilities, it is better to choose another breed with a coat that requires less attention.

Coton de Tuléar

Coton de Tuléar

COUNTRY OF ORIGIN
Madagascar.

APTITUDE
Family pet.

SIZE
The shoulder-height is 25 - 32cm ($9^1/_2$ - $12^1/_2$in) for dogs and 22 - 28cm ($8^1/_2$ - 11in) for bitches.

COAT
The fine, long hairs create a curly coat with a cotton-like texture. There is no undercoat. The colour is always white with a few yellow to dark grey patches (especially by the ears).

CARE REQUIRED
The coat needs grooming with brush and comb several times each week. They do not shed hair but the dead hairs can be brushed out and then removed from the brush.
Remove excess hair between the pads of the feet and in the inner ear. The Coton de Tuléar does not need a bath more than once or twice

COAT
The coat, which is always white, consists of a mass of long, erect locks. There is no undercoat.

CARE REQUIRED
Because the hair tangles easily, the coat should be combed out every day, especially on the belly, behind the ears, and between the legs. They need to be bathed regularly to keep the coat white. One advantage of the coat is that it does not shed its hair - dead hairs should be removed by brushing.

Check the ears to ensure they are clean and free of any loose hairs.
When necessary, clip excess hair between the pads of the feet.

CHARACTER
This is a cheerful, intelligent, and obedient dog that is very affectionate, calm, yet vigilant.

TRAINING
Training this breed usually passes off without any difficulty.
These dogs like to do things for their handler and they find it easy to learn.

a year - which is adequate to keep the coat clean.

CHARACTER
These dogs are friendly, intelligent, vigilant, playful, and sometimes they can be a little bit obstinate.

TRAINING
The Coton de Tuléar learns quite quickly but do not forget that, although they are intelligent and eager to work, they can have minds of their own. They do well in various areas of dog sports such as agility skills trials and fly-ball.

SOCIAL BEHAVIOUR
These are very sociable dogs that are happy to live in friendship with other dogs and animals. They are usually first-class playmates for children.

EXERCISE
The dogs of this breed adapt seamlessly to the family requirements. They like to swim and play ball games.

Coton de Tuléar

Havanese

COUNTRY OF ORIGIN
Cuba.

APTITUDE
Family pet.

Havanese with puppies

Havanese

WEIGHT
The Havanese should not weight more than 6kg
(13$^1/_2$lb).

COAT
The long-haired coat has no undercoat. Any
colour is accepted, with the exception of black
which is not recognized by some countries.

CARE REQUIRED
The coat needs considerable grooming. These
dogs need to be thoroughly brushed and be
combed at least twice per week.
This is best done with a coarse comb. There is
a lotion available to prevent the hair from splitting. Clip excess hair between the pads of the
feet.
The feet themselves may be clipped to a round
form so that they do not walk around with
"floss" on their feet. This breed does not shed
hair; dead hairs are best removed with a brush.
Check the eyes regularly.

CHARACTER
These are cheerful, very affectionate, playful,
gentle-natured dogs which are highly intelligent, sociable, and sensitive.

TRAINING
The Havanese learns quickly and enjoys doing
things for you - this is why the breed used to be
so widely found as circus dogs. It is very sensitive to the intonation of your voice and harsh
words will achieve very little except to upset the
dog unnecessarily.
Some of them tend to bark more than necessary, so teach them early not to do so before it
becomes a habit.

SOCIAL BEHAVIOUR
The Havanese gets along well with all-comers -
dogs, cats or other pets, and they can be fine too

with children but they do not like to be pestered
by them. If this does happen, the dog will tend
to become withdrawn for quite some time.

EXERCISE
They have an average need for exercise - so that
three short outings a day will keep them happy.

Löwchen (Little Lion Dog)

COUNTRY OF ORIGIN
France.

APTITUDE
Family pet.

SIZE
The shoulder-height is 20 - 35cm
(7$^1/_2$ - 13$^1/_2$in).

Löwchen or Little Lion Dog

Löwchen or Little Lion Dog

COAT
The coat is long and wavy but should not curl. Löwchen do not have undercoats. Any colour is acceptable.

CARE REQUIRED
Brush and comb the coat regularly to prevent tangles forming. This dog is usually clipped out in the breed-style regardless of whether they are to be shown. The hindquarters, the section of the tail closest to the body, and part of the front legs are close-clipped. The coat does not shed hairs so any dead hairs are removed by brushing.

CHARACTER
This is a cheerful, playful, and companionable dog that is intelligent, eager to learn, gentle-natured, and sensitive.

TRAINING
These dogs usually learn quickly and present little difficulty in their training.

SOCIAL BEHAVIOUR
The company of children and other household animals causes no problems of any kind.

EXERCISE
They have average needs in terms of exercise and normally adapt to your circumstances. When you want to go for a longer walk, this dog will happily accompany you.

Maltezer

COUNTRY OF ORIGIN
Italy/Malta.

APTITUDE
Family pet.

SIZE
The shoulder-height is 21 - 25cm ($8^1/_2$ - $9^1/_2$in) for dogs and 20 - 23cm ($7^1/_2$ - 9in) for bitches.

COAT
The Maltese has a white coat of long silken hair without an undercoat, which is worn with a parting down the centre of the back.

CARE REQUIRED
Grooming requirements for this breed are substantial, including daily brushing and combing and regular washing. There is a special lotion to remove the ugly "tear" stains.
Hairs can grow in the corner of the eyes which cause irritation. Prevent this by removing them. These dogs do not shed hair, the dead hairs can

Maltese

Maltese puppy

be removed from the brush after grooming. The coat is supposed to be long, reaching the ground.
The hair in front of the eyes is usually held together with a hair band. Keeping the coat in show condition requires considerable effort.

Owners of show dogs oil the hair and wind the hair in curling papers to prevent it from splitting.

CHARACTER
These are friendly, lovable, and playful dogs which besides being sociable, are eager to learn, but sensitive.

They can get along really well with children and bond very closely with their handler.

TRAINING
Training these dogs is relatively easy because they like to be with their family and will adapt to almost any circumstance.

They are very sensitive for harsh words and should never be trained with a hard approach.

SOCIAL BEHAVIOUR
The Maltese likes to avoid causing any problems and therefore usually gets on well with other dogs, household animals, and children. The breed causes no difficulties with visitors.

EXERCISE
It is not necessary to take this dog for lots of long walks but if you like doing so, it will happily accompany you.

Poodles

Poodles

Toy and Miniature Poodles

COUNTRY OF ORIGIN
France.

APTITUDE
Family pet.

SIZE
The minimum shoulder height for the Toy Poodle is 25cm ($9^1/_2$in) and should not be more than 28cm (11in).
The shoulder-height for the Miniature Poodle is 28 - 35cm (11 - $13^1/_2$in).

COAT
The coat consists of fine, woolly but frizzy hair. Acceptable colours are monotone white, black, apricot, brown, and grey.
Poodles that form corded coats after a time are very exceptional.

CARE REQUIRED
Show dogs have to be clipped out according to the breed-style. This requires considerable skill and knowledge and is best left to a professional specialist salon.
Keeping a dog in this condition requires not only considerable time but also costs a great deal of money.

The Poodle is regarded as one of the most difficult breed-standard patterns to achieve - if not the most difficult. The competition is usually considerable in the show-ring. Poodles that are kept as pets are usually closely trimmed, leaving longer hair on the head, the ears, and the legs.

The grooming requirements for these household pets is considerably easier than with show dogs. They do not shed hair. Check the teeth for tartar and clean the ears regularly. Poodles can be washed quite often.

CHARACTER
These are lively, playful dogs that are intelligent, keen to learn, but sensitive, and they bond closely with their owner and family.

TRAINING
Miniature and Toy Poodles are very intelligent dogs, which if handled properly, quickly learn what is required of them.

The best results are achieved with a gentle but consistent approach.

SOCIAL BEHAVIOUR
These are generally trouble-free dogs in terms of getting along with other dogs, and pets. They announce visitors but that is all.

EXERCISE
Although these Poodles can happily live in a flat, they do need to get sufficient exercise.

Brown Toy Poodle

Black Large Poodle clipped out in the style of a lion

Grey Miniature Poodle

Giant Poodle

COUNTRY OF ORIGIN
France.

APTITUDE
Hunting dog by origin, now a family pet.

SIZE
The shoulder-height is 45 - 58cm ($17^1/_2$ - $22^1/_2$in).

COAT
The coat consists of fine, woolly but frizzy hair. Acceptable colours are monotone white, black, apricot, brown, and grey.
Poodles that form corded coats after a time are very exceptional.

Black Giant Poodle with corded coat

CARE REQUIRED
See Miniature and Toy Poodles.

CHARACTER
These are high-spirited and highly intelligent dogs that are sportive, companionable, loyal, pliable, active, careful, curious, and vigilant, and they are also eager to learn.

TRAINING
The Giant Poodle learns quite quickly and training should present few if any difficulties. Be clear with them and ensure that you are consistent.
Poodles are very sensitive to the intonation of your voice.

SOCIAL BEHAVIOUR
These are sociable animals by nature and they get on well with dogs and other pets. The company of children will be equally trouble-free. They are usually vigilant but not unfriendly towards strangers.

EXERCISE
These dogs need fairly substantial levels of exercise. Play ball with them in the garden or take them for a long walk to keep them fit. They usually do well at activities such as fly-ball, activity skills trials, and obedience competitions. The Giant Poodle is one of the most intelligent breeds in the world.

Grey Standard Poodle

Standard Poodle

COUNTRY OF ORIGIN
France.

APTITUDE
Hunting dog by origin but now a family pet.

SIZE
The shoulder-height is 35 - 45cm (13$^{1}/_{2}$ - 17$^{1}/_{2}$in).

COAT
The coat consists of fine, woolly but frizzy hair. Acceptable colours are monotone white, black, apricot, brown, and grey. Poodles that form corded coats after a time are very exceptional.

CARE REQUIRED
See Miniature and Toy Poodles.

CHARACTER
These are extremely intelligent, high-spirited dogs which are lively, affectionate, sociable with other dogs, that are loyal to their handler. Most of them love to swim.

TRAINING
This breed is fairly easy to train because they learn so quickly.
They can win the attention of the top people in various dog sports such as fly-ball and agility skills trials.

SOCIAL BEHAVIOUR
These dogs get on well with their own kind and with other household pets; there is also unlikely to be any problem with children. You will always be warned of visitors.

EXERCISE
This Poodle needs fairly substantial exercise. Most of them like to swim and to retrieve.

Belgian Griffons

Griffon Bruxellois, Belgian Griffon and Petit Brabançon

COUNTRY OF ORIGIN
Belgium.

APTITUDE
Family pets.

WEIGHT
These dogs weigh about 5kg (11lb).

COAT
The Griffon Bruxellois and the Belgian Griffon are rough-haired The Griffon Bruxellois is reddish pink, perhaps with black on its nose and chin.

Griffons and Petit Brabançons

Belgian Griffon (Griffon Belge)

The Belgian Griffon is completely black, black and tan, or red. The Petit Brabançon is short-haired and is accepted in the same colours as the other Griffons.

CARE REQUIRED
The rough-haired Griffons are usually plucked by hand at regular intervals, leaving the moustache, beard and other facial hair features alone. Comb the beard frequently to remove food remnants and such like and to prevent tangles. The hairs in the corners of the eye must be removed if necessary to prevent them pricking the eyeball and causing irritation.

CHARACTER
These are curious, mischievous dogs that are playful, straightforward, calm, eager to learn, that are also good with children.
They keep a good vigil and like to be close to their handler.

TRAINING
Training should run smoothly because these are very intelligent dogs that are keen to learn. They do well in various areas of dog sports.

Griffon Bruxellois (Brussels Griffon)

Petit Brabançon

SOCIAL BEHAVIOUR
The dogs of these breeds get on well with children, dogs, and cats because they are naturally sociable and enjoy company.

EXERCISE
Although Griffons can be perfectly happily kept in a flat, they do like to be taken to woods and other country places.

Do this regularly even though they adapt so well to town life.

Hairless dogs

Chinese Crested

COUNTRY OF ORIGIN
China.

APTITUDE
Companionship dog.

SIZE
The shoulder-height is 28 - 33cm (11 - 13in) for dogs and 23 - 30cm (9 - 11$^1/_2$in) for bitches.

COAT
There are two sorts of Chinese Crested. One only has hair on its head, ears, the tip of the tail, and a little on the feet. The hairless body feels soft to the touch.
The other type, is known as the 'Powder Puff.' This type has an undercoat and a veil-like top-coat of silken hair. Any colour is acceptable. These two varieties are interbred with each other.

CARE REQUIRED
The skin of the Chinese Crested requires careful attention. Those with show dogs wash the skin regularly with skin exfoliating creams made for humans, to remove the dead cells and to soften the skin. The important point is for the skin to be supple and smooth and protected against becoming dry.
There are excellent lotions and creams for this purpose. The unpigmented areas of skin are especially sensitive to the sun and it is advisable not to expose the dog for long to the sun, or to use a quality suntan lotion.
The 'Powder Puff' should be brushed now and then and washed more frequently. Usually these dogs have the hair on the face clipped to form

Chinese Crested 'Powder Puff'

downward-facing points to achieve the typical style of this type of dog.

CHARACTER
These are high-spirited, cunning, and playful dogs that are sensitive, vigilant, very lively, and active.
They are somewhat cautious with people they do not know.

TRAINING
The Chinese Crested is not difficult to train because they are intelligent and quickly grasp what is required of them.

SOCIAL BEHAVIOUR
Provided children do not disturb the dog in its own territory, they will have no problems with this dog.
They also rarely cause problems in the company of other dogs and pets.

EXERCISE
They adapt to the family circumstances in terms of their exercise needs.

SPECIAL REMARKS
Skin wounds hardly show up on dogs with hair but the opposite is the case with the Chinese Crested.

An advantage of them is that they are very clean and there are no loose hairs to litter the carpet.

Chinese Crested

Head of a Chinese Crested

Mexican Hairless or Xoloitzcuintli

Mexican Hairless or Xoloitzcuintli

Mexican Hairless or Xoloitzcuintli

COUNTRY OF ORIGIN
Mexico.

APTITUDE
Watchdog and family pet.

SIZE
The Mexican Hairless is bred in two sizes: one
has a shoulder-height of 25 - 33cm ($9^1/_2$ - 13in),
the other is 33 - 56cm (13 - 22in).

COAT
This breed has no hair except for a tuft of short
straight hairs on the forehead and longer hair
on the tip of the tail.

The skin is a variety of colours including black,
elephant grey, dark bronze, and grey-black.

CARE REQUIRED
The fact that this breed has no hair does not
mean that its skin requires no care!
The skin must be protected as much as possible
from the sun to prevent sunburn.

People who show these dogs scrub them regularly to remove dead skin and to keep the skin
soft, with special exfoliating creams intended
for use by humans.

It is most important to keep the skin supple
and smooth and to prevent it becoming dry.
This is usually done with a lotion or cream.
Sometimes the skin is rubbed with oil.

CHARACTER
They are affectionate towards their own people
and get on well with children.

These dogs are also intelligent, peaceful, and
noble, and are extremely adaptable. They cannot bark but let out a howl of sorts.

TRAINING
The Mexican Hairless is not difficult to train.

SOCIAL BEHAVIOUR
These highly noticeable dogs generally get on
with other dogs, all household animals, and
with children.

EXERCISE
This breed does not require much exercise. If
you let them romp and play regularly, they will
be quite contented.

They are happy to walk on the lead every-where their handler goes.

SPECIAL REMARKS
The Mexican Hairless or Xoloitzcuintli is an extremely rare and special dog which could do with being better known and with more enthusiasts to prevent the breed from dying out.

Tibetan breeds

Lhasa Apso

COUNTRY OF ORIGIN
Tibet.

APTITUDE
Family pet.

SIZE
The shoulder-height is about 25cm (9$^1/_2$in).

COAT
The very long topcoat has no curls and is quite hard. The undercoat is medium-length and somewhat softer.

Almost any colour is acceptable, including blue, black, all manner of shades of beige, red, grey, white, brown, and multi-coloured.

CARE REQUIRED
It is necessary to groom this breed thoroughly with brush and comb every week, paying attention not only to the topcoat but especially removing and preventing tangles in the undercoat.
Do not pull too hard during combing to prevent breaking the hairs and, if required, use a special lotion to stop them becoming too brittle. Check the eyes regularly for dirt and for any irritant hair, clip excess hair between the pads of the feet, and keep the ear passages clean.

Getting the coat into show condition and then keeping it so requires much attention. Dogs kept as pets are often clipped short, and although breed enthusiasts will frown at this, it is preferable to a long-haired dog going through life with its coat full of tangles.

CHARACTER
These are calm, loyal, lovable dogs, which are equable, cheerful, and independent, and distrustful of strangers. The Lhasa Apso likes company but it will not cling to you.

In common with other Eastern breeds, the Lhasa Apso is somewhat obstinate. Do not expect any tricks from it and lead its character in the right direction by rewarding it when it does well.

Harsh words can touch them deep in the soul and cause them to feel insulted and be very disconcerted and withdrawn. They are intelligent enough to understand your rules.

SOCIAL BEHAVIOUR

The Lhaso Apso gets on well with dogs and other household pets, and children. They are rather cautious towards strangers.

EXERCISE

They have normal exercise needs. The dogs are quite happy by nature indoors and there is no need to go for long walks on their account.

SPECIAL REMARKS

Provided you do not regard grooming as a little job to be fitted in when you can, the Lhasa Apso is an excellent dog for a family.

Shih Tzu

Shih Tzu

Shih Tzus

Shih Tzu

COUNTRY OF ORIGIN
Tibet.

APTITUDE
Family pet.

SIZE
The shoulder-height is about 25cm ($9^1/_2$in) and the weight is 5 - 6kg (11 - $13^1/_2$lb).

COAT
The long-haired coat is accepted in any colour, including beige, black, and red, often with white.

CARE REQUIRED
A Shih Tzu requires a lot of grooming. Comb the coat thoroughly every day to prevent tangles. A hair band is essential to keep the hair out of the eyes. Because the eyes are a sensitive spot for these dogs, you need to make sure they are kept clean. Use the special eye drops prepared for this purpose. Clean the ear passages

regularly too. If you do not have the time to keep the coat in good condition, you will need to take the dog about every two months to be clipped, which will spare the dog a lot of misery.

CHARACTER
These are intelligent, lovable, affectionate, cheerful, and sociable dogs that are also independent and not friends to all. The Shih Tzu rarely barks.

TRAINING
If you approach this somewhat obstinate breed with plenty of patience and remain consistent at all times, it is possible to achieve a reasonable level of training.

SOCIAL BEHAVIOUR
Dogs of this breed usually get on well with other household animals and children. No matter what company they keep, they always behave with dignity.

EXERCISE
The Shih Tzu is content with short walks.

SPECIAL REMARKS
The true beauty of this breed is only fully appreciated when the coat is immaculately groomed. It is difficult to attain and maintain the level of condition required for showing.

Tibetan Spaniel

Tibetan Spaniel

COUNTRY OF ORIGIN
Tibet.

APTITUDE
Family pet.

SIZE
The shoulder-height is about 25cm (9$^1/_2$cm) and the weight is 4 - 6.5kg (8$^1/_2$ - 14$^1/_2$lb).

COAT
The Tibetan Spaniel has a double, long, silken-haired coat.
Any colour is acceptable but the most common colour is golden.

CARE REQUIRED
The coat is fairly easy to care for. Brush the dog regularly and keep the ear passages clean.

CHARACTER
These self-assured dogs are brave, vigilant, and cautious with strangers but they are not yappy. They are also blessed with a strong constitution and intelligence.

TRAINING
Tibetan Spaniels are quite easily to train because they quickly grasp what you intend.

Remain consistent with them because they can sometimes be obstinate.

SOCIAL BEHAVIOUR
These dogs are lovable with children and can also get on well with other dogs and cats provided they have met them when they were young. They always warn of danger.

EXERCISE
They do not need that much exercise to keep them in good condition.

It is sufficient to take them for three short walks each day and then to let them run and play off the lead in the garden.

Tibetan Terriers

Tibetan Terriers

COUNTRY OF ORIGIN
Tibet.

APTITUDE
Family pet.

SIZE
The shoulder-height is 35.5 - 43cm (14 - 17in) for dogs. The bitches are slightly smaller.

COAT
They have a double coat: the topcoat is long, luxuriant, fine, and either straight or wavy; the undercoat is dense and woolly.
The colours are black, white, various shades of beige or grey, and multi-coloured.

CARE REQUIRED
To prevent tangles and to remove loose hair, it is necessary to brush this dog every day. Do not overlook those places where tangles form most readily, such as beneath the leg joints, the beard, and the hindquarters.
Bath regularly and remove excess hair from the ear passages. Clip any build-up of hair between the pads of the feet.

CHARACTER
Beneath the cuddly appearance this is a tough, brave dog, that is lively, vigilant, equable, intelligent, noble, and cheerful.
They are dedicated to their handler and somewhat cautious with strangers, and can be dominant towards other dogs. They do not cope well with being left alone.

TRAINING
Train them in a calm, equable manner. They are sensitive by nature and react very well to the intonation of your voice.

SOCIAL BEHAVIOUR
In company with other dogs, this breed can be rather dominant.
They need to be socially trained when young with cats and other household animals if they are to live in harmony with them. Provided children do not pester them, it will in turn cause no problem for them.

EXERCISE
This breed has lots of energy and the dog must have regular opportunities to enjoy itself. Agility skills trials and fly-ball are suitable activities for them.

Tibetan Terrier

Chihuahua

Chihuahua

COUNTRY OF ORIGIN
Mexico.

APTITUDE
Family pet.

SIZE
The Chihuahua is the world's smallest dog, weighing between 500 - 2,500g (1 - 5$\frac{1}{2}$lb).

COAT
There are long-coat and short-coat Chihuahuas. Their colours include black, white, blue, red, or wheaten, with or without dark or white markings.

CARE REQUIRED
The long-haired type should be groomed normally with brush and comb while the short-haired ones should be groomed occasionally with a rubber brush. Administer eye-drops regularly to prevent "tear" stains, and check the teeth frequently for tartar, and to ensure with young dogs that new teeth are forming properly. Keep the claws trimmed.

CHARACTER
They are intelligent, brave little dogs but sometimes they are too brave for their own good. They can be stubborn, and can also be sensitive, and playful. Chihuahuas usually bond with one person.

Short-coat Chihuahua

Long-coat Chihuahua

Long-coat Chihuahua

TRAINING
Because these little dogs can do little damage, they are usually not trained. This is a shame because the Chihuahua is an eager pupil.

SOCIAL BEHAVIOUR
Chihuahuas are sociable animals so that living together with dogs and cats does not usually cause any difficulty.

Do not forget that they are so small that they can easily be trampled underfoot by larger dogs. They are not suitable for small children who will tend to regard the dog as a toy.

EXERCISE
Because these dogs are so small, they usually get sufficient exercise indoors.

If taught to do so, they can use a cat litter tray for their toilet. They feel the cold, damp and draughts, and a small coat is not an unnecessary luxury for them in wet weather.

The Chihuahua is a perfect choice for people who do not have much space in their home. You can easily take them with you everywhere and the cost of feeding will not break the budget. It is a shame that this little creature is regarded as a toy. Try not to forget that this animal is a real dog, in spite of its size, complete with the needs of all dogs.

Short-coat Chihuahua puppies

Dwarf English Spaniels

Cavalier King Charles Spaniel

COUNTRY OF ORIGIN
England.

APTITUDE
Family pet.

SIZE
The weight is 5.4 - 8.1kg ($11^1/_2$- $17^1/_2$lb).

COAT
The coat consists of light to firmly waved soft hair. The recognized colours are black and tan, ruby, and Blenheim (chestnut markings on a pearl white ground). There is a three-coloured coat too (black and white with russet brown markings).

CARE REQUIRED
Comb the coat regularly with particular care given to the chest, ears, and between the legs.

Cavalier King Charles Spaniels

Cavalier King Charles Spaniel

Check the ears frequently for dirt or loose hairs.

CHARACTER
These are lovable engaging dogs that are high-spirited and active, intelligent, obedient, gentle-natured, sociable, and very adaptable.

TRAINING
Since these dogs want to learn and are intelligent enough to understand what you want, there is little difficulty to be encountered in their training.

SOCIAL BEHAVIOUR
These are uncomplicated household companions that happily get along with children, other dogs, and any other animals you may have.

EXERCISE
The Cavalier King Charles Spaniel will adapt itself to your family circumstances.

Cavalier King Charles Spaniel

King Charles Spaniel

Head of a King Charles Spaniel

King Charles Spaniel

COUNTRY OF ORIGIN
England.

APTITUDE
Family pet.

SIZE
The shoulder-height is 25 - 30cm ($9^1/_2$ - $11^1/_2$cm) and the weight is about 5kg (11lb).

COAT
The coat consists of lightly waved, long, soft hair. The colours are black and tan, ruby, and Blenheim (chestnut markings on a pearl white ground).
There is also a three-coloured coat (black and white with reddish brown markings).

CARE REQUIRED
Take care of the folds of the face from time to time with a special lotion for this purpose and brush the coat well twice each week, with particular attention to the hair on the chest, behind the ears, and between the legs.
Remove any dirt or loose hairs from the ear passages.

CHARACTER
These dogs like to be with the family and to receive lots of attention. They are playful, intelligent, cheerful, and are also very adaptable. They rarely bark.

TRAINING
Training passes off virtually without difficulty because these dogs are intelligent enough to quickly grasp what is expected of them.

King Charles Spaniels

240

SOCIAL BEHAVIOUR

The dogs of this breed are almost exclusively sociable animals which usually get on with other dogs and household pets.
Children which approach calmly will not have any problems.

EXERCISE

They adapt themselves for their exercise needs to the family of which they form a part.

Japanese Chin and Pekingees

Japanese Chin (Japanese Spaniel)

COUNTRY OF ORIGIN
China.

APTITUDE
Family pet.

SIZE
The shoulder-height is 20 - 25cm ($7^1/_2$ - $9^1/_2$in), although the dogs may be slightly taller. The weight is 2.5 - 3kg ($5^1/_2$ - $6^1/_2$lb).

Japanese Chin or Japanese Spaniel

COAT

The silken coat consists of soft, long hair which should not be curly. The accepted colours are black with white or red with white. The red with white combination is permitted to vary from lemon to dark red.
The most usual colouring is black with white. There are also three-colour dogs and sable and white but these are not recognized in every country.

CARE REQUIRED

The beautiful coat fortunately does not easily tangle so that grooming twice per week with a brush and comb is sufficient. To keep the beautiful white of the coat, it will be necessary to wash them from time to time. Keep the ear passages clean and clean the facial creases with acid-free petroleum jelly to prevent dark staining.

CHARACTER

These engaging dogs are affectionate, playful, but also calm, straightforward and cheerful. They can have minds of their own and they like to be the centre of attention. They do not bark often. They like to be close to their handler.

TRAINING

Provided you make allowances for their obstinate streak, there should be few problems in their training. The breed is usually quickly house-trained.

SOCIAL BEHAVIOUR

These are not difficult dogs and they usually get on extremely well with children, cats, and other dogs. It is surely obvious that a dog of this size cannot cope with rough handling by larger dogs or children. They will not readily bite.

EXERCISE

Running, romping, and playing are the activities this breed enjoys. Some people insist they can also climb.

They will be perfectly happy in a flat and they can be taught to use a cat litter tray. In such cases make sure they do get sufficient exercise and fresh air.

Japanese Chin

Japanese Chins

Pekingees

Pekingees

COUNTRY OF ORIGIN
China.

APTITUDE
Companion dog.

SIZE
The shoulder-height is about 20cm ($7^1/_2$in) and these dogs weigh 4 - 5kg ($8^1/_2$ - 11lb).

COAT
The abundant long-haired coat has a copious undercoat.

A wide range of colours are known for the breed with the most usual being black and beige, sometimes combined with white. There are no albino or liver-coloured Pekingese.

CARE REQUIRED
This breed requires intensive grooming of its coat. Teach them when young to regard it as something enjoyable, to prevent wrestling matches every time you use a brush and comb when they grow up.

Pay special attention to the hair under the leg joints, on the belly, and the legs, where tangles form most readily. Before, during, and after grooming you can use talcum powder or dry shampoo. Give attention to the facial creases where infections are otherwise likely to occur. Clip the excess hair from between the pads of the feet.

CHARACTER
These are affectionate, noble dogs that possess a winning way. They can be both self-centred and stubborn, but they are intelligent, brave, and not particularly fond of strangers. They choose who will be their "boss."

TRAINING
Although a Pekingees will not let you lay down

the law to it, it is essential to teach it some basic principles if you do not want to be saddled with a bad-tempered dog that wants its own way. Praise it when it does something well but do not punish too harshly when it gets it wrong - this is the best way to achieve anything.
A Pekingees that has been punished will withdraw feeling very hard done by and affronted.

SOCIAL BEHAVIOUR
Pekingese do not generally have problems in mixing with other animals although this has a lot to do with the extent to which they have been socially trained. Since they do not like to be disturbed when they are resting, they are less suitable for a household with young children.

EXERCISE
Because of their physique, the majority of these dogs are not too fond of long walks.

Since they have relatively small demands for exercise, they make an ideal dog for those living in towns or for people who are themselves less active.

SPECIAL REMARKS
If you regard grooming as a necessary evil, a breed such as this is best avoided.

Continental dwarf Spaniels

Papillon and Epagneul Phalene

COUNTRY OF ORIGIN
Belgium/France.

APTITUDE
Family pet.

SIZE
The shoulder-height for both breeds is about 28cm (11in).

COAT
The long-haired coat is usually white with coloured patches. A white blaze on the head is desirable.

CARE REQUIRED
Brush regularly and thoroughly and remove loose hairs from the ear passages.

Papillon

CHARACTER
These are affectionate, lovable, lively little dogs that are playful, intelligent, and keen to learn. They can be jealous of and withdrawn with strangers.

TRAINING
Teach this breed, which is always eager to learn something new, with a gentle hand. Vary instruction by playing ball or with some such reward.
These are very intelligent and obedient dogs, that with the right training can perform outstandingly in obedience and agility skills trials, or at fly-ball.

SOCIAL BEHAVIOUR
Some of these dogs can be jealous if their owner's attention is directed elsewhere but this does not apply to every dog and is largely dependent upon the way their social training was carried out. In general they get on well with other pets and children.

Epagneul Phalene

Dwarf Mastiffs

Boston Terrier

Boston Terrier

COUNTRY OF ORIGIN
England/United States.

APTITUDE
Family pet.

SIZE
Boston Terriers are bred in a variety of sizes. The largest of them should not weigh more than 11kg (24lb).

COAT
The short-haired coat can be a black roan or black with white markings. The preference is for the roan.

CARE REQUIRED
These dogs do not require much grooming. Run a smooth glove or brush across the coat.

Keep the ears clean and the claws trimmed. Attend to the facial creases occasionally with a special lotion made for this purpose.

CHARACTER
These are intelligent, enthusiastic, occasionally boisterous dogs, that have a sense of humour, are playful, self-confident, affectionate, and make good watchdogs without being yappy.

TRAINING
The breed is not difficult to train because they like to learn and their intelligence ensures they pick things up quickly. They are very sensitive to the intonation of your voice.

SOCIAL BEHAVIOUR
Generally these dogs can get along very well

Boston Terriers

with other dogs and pets, and also with children.

EXERCISE
This Terrier has no desire for long walks but does like to go with you everywhere. They are not heavy and when it is hot or the distance too great, they can easily be carried. They love to play.

French Bulldog

COUNTRY OF ORIGIN
France.

APTITUDE
Family pet.

SIZE
The shoulder-height is about 30cm (11$^1/_2$in) and the weight is 8 - 13kg (17$^1/_2$ - 28$^1/_2$lb).

COAT
The coat is made up of short, shiny hairs which lie one upon another to form a dense layer.

They can be a roan but fawn and white with streaked patches is the most usual combination.

CARE REQUIRED
There is little to the grooming of this breed. Brush them occasionally with a rubber brush and keep the ear passages clean - do not use cotton buds! Clip the claws to keep them short and treat the facial creases with a special lotion occasionally (although petroleum jelly seems to be a good substitute).

CHARACTER
These are intelligent, very affectionate, lovable dogs that are tolerant of children, and also playful, cheerful, sensitive, sometimes boisterous, with a strongly developed sense of humour, that are persistent, tough on themselves, and can be obstinate. French Bulldogs can be jealous if their owner's attention is directed elsewhere. They like to be part of the family and should not be left alone too often.

TRAINING
This breed is not difficult to train because they are bright and learn quickly. Their expressive

245

face can easily lead you astray so it is important to be consistent with them. They are not only sensitive to the intonation of your voice but will pick up on any bad atmosphere in your house.

SOCIAL BEHAVIOUR

It is often said that these dogs are mad about children but that is not true - it is more the case that the children are crazy about the dog. Some of them can be rather dominant towards other dogs, although there are never problems with other household pets - provided these dogs have met them when they were young and grown up with them. Most of them are fond of people and visitors are mostly enthusiastically welcomed, although some of the dogs can be quite vigilant.

EXERCISE

Provided they get enough attention, no long walks are necessary. In hot weather, because of their short nose, exercise is best avoided.

They usually are content with three turns around the neighbourhood provided they also have a chance to run and play in the garden. They make ideal companions for flat dwellers.

SPECIAL REMARKS

The French Bulldog likes to be part of the family and can be taken everywhere with you. They do not belong in a kennel.

Pug

COUNTRY OF ORIGIN
England.

APTITUDE
Family pet.

SIZE
The shoulder-height is about 35cm (13^1/$_2$in) and the weight is about 7kg (15^1/$_2$lb).

Pug

COAT
The short-haired coat can be black, silver-grey, or beige, all with a black mask.

CARE REQUIRED
Attend to the facial creases now and then with the special lotion intended for this purpose. Loose hair can be easily removed with a rubber brush.
When necessary, apply drops to the eyes.

CHARACTER
These straightforward, pliable, dogs are calm indoors, sociable, sensitive, have a well-developed sense of humour, are very affectionate and intelligent, and they are physically demanding of themselves. Most of them snore.

TRAINING
Train them with a gentle-handed approach. The are sensitive to the intonation of your voice, making harsh punishment unnecessary.

SOCIAL BEHAVIOUR
Pugs get on well with other dogs and pets, and they behave impeccably with both children and visitors.
Do not forget though that they require lots of attention and become jealous if their owner's attention goes elsewhere.

EXERCISE
In fine weather they love to romp and play out of doors.
If it is very hot, do not leave them out too long and make sure they have a cool shady place where they spend the rest of the day.

The expressive face of a Pug

French Bulldogs are kind with children

Pug

10. Sighthounds

Breeds with feathering or long coats

Afghan Hound

COUNTRY OF ORIGIN
Afghanistan/England.

APTITUDE
Hunter by sight of large and small wild game, also watchdog, racing dog, and companion.

SIZE
The shoulder-height is 68 - 74cm ($26^1/_2$ - $29^1/_2$in) for dogs and 63 - 69cm ($24^1/_2$ - $27^1/_2$in) for bitches.

COAT
The Afghan Hound has a very long, fine coat. The hair on the face is short. Any colour is accepted but the most common colours are red through to shades of beige, often with a darker mask.

CARE REQUIRED
The grooming of the coat of these dogs requires a full hour each time, twice a week. The best method is to comb each handful of hair from the skin outwards so that no tangles can be overlooked, but take care not to break the hairs. Keep the ear passages clean.

Afghans should be bathed about every two months, using a good quality dog shampoo which does not dry the skin. Do not consider an Afghan Hound if you have no time or interest in the careful grooming required.

CHARACTER
These are independent, proud, and noble dogs that are calm indoors but very active and quick as lightning out of doors. This intelligent animal is not slavishly compliant, and they are brave, vigilant, though not noisy, and cautious with strangers.

It is instinctive for them to chase anything that moves quickly. The males can be rather dominant.

Afghan Hound

TRAINING
These dogs are not suitable for inexperienced people. Their independent nature makes them difficult to train and they never will obey totally. They respond adversely if you hit or shout at them - this merely lowers their respect for you. The best way to achieve anything with them is to use a firm yet soft hand with them.

SOCIAL BEHAVIOUR
The dogs can be rather dominant towards other males. They get along fine with children provided the dog is not pestered by them and is left alone in its own territory. They are probably better for a family with older children.

An existing cat will be accepted but do not forget that Afghan Hounds chase anything that runs quickly - it is in their blood.

EXERCISE
The Afghan Hound needs lots of exercise. Cycle with the dog every day to give it the chance to get rid of its energy, but do not forget their hunting instinct.
Only allow an Afghan to run freely off the lead on land where it cannot run off or it probably will.

The laborious task of grooming a show dog makes it impossible to combine showing these dogs with racing them.

Afghan Hound

A well groomed Afghan Hound is a marvellous sight and the dog knows it. This is a dog for the real enthusiast; you must appreciate its independent and sometimes unfathomable eastern character.

Borzoi

Borzoi

COUNTRY OF ORIGIN
Russia.

APTITUDE
Hunting by sight of large and small game, companion.

SIZE
The shoulder-height is 70 - 82cm ($27^1/_2$ - $32^1/_2$in) for dogs, and about 5cm (2in) shorter for bitches.

COAT
The coat consists of soft, medium-length wavy hair. Accepted colours are white, gold, red, grey, black, black roan, and patched.

CARE REQUIRED
The coat needs regular grooming. Trim excess hair between the pads of the feet. During the growing stage, these dogs need a high nutritional diet; do not scrimp on it.

CHARACTER
These are proud and self aware dogs that are loyal to their family. They are also good-natured, equable, calm when indoors, and more likely to be distant than to want to follow you about.

The Borzoi can be difficult to fathom. When necessary, they will protect your home.

TRAINING
The training of this breed has to be based upon mutual respect. They are not very obedient, so expect no miracles, but teach them the basic requirements.

SOCIAL BEHAVIOUR
These dogs do not like intrusive strangers. They are noble animals that get on fairly well with children but they are certainly not playmates.

They prize their rest and do not like rough play. They are usually fine with like-minded dogs. It is advisable to train them socially with cats and other pets as young as possible but they will always be hunters that tend to react to the sight of a fleeing animal.

Borzoi

EXERCISE
Indoors the Borzoi can be so peaceful it might escape notice but out of doors it needs lots of space to walk and run. In some countries it is forbidden to allow all the dogs in this fleet-footed hunting category off the lead.

They usually enjoy running alongside a cycle but beware - a Borzoi is quite likely to shoot off after any prey it catches sight of. You will need to react very quickly if this happens.

SPECIAL REMARKS

These majestic dogs are at their best with an owner who has a large area of fenced ground in which they can run all day to their heart's content.

Indoors they like to be close to the family and are fond of rest and comfort, making them unsuitable for life in a kennel.

Head of a Saluki

Saluki

COUNTRY OF ORIGIN
Iran.

APTITUDE
Hunter by sight of large and small game, and a companion.

SIZE
The shoulder-height is 58 - 71cm (22$\frac{1}{2}$ - 28in) for dogs, and slightly less for the bitches.

COAT
The coat is smooth and silken. The hair on the tail, ears, and rear of the legs should be feathered and longer.

Salukis are white, cream, sandy, golden, red, grey-on-grey, three-coloured (black, brown, and white), black with brown, and variations of these colourings.

CARE REQUIRED
The coat is kept in condition with an occasional thorough brushing, especially of the longer-haired parts of the dog. Check the ear passages to ensure they are clean.

CHARACTER
These are independent dogs with minds of their own but they are noble, peaceful, and need the company of their owner. They are cautious with strangers and have strong hunting instincts.

TRAINING
A degree of care is needed in the rearing of a young Saluki. This breed will never be perfectly obedient so do not set your sights too high. With much patience and insight you can get the dog to be fond of you and not an embarrassment to you.

SOCIAL BEHAVIOUR
Salukis can get along perfectly well with like-minded dogs and it is possible to put them together with children.

Other animals are better kept well away from them, regardless of whether these are rabbits or goats because their hunting instincts are very strong.

With a few exceptions it has proven quite impossible to train such dogs not to hunt.

EXERCISE
Salukis hunt on sight which means that they may not be let of the lead in some countries. In the grip of their passion for the chase they tend to be deaf to your calls.

Trotting alongside a cycle or coursing are excellent ways for them to get rid of their energy.

Saluki

Rough-haired breeds

Deerhound

COUNTRY OF ORIGIN
Great Britain.

APTITUDE
Hunter by sight of large game and family pet.

SIZE
The shoulder-height is a minimum of 76cm (30in) for dogs and 71cm (28in) for bitches.

COAT
The rough, medium-length coat should not feel woolly. The most common and the most prized colour is a dark blue-grey.
Yellow, sandy red, light grey, and roans of these colours are also possible, with dark mask and ears. A small amount of white on the tip of the tail, chest, and feet is acceptable.

CARE REQUIRED
The coat should be brushed thoroughly on a regular basis. Pluck excess hair from the ear passages from time to time and remove surplus hair between the pads of the feet.
Depending on the condition of the coat it may require plucking by hand once or twice per year.

CHARACTER
These are friendly, gentle-natured, sensible, and straightforward dogs that are noble, intelligent, kind to children, and not particularly vigilant. They rarely bark but are rather hard on themselves physically.Most of them have very strong hunting instincts.

Deerhound

TRAINING
The Deerhound learns quite quickly providing the handler and dog understand each other. A friendly request is often all that is needed to get the dog to do what you want of it.

SOCIAL BEHAVIOUR
With other similar dogs the Deerhound can get along fine and there are few difficulties with children.
Some of the dogs of this breed have stronger hunting instincts than others and this will have to be borne in mind if you have cats and other animals.

EXERCISE
This dog needs lots of exercise. Once you have seen how much enjoyment they get when they are allowed to run freely you will understand that these dogs cannot be limited to three short circuits of the neighbourhood every day.
Coursing is an excellent way for them to rid themselves of their energy but trotting alongside a cycle will also keep them both mentally and physically fit.

Irish Wolfhound

COUNTRY OF ORIGIN
Ireland.

APTITUDE
Hunter by sight of large game and family pet.

SIZE
The shoulder-height is a minimum of 79cm (31$^1/_2$in) for dogs and 71cm (28in) for bitches.

COAT
The coat consists of rough, coarse, hard, and rather unkempt-looking hair.
They can be grey, grey roan, red, black, roe deer coloured, and plain white. Grey is the most common colour.

CARE REQUIRED
Regular and thorough grooming with brush and comb will keep the coat in good condition. About once or twice a year the coat will need to be plucked to remove excess hair.

CHARACTER
These are friendly, gentle-natured, dogs that are kind to children, unconditionally loyal to their owner and family, pliable though not slavishly so, calm, and not yappy.

TRAINING

The Irish Wolfhound is relatively easy to train. A gentle approach with plenty of understanding will go a long way, because this dog quickly grasps what you intend. Ensure that the young dog is given as much self-confidence as possible and make sure you are always consistent with it, so that it can develop into an equable, confident dog.

Do not forget to teach it not to pull on its lead - preferably before it gets big and strong. These dogs grow rapidly and during this stage high-quality food is essential. During this time let the dog decide for itself how much exercise it wants.

Forced exercise and long-distance walks are too taxing for their bodies during this time. It takes two whole years before they are fully grown.

SOCIAL BEHAVIOUR

This breed normally gets on well with children and there should be no difficulty with other dogs.

This is also true for other animals if the dog has got to know them when it was young. They need to be at the centre of a family and will pine away in a kennel.

They are not usually vigilant, giving a friendly greeting to allcomers.

EXERCISE

These dogs adapt to your family circumstances and will not misbehave if the odd week passes with fewer chances to enjoy exercise.

But that does not mean they do not adore being taken for a lengthy trek in the countryside.

Smooth-haired breeds

Azawakh

COUNTRY OF ORIGIN
Mali.

APTITUDE
Hunter by sight of small and large game.

SIZE
The shoulder-height is 64 - 72cm ($25^1/_2$ - $28^1/_2$in) for dogs and 61 - 71cm (24 - 28in) for bitches.

COAT
The Azawakh has a short-haired coat which is sandy, red, or a roan of these colours. A white blaze and some white on the chest are acceptable, and white feet are a breed requirement.

CARE REQUIRED
The coat of this breed does not require much attention. It is sufficient to brush them now and then. Keep the claws trimmed, the ears clean, and check from time to time to see if there is tartar on the teeth.

CHARACTER
These are temperamental, lively, independent, and proud dogs, that have considerable stamina, and are vigilant. These dogs only let people they like see their affectionate and gentle nature. Because their original natural behaviour has not been bred out of them, it will defend its own people if they are threatened.

Head of an Azawakh

TRAINING
It is not easy to train this dog. The most success is achieved with lots of patience and much insight into the dog's character. Corporal punishment will not force the dog to respect you - quite the opposite. In spite of this you must make sure it does not take liberties with you.

SOCIAL BEHAVIOUR
The company of similar dogs is not a problem, and that is also true of mixing with children, as long as they respect the dog.
In view of their strong hunting instincts, they should not be trusted with cats and other household animals. They are usually rather distrustful of strangers.

EXERCISE
This breed cannot be restricted to a daily trot around the block. They must be able to run in order to get rid of their unbridled energy. This is an ideal dog for the really keen cyclist since they can cover considerable distances without tiring. In some countries it is forbidden to let dogs which hunt by sight such as the Azawakh to run freely off the lead.

Azawakh

Galgo Español

COUNTRY OF ORIGIN
Spain.

APTITUDE
Hunting of small game by sight and family pet.

SIZE
The shoulder-height is 65 - 70cm ($25^1/_2$ - $27^1/_2$in) for dogs and 60 - 68cm ($23^1/_2$ - $26^1/_2$in) for bitches.

Head of a Galgo Español

COAT
This breed has both a short-haired and rough-haired version. The majority of dogs are black, sandy, white, red, brown, yellow, or a roan.

CARE REQUIRED
Little grooming is required. In common with other dogs, the ears should be checked regularly and the claws kept short.

CHARACTER
These are intelligent, curious, and affectionate dogs, which are kind to children, and are very loyal to their handler and family. If necessary they will protect their family.

TRAINING
With a very consistent approach and much patience and insight, these relatively untamed dogs can be basically trained.
Direct its natural character in the desired direction but do not try to create a perfectly respon-

sive machine because this is the wrong dog for that.
It is extremely important that the young dog becomes acquainted with other people and different situations.

SOCIAL BEHAVIOUR
These dogs will rarely cause any problems with children because they are still close to nature and instinctively know that small persons need to be taken care of.

They like to play with other dogs and enjoy showing off their speed. They are not the most ideal choice if you have cats or other small animals because they have strong hunting instincts which make them chase anything which suddenly moves - and they cannot resist the urge.

EXERCISE
If these dogs have the freedom of a fair-sized piece of ground which is well fenced in, an outing twice a week with the bike for a change of background will be sufficient.
If not, they will need a considerable amount of exercise.
If this is not available for the dog, it is likely to become very frustrated and to make this obvious.

Greyhound

Greyhound

COUNTRY OF ORIGIN
England.

APTITUDE
Racing dog, hunter by sight of large and small game, and family pet.

Size
The shoulder-height is 71 - 76cm (28 - 30in) for dogs and 68 - 71cm (26$^1/_2$ - 28in) for bitches.

Coat
Greyhounds have a smooth, close coat of short hairs most commonly seen in black, white, fawn, orange, and roans of these colours or with other white markings.

Care required
It is sufficient to groom the Greyhound occasionally with a soft brush. However, the ears should be checked regularly and the claws kept trimmed.

These dogs are suitable for living in an outdoor kennel because they are reasonably resistant to the cold. Make sure that where they sleep is dry and draught-free.

Character
They are calm and sociable indoors, perhaps even downright lazy. These dogs are intelligent, sensitive, bond strongly with their own people, have tremendous stamina, and do not bark much. Greyhounds are not particularly vigilant.

Training
Compared with the other fleet-footed keen-eyed hunters, the Greyhound is reasonably easy to train. They can learn almost all commands and are fairly obedient, except when they have set their eyes on a prey. At these moments they ignore all your commands.

In some countries dogs of this entire group are not allowed out unless they remain on a lead, not just because of the danger they could pre-sent for wild animals but also the danger to themselves and road-users.

Social behaviour
It is instinctive for these dogs to chase anything that moves quickly, which means that they are not really suitable companions for people with one or more cats.

They seldom present difficulties with other dogs and are normally good with children. With strangers, they tend to be rather cautious.

Exercise
The dogs of this breed want to cover long distances, running and walking. Consider joining a Greyhound racing association because the dogs can really express their natural selves on a race track.

Trotting alongside a cycle is a good alternative for working off the dog's energy. It does not really matter how the dog gets its exercise provided it gets enough.

Special remarks
Greyhounds which race differ quite a bit from those which must do well in the show ring. They are a very healthy breed and can live quite long.

Italian Greyhound

Country of origin
Italy/Egypt.

Aptitude
Hunter by sight of rabbits and other game; also a family pet.

Size
The shoulder-height is 32 - 38cm (12$^1/_2$ - 15in).

Coat
The coat is fine and short. The colour of this breed is frequently a greyish yellow, black, or slate, perhaps with white on the chest and feet. Flecked versions also exist but are not accepted in all countries.

Care required
These dogs need little grooming. It is usually sufficient to wipe the dog with a cloth to make the coat shine.

It is necessary though to check the teeth regularly because tartar is prevalent with this breed. The adult dog is certainly not delicate but until they are about eighteen-months old, they can break a leg rather easily.

Greyhounds are suitable for dog racing

Italian Greyhound

Italian Greyhounds

CHARACTER
These are gentle, affectionate, and cheerful dogs that are quick and active, intelligent, and compliant.

TRAINING
Generally these are not difficult dogs to train provided their handler is consistent with them. They are often naughty and are aware that they are.
It is important that you can see the funny side when things go wrong but this does not mean allowing them to take liberties.

SOCIAL BEHAVIOUR
These dogs get on well with other dogs and cats and they normally also get on well with children, but do not let children treat the dog as a toy.

It is obvious that they do not make good playmates for Rottweilers. Italian Greyhounds usually get on well with each other and it is recommended that you have more than one of them.

EXERCISE
This active breed likes to run. If possible, let them run freely on an enclosed patch of land.

Sloughi

COUNTRY OF ORIGIN
Morocco.

APTITUDE
Hunter by sight of large and small game, and companion.

SIZE
The shoulder-height is 66 - 72cm (26 - 28$\frac{1}{2}$in) for dogs and 61 - 68cm (24 - 26$\frac{1}{2}$in) for bitches. The ideal height is 70cm (27$\frac{1}{2}$in) for dogs and 65cm (25$\frac{1}{2}$in) for bitches.

COAT
The Sloughi has a soft, short-haired coat, usually seen in various shades of sandy colourings or a roan, with or without a darker mask.

CARE REQUIRED
They require little grooming. An occasional brushing is adequate.
Keep the claws trimmed and check the teeth for tartar.

CHARACTER
These are proud, temperamental, and somewhat obstinate dogs with considerable stamina, that are vigilant, and cautious with strangers.

They only show any affection towards people they like.

Sloughi

TRAINING
This independent-minded dog is not easy to train, but that does not mean it cannot be taught anything.

A handler with sufficient insight into the dog's character and lots of patience can teach the Sloughi much, creating a bond of mutual respect between them.

SOCIAL BEHAVIOUR
It is necessary to introduce this breed when quite young to all manner of situations, different people and animals.

Properly trained, it is possible for a Sloughi to live together with one or more cats.

EXERCISE
This breed has an enormous desire for exercise.

In some countries breeds such as this that hunt by sight are not allowed to run freely off the lead and in these circumstances, the race track is the only place where they can rid themselves of their energy. These dogs have outstanding levels of stamina.

Head of a Sloughi

Whippet

COUNTRY OF ORIGIN
England.

APTITUDE
Racing dog and family pet.

SIZE
The shoulder-height is 47 - 51cm ($18^1/_2$ - 20in) for dogs and 44 - 47cm ($17^1/_2$- $18^1/_2$in) for bitches.

COAT
The short-haired coat is fine and dense. It comes in many colours but the most common are white with streaked or yellow patches, black, black with white, blue, roan, or beige with darker mask.

CARE REQUIRED
Little grooming is required for these dogs. It is sufficient to brush them from time to time to remove dead and loose hairs. Some examples have a predisposition for tartar but this can be kept in check by regularly giving them something to chew. Keep the claws trimmed short.

Whippet

CHARACTER

These dogs are affectionate, cuddly, and lovely with children. They are also intelligent but not particularly obedient, cheerful, peaceable, playful, a touch obstinate, and sometimes also vigilant.

TRAINING

Introduce plenty of variety into a Whippet's training. The best results are achieved by interspersing games and running but remember that this will never be an unreservedly obedient dog.

SOCIAL BEHAVIOUR

Whippets are usually very good with children but they tend not to be too fond of strangers. They will invariably warn you of visitors. They are very tolerant of other dogs and there is rarely any difficulty.

The tendency to chase everything that moves quickly is inborn in them. The household cat, to which the dog has grown accustomed, will be left alone.

EXERCISE

The Whippet is a small Greyhound, meaning that its entire body is built for racing and hunting. Understandably they need plenty of exercise. In some countries they may not be allowed to run freely off the lead, in common with other dogs that hunt by sight.

In these circumstances cycle with the dog or join an organization that races Whippets so that you can let the dog live its life fully on the race track.

Whippets

11. Breeds that are not recognized

American-Canadian White Shepherd

COUNTRY OF ORIGIN
United States/Canada/Europe.

APTITUDE
Family pet.

SIZE
The shoulder-height is 60 - 65cm ($23\frac{1}{2}$ - $25\frac{1}{2}$n) for dogs and 55 - 60cm ($21\frac{1}{2}$ - $23\frac{1}{2}$in) for bitches.

Variation of 2cm ($\frac{1}{2}$in) on these dimensions is permitted provided the overall proportions of the dog are correct.

COAT
This breed has stiff-haired, long stiff-haired, or long-haired coats. The long-haired types do not have an undercoat. The colour is always white.

CARE REQUIRED
Brush and comb these dogs every day during the moult. Check the ears regularly and keep the claws trimmed short.

CHARACTER
These are friendly, intelligent, attentive, and loyal dogs that are eager to work. They like to be close to their handler.

TRAINING
These dogs are difficult to train because they like to work for their handler and they learn quite quickly.
It is very important that the young dog has lots of positive encounters with all manner of animals, people, things, and situations, to help it grow up as a well-balanced animal.

SOCIAL BEHAVIOUR
These dogs generally get on well with other dogs and children. If they have the chance to get to know them when they are young, they will also get along with cats and other pets.

EXERCISE
This breed has an average demand for exerci-

American-Canadian White Shepherd

se, but three short trots around the neighbourhood is not adequate, and the dog would quickly become bored with this routine. These dogs are very suitable for various sporting activities such as obedience, fly-ball, and agility skills trials.

American-Canadian White Shepherd

Short-haired Jack Russell

Short-legged Jack Russell

COUNTRY OF ORIGIN
England.

APTITUDE
Hunting dog and family pet.

SIZE
The shoulder-height is 25 - 30cm ($9\frac{1}{2}$ - $11\frac{1}{2}$in).

COAT

There are two types of coat: the rough-haired and the smooth-haired. With both types the hair is wiry, close, and dense.

The colour is either wholly white or it can be marked with tan, lemon, or black markings, or with all three. The markings are preferably restricted to the root of the tail and the head.

CARE REQUIRED

This Jack Russell needs little grooming. Brush occasionally to keep the coat in good condition.

CHARACTER

These are animated, very brave and temperamental dogs, that are vigilant, lively, enterprising, intelligent, and playful, but they can also be hard on themselves, have minds of their own, be dominant, and independent.

TRAINING

This healthy breed is not difficult to train for handlers who are kind, very consistent, and confident of themselves. They are brimming with self-confidence and if you and your family let them, they will do what pleases them.

SOCIAL BEHAVIOUR

Provided they are socially trained when they are young, there should be no difficulties with other dogs and pets. These dogs are independent hunting dogs by nature, which accept the cat from its own house but will chase any others. They are normally good with children and can accept a knock or two.

EXERCISE

These dogs have tremendous energy and they like to work. Not surprisingly, they are not content to be hurried three times each day for the shortest of outings. They want to run and play, and they love to dig.

They happen to be first-class destroyers of vermin, making them ideal dogs to live on a farm. They can be quite impressive in sports such as fly-ball.

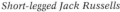

Short-legged Jack Russells

Important addresses

For all questions regarding breeds in general you can contact your national cynological or dog institution.

In the United States this is:
The American Kennel Club
51 Madison Avenue
New York NY 10010

In Great Britain this is:
The Kennel Club
1 - 5 Clarges Street
Piccadilly
London WIY 8AB

Photograph acknowledgements and thanks

All the photographs were taken by Esther J.J. Verhoef-Verhallen. Additional material was provided by:
Sandra Arts; H. Settelaar: R. van Riet; C.C. Asselbergs; A. Christiansen; Archief Pystykorva; Joenpolvi; J.W.A. Snel; Lochs-Romans; Reina Jansen; Willemien Dubislav-Tol; Henk and Ine Hartgers-Wagener.

The publishers and author would like to thank the following owners for making their dogs available:

1. Sheepdogs and cattle herders
The Avontuur family, F.H.M .Backx, the Beenen-Sluijters family, Mascha Bollen, the van Boven family, Bea and Gerrit Enthoven, P.B.T. Gerritsen, J. de Gids, D. Griffin, H. ten Haaf, the De Haas family, T. van der Heijden, W.L. van der Hoek, C.A. Keizer, the Klein family, D.van Klingeren, H.M. Luijken, Yvonne Maas, Jacky Marks, M. and J. van Mook, Mr Van de Meijden senior, M.A. van Mierlo, Laura van den Nieuwenhuijzen, A. van Noorda, M.E. .Spiering, M. Olsthoorn, the Van Ooijen family, R. Peschier, the Prins family, Bert Reintjes, T.A. Scherbeyn, Yvonne Schultz, H. Settelaar, H.Smits, R. and A. Tetteroo, H.P.P. Verbakel, Jet Vermeulen, the Welvering family, Nancy Wijnhoven.

2. Pinscher, Schnauzer, Molossian, Mastiff, and Swiss Sennenhunds breeds
J.M.W. van de Berg, J. Bouland-Planken, Arie and José den Dekker-Bragt, M. van Deursen, the Gest family, M.I.J. van Goethem-Jagt, H. and I. Hartgers-Wagener, P. Hendriks, Louis Hillebrand, the Hoendervanger family, J.C.G. van der Kant, Frans Kappe, G.Kemps, J. and E. Kloosterhof, E.Kluijs, H.T.J. van Laar, M.C .Langendoen,L.J. Lodders, J. Luyks, B. Martens, the van de Mierden family, the Nettenbreijer family, the Oudendijk family, the Plattje family, Pranger, the Reijnen-Labee family, J .Rutten, Schellekens, J.M. Stramer, Joke and Jan Verberkt, E. Verhoef, the J. Westerhoven family, A. van Wijk, F. and L. van Wijk, G. van Wijk, Annette Wijnsouw, C. Zuydeweg-Roxs.

3. Terriers
J.H. Albers, Atilla and Nancy, Marianne Baas-Becking, R. Bomers, Laurens and Sandra van de Burgt, J. Dekker and J. Roskam, Charlotte Froon, A. Hartmann-Tibbe, A. van Hoorn, Peter Jaspers, Colette de Jong, R. and I. Kelleter, E. Lahaye, B. and P. Langemaat-Oudkerk, J. van Lieshout, G.H.J. Lustigheid, C. Meijer, W. Pul, W. de Reus and R. Bomers, Irma de Roo-Strous, R.P. Snip and J. Bourret, Marga Steenvoorden, C.C.E. Thomas, P. Koolen, W. Tijsse-Claase, T. Hoffman-Winkels, Jet Vermeulen, Th. and W. van Vessem, Lily Weber, the De Wolf family.

Dachshunds
Mrs Blom, Jeanine van de Heuvel, P. van Leeuwen, the van Oers family.

Spitz and other primitive breeds
J.A. van de Berkmortel, A.W.Bruynzeel, Michel Cayol, M. van Deursen, Chris Eizenga, R. and M. Fisher, Jennifer Gielisse, Sandra van de Graaf, Cornelis Koot, Marjo van Oers-van Mimpen, Ronny van Riet, H. Vrieze, J.W.A. Snel, A.M.M. Konijnenburg, Jet Vermeulen, the De Wolf family.

Hounds
Thea Bouman, M. van de Broek, N. Horsten, H. and F. Huikeshoven, Mrs De Jong-Van Wijngaarden, G.M. Koenraadt, B. and P. Langemaat-Oudkerk, R. Morgans, the Rust family, R. Smits.

7. Pointers

J.F.H. Brocken, Anneke Cornelissen, A. Dekker, Lianne Eekman-Lampio, Margriet Gijsen-van de Bosch, Jan van Haren, A. Harduin, N. Hoogervorst-Hazenoot, J. Kamsteeg, G. Kemps, R. Key, Marianne Krans, B.G.A.W. Maton, M.B. Melchior, I. Nannings-Balvert, the Roks family, the Van Son family, A. Vorstenbosch, M.J.A.H.M. van Wanrooij, J. van Dommelen, Annette Wijnsouw.

Gundogs and retrievers

Cat, Jolanda van Gils, A. de Goede-van den Burg, Ellen Hagendijk, M. Hoogendorp, Hazel Huybregts-Kingham, A.T. Kramer, the Knol family, Ge and Ria Kleynen, H. Konings, R. Lochs-Romans, J. Luyks, R. Notenboom, J-P and V. Perennec, the Smits-Steenbakkers's, Van der Linden-Steenbakkers, J. Tresoor-Homan, Marc Wynn, Ton and Louise van Zoom, C. Zuydeweg-Roxs.

Toy and other miniature dogs

Hans Bleeker, Jan den Otter, M.W.A.H.Cooymans, A.M. and T. van Dongen-Ribberink, Willemien Dubislav-Tol, A.P.M. van de Horst, H.R. Jacobs, Reina Jansen, Wim and Ria Jansen, Reina Janssen-Spits, M. Kavelaars, J. and E. Klooster-hof, T.J. Koster, T.J. Koster and A. Leliveld, J. van Lieshout, H.M. Luijken, Erwin Manders, Jo and Majorie Nelissen, B. and Chr. Schiltman, J. Tekelenburg, J. Timmers, H. Verhees, the De Wit-Meemen's, F. Voogt, R. Rullens.

Sighthounds

The Ferber-Llinares family, Anita, M.T.H Gielisse, Jennifer Gielisse, Sandra van de Graaf, E. van de Have-van Dipten, Annemie and Jo Hoffman, Phil Morgan, the Oudendijk family, Sonja van Rij-van Baarle.

Breeds that are not recognized

Klerken, H.L. Noordhoek.

The author particularly wishes to thank C.C. and T.J. Asselbergs for the provided information they provided and their input regarding the Scandinavian breeds.

Thanks are also due to all the breed societies, breed specialist, breeders, owners, and enthusiasts not named above who made equally important contributions to ensure accurate descriptions of the breeds in question.

Index

Labrador Retriever

Grand Basset Griffon Vendéen

Glen of Imaalterriër

Tervuerense herder